Laird of the West

John W. Chalmers

Detselig Enterprises Ltd.
Calgary, Alberta

© 1981 by **John W. Chalmers**

Canadian Cataloguing in Publication Data

Chalmers, John W., 1910-
  Laird of the West

  Bibliography: p.
  Includes index.
  ISBN 0-920490-18-2

  1. Laird,David, 1833-1914. 2. Canada. Bureau of Indian Affairs
- Officials and employees - Biography. 3. Cabinet ministers - Can-
ada - Biography.* 4. Lieutenant-governors - Northwest Territo-
ries - Biography.* 5. Journalists - Prince Edward Island -
Charlottetown - Biography. 6. Indians of North America - Can-
ada - Treaties. 7. Northwest, Canadian - History - 1870-1905.*
I. Title.
FC506.L34C49   971.05'092'4   C81-091337-2
F1033.L34C49

Detselig Enterprises Ltd
P.O. Box G399
Calgary, Alberta T3A 2G3

Printed in Canada   ISBN 0-920490-18-2

*For Elizabeth Laird, David Laird Mathieson,
and all the other descendants of the
Hon. David Laird*

Contents

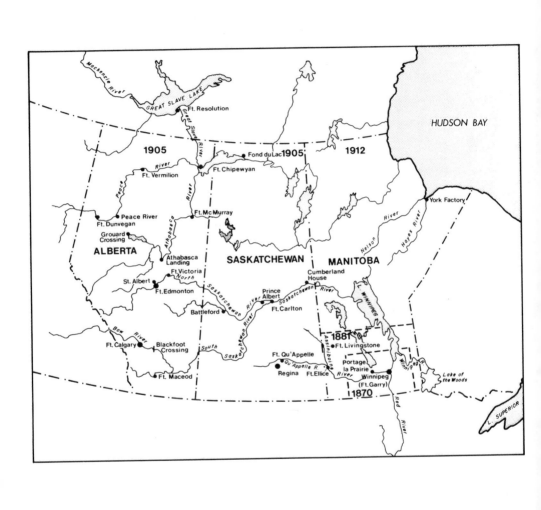

HUDSON BAY

1905   1912

Mackenzie River

GREAT SLAVE LAKE

Ft. Resolution

Fond du Lac

Peace River

Ft. Vermilion

Ft. Chipewyan

Ft. McMurray

Peace River

Ft. Dunvegan

Grouard Crossing

ALBERTA

Athabasca Landing

Ft. Victoria

St. Albert

Ft. Edmonton

Battleford

Ft. Calgary

Blackfoot Crossing

Ft. Macleod

SASKATCHEWAN

Cumberland House

Prince Albert

Ft. Carlton

Saskatchewan River

South Saskatchewan River

Ft. Qu'Appelle

Qu'Appelle R.

Regina

Ft. Ellice

MANITOBA

York Factory

Nelson River

Hayes River

L. WINNIPEG

1881

Ft. Livingstone

Portage la Prairie

Assiniboine River

Winnipeg (Ft. Garry)

L. WINNIPEG

Lake of the Woods

Red River

1870

L. SUPERIOR

Bow River

Acknowledgements

The Hon. David Laird's descendants had long considered the preparation of a biography of their illustrious ancestor, and to that end have long collected and preserved letters, diaries, newspaper clippings, and other relevant material. It remained for his granddaughter, Elizabeth Laird, however, to initiate the present project, to make family papers available to the undersigned, and to do a great deal of additional research. The author is accordingly greatly indebted to her and to her cousin, David Laird Mathieson, Q.C., for such and additional information, to both of them for reading the manuscript, making valuable suggestions, correcting factual errors, and assembling pertinent material from other Laird descendants.

Other relevant material was obtained from or through the help of the Public Archives of Canada, Public Archives of Prince Edward Island, Provincial Archives of Manitoba, Archives of the Hudson's Bay Company, Provincial Archives Board of Saskatchewan, both Regina and Saskatoon offices, Battleford National Historic Park, and the Library of the University of Alberta.

Financial assistance from Alberta Culture was greatly appreciated, particularly as it made possible travel for the collection of basic information and its photographic reproduction.

John W. Chalmers

Sincere appreciation is tendered to the following for permission to quote from the sources indicated below.

Canada, Minister of Supply and Services for excerpts from Don W. Thomson, *Men and Meridians,* vol.2.

The Country Guide for excerpts from D.C. Harvey, "David Laird The Man whose Tongue is not Forked," in *The Grain Grower's Guide,* 20 August 1919.

The Dalhousie Review for excerpts from Frank McKinnon, "David Laird of Prince Edward Island," in vol. 26, no. 4.

H.A. Dempsey for excerpts from his *William Parker Mounted Policeman, Jerry Potts Plainsman,* and *Crowfoot, Chief of the Blackfeet.*

Houghton Mifflin Co., Boston, for excerpts from *The Scotch,* by John Kenneth Galbraith, (c) 1964 by John Kenneth Galbraith.

Hudson's Bay Company for excerpts from *The Beaver*: Margaret Complin, "Calling Valley of the Crees," (March, 1935), Clifford Wilson, "Indian Treaties," (March, 1939); R.C. Fetherstonhaugh, "March of the Mounties," (June, 1940); Molly McFadden, "Steamboats on the Red," (September, 1950); R.C. Russell, "A Minister Takes the Carlton Trail," (Winter, 1950); Ron Vastokas, "The Grand Rapids Portage," (Autumn, 1961); James McCook, "Frontiersman at Fort Ellice," (Autumn, 1968).

Hurtig Publishers, Edmonton, for excerpts from J.G. MacGregor, *Edmonton, A History,* and George Woodcock, *Gabriel Dumont.*

The Island Magazine for an excerpt from Lewis Fischer, "The Shipping Industry in the Nineteenth Century Prince Edward Island: A Brief History," in vol. 1, no. 4.

Elizabeth Laird, for material from numerous letters and other documents.

Jean Larmour and *Saskatchewan History* for an excerpt from her "Edgar Dewdney Indian Commissioner in the Transition Period of Indian Settlement 1879-1884," in vol. 31, no. 1.

Maclean's for excerpts from Frank Oliver, "The Blackfoot Indian Treaty" in issue of 15 March 1931.

Manitoba Historical Society for excerpts from Molly McFadden, "Steamboats on the Red," *Transactions,* Series III, No. 7.

Manitoba Public Archives for excerpts from letters, David Laird to Alexander Morris Papers, Ketcheson Collection, item 132) and 7 July 1875 (MG 12, B1, Alexander Morris Papers, Lieutenant-Governor Collection, item 1033).

David Laird Mathieson for material supplied in letters and interview.

McClelland and Stewart, Ltd., Toronto, for excerpts from René Fumoleau, *As Long as this Land Shall Last*.

F.J. Newson for excerpt from "Reminiscences of Seaside Hotel, Rustico Beach, P.E.I." (unpublished typescript).

Bruce Peel for excerpt from *Steamboats on the Saskatchewan*.

Prince Edward Island Public Archives for excerpts of letters, David Laird to David Rennie Laird, 30 August 1879, 9 December 1880 (2979, 1-8), 1 May 1908 (2979-148), to Mr. Moffatt, 8 January 1903 (2545,2), and William Dawson to David Laird, 17 April 1889 (2541, 66), also the document entitled "Mr. Mair's Account of the Meeting with the Sioux Chiefs," (1279, 9).

Public Archives of Canada for excerpts from letters, Constantine Scollen to A.G. Irvine, NWMP, 15 April 1879 (RC10 v. 3695 f. 14942), David Laird to D. MacLean, 15 March 1899, telegrams David Laird to J.S. Dennis, 9 August 1880 (No. 204, 1880, Department of the Interior) and Lindsay Russell, 9 August 1880, and "Statement of an Interview between Lieutenant-Governor and 'Ocean Man'," 15 March 1899 (10846 and 10484, No. 207, Department of the Interior, 1880).

Ian Ross Robertson for excerpts from "Pope, William Henry," in *Dictionary of Canadian Biography*, vol. 10; "The Bible Question in Prince Edward Island," in *Acadiensis*, vol. 5, no. 2; "Party Politics and Religious Controversialism in Prince Edward Island from 1856 to 1860," in *Acadiensis*, vol. 7, no. 2.

Saskatchewan Archives Board, Regina, for excerpts of letters, David Laird to Col. Macleod, 18 February 1878; to Alexander McKenzie, 20 April 1879; to Mr. Palmer, 18 October 1879; to Deputy-Minister of the Interior, 29 June 1880 (all in Laird Letter Book), also "Hon. David Laird" and "Early Days in the North-west," by Mary Alice Mathieson (unpublished typescripts SHS 32).

Saskatchewan History for excerpts from Jean E. Murray, "The Early History of Emmanuel College," vol. 9, no. 3, and G.K. Kinnaird, "An Episode of the North-West Rebellion," vol. 20, no. 2.

Star-Phoenix, Saskatoon, for an excerpt from A.N. Wetton, "Christmastide in Old Barttleford," in issue of 24 December 1958.

L.H. Thomas and *Saskatchewan History* for an excerpt from "Governor Laird's Thanksgiving Day Address," vol. 5, no. 3.

1

New House
to New Glasgow

Laird, Lang, Scott and Holm,
The chief names in Kilmacolm.

According to the historian the Rev. James Murray, certainly as early as the Battle of Bannockburn in 1314, such were the principal names in the Parish of Kilmacolm, four miles south of the Clyde River and perhaps twenty miles west of Glasgow. Six centuries later, Laird was still a common name in Kilmacolm.

> The River Gryfe runs through the Parish, and on either side of the valley the grounds rise in a series of hills. At the beginning of the nineteenth century the population of the Parish was 951, 443 males and 508 females. In the hamlet there were 45 houses and 126 persons.
>
> Part of the present church was built in the 12th century. It was enlarged and restored several times. . .
>
> An old stone terrace of two stories was built in 1817 with three separate doors and passages with rooms opening off the passages still in use. Some of the streets are very narrow, and hedged in between old and high stone walls. There are several fine streets and residences and public buildings.[1]

About three miles from the hamlet and in the Barony of Duchald are two farms, North and South (once High and Low) Newton. In 1695, the earliest year for which parish records are available, one or both of these farms were known as Newtoun or Newtoune (New House). The occupant and tenant farmer was one John Laird, married to Margaret, née Hatrick. Possibly but by no means surely, John Laird was an ancestor of the Prince Edward Islander who came to be known as Laird of the West. Certainly the Alexander Laird who was David Laird's great-great-great-grandfather occupied the same farm in the early or mid-1700's, as did his son and his

1

grandson, also named Alexander, and his great-grandson James. James sired a number of sons and daughters, one of whom inevitably was named Alexander.

Little is known of these early Lairds beyond some dates of their baptisms, marriages, and deaths. They were tenant farmers with families often quite large, and probably as a result lived in very modest circumstances. That they were Presbyterians is indicated by the ordination of Alexander Laird (the second in this record) as an elder in 1715. Five years later, he (or another Alexander Laird) signed a protest from the Session to the Presbytery against the settlement and conduct of the parish minister.

In 1745 and 1746, Scotland was wracked by civil war, when Bonnie Prince Charlie, as he was called by his romantic and feckless Highland followers, tried to regain the United Kingdom crown for the Stuarts. But the dour, hard-headed Lowlanders, such as the inhabitants of Kilmacolm, would have none of such nonsense — the agony of Bannockburn was not forgotten, even after four centuries. And so the Uprising of 1745 did not disturb the even if unexciting tenor of Kilmacolm's ways.

But by the turn of the century the Lowland rhythms and routines, some of which had endured for hundreds of years were changing. As early as 1791, James Boswell had quoted the great Samuel Johnson as saying, "The noblest prospect which a Scotchman ever sees, is the high road which leads him to England."[2] Certainly the meagre resources of Caledonia stern and wild had for a long time been unable to support its fecund families, and especially after the enclosures following the Rebellion of '45. Then the Campbells and others, rewarded for their loyalty, were granted the forfeited estates of rebellious Highlanders. The new owners found it more profitable to raise sheep rather than Scottish ragamuffins. But ambitious Scottish lads, especially younger sons, had long found careers in the British army, but with the end of the Napoleonic Wars, such opportunities had virtually ceased. The alternative seemed to be emigration, as with the Hudson's Bay Company, or to that Promised Land, America. Thus in 1819 Alexander Laird, aged twenty-two, had decided that his future lay across the Atlantic in the British colony of Prince Edward Island.

Until 1763, the Island of St. John was a French possession. In that year, by the Treaty of Paris, which ended the Seven Years' War, it was ceded to Great Britain, and in 1780 renamed Prince Edward Island. Beginning in 1765 it was surveyed into sixty-seven townships (commonly called lots), each of approximately twenty thousand acres. These were granted, in fee simple, to Men of Valor and Worth who had contributed to the successful prosecution of the war with France. Mainly they were army and navy officers, plus a sprinkling of Members of Parliament, civil servants, and prominent merchants. It was the government's intention — perhaps, more accurately, its hope — that the owners of these sinecures would subdivide them and sell them on easy terms to sturdy British yeomanry — such was a condition of the grants — all for the greater security, glory, and affluence of the British Empire.

Instead, from the beginning, most proprietors showed no interest in promoting settlement, and certainly none in leaving the comforts of Olde England to visit this wilderness. Some disposed of their Island estates as rapidly as possible; others, original grantees or purchasers, appointed agents to extract the highest possible revenue through rents from their holdings, or to sell them under terms which poor and struggling farmers found impossible to meet. An honorable exception was Thomas Douglas, fifth Earl of Selkirk, not an original grantee. In the Canadian West he is usually remembered for his Red River Colony which grew into the city of Winnipeg. But his first settlement, established in 1803 under his personal supervision, was on the Island. His leases were generous, and he encouraged freehold (title) by generous purchase terms.

Many years were to pass after Selkirk's venture before some townships, such as No. 23, were settled. This one, like most, was rectangular, rather narrow, just north-west of Charlottetown, but on the opposite side of the Island. Unlike many of the lots, it was not land-locked but ran, in a direction just west of north, from the centre of the Island to the beautiful Cavendish beaches. Through the township meanders the lovely little Clyde River, known in its upper reaches as the Hunter. Today, readers of L.M. Montgomery know the whole area as "Anne" country.

Grantees of Lot 23 in 1767 were Allan and Lauchlin MacLeane, but in 1771 its owner was a military man by the name of Winter. In 1805 the property came into the possession of David Rennie, a Glasgow merchant. Evidently Rennie was a colonizer of Selkirk's stamp. Many years later the Hon. David Laird was to call his eldest son David Rennie, and the second rather than the first given name was used throughout his life.

Rennie very carefully chose as his agent a Newfoundlander by birth, Scot by up-bringing, M.A. of the University of Edinburgh by education, one William E. Cormack. Cormack, only twenty-two himself in 1818, sought in the Glasgow environs for young, sturdy, and intelligent settlers for Lot No. 23. Among them he recruited Alexander Laird, born in 1797, who arrived on the Island in time for his twenty-third birthday. On the same vessel and bound for the same destination was William Orr, of Glasgow, and his seventeen-year-old daughter Janet. After a year on the Island, spying out the land like Caleb and Joshua, young Alexander sent for the rest of the family: brother James, several sisters, and his father, now widowed.

Converting the wilderness of Prince Edward Island to farms was more than merely putting a plough into the soil. Before the land could be cultivated, it had to be cleared of the timber on it. But that process itself led to two other industries: lumbering and ship-building. As early as 1783 the schooner *Betsey* was built at Rustico, on the mouth of the Clyde, an indication of the timber resources of the area. For nearly a hundred years thereafter, lumbering and ship-building remained important industries on the Clyde, at Rustico and New Glasgow, that amibitiously-named hamlet in the centre of Lot. No. 23.

> At the beginning of the fifth decade of the nineteenth century, all of the prerequisites for a major shipping industry were present on the Island. Local shipwrights and shipbuilders, such as . . . the Orrs in New Glasgow and Rustico . . . had accumulated sufficient expertise and capital to construct durable yet inexpensive vessels for overseas sale.[3]

David Laird Mathieson, Alexander Laird's grand-son-in-law, writes:

> My father's father, Ronald Mathieson, bought a farm in Lot 33 in the 1840's. His sister was married to Captain John Matheson, a shipbuilder near Rustico. John would build a ship and have it loaded with produce , some from Ronald's farm. Ronald would then return to his former vocation as a master mariner, sail the ship to Courok or Liverpool and sell both ship and cargo. This went on for years . . .[4]

Such sophisticated enterprises of the 1840's were no doubt well advanced in the 1820's. Thus, like many another pioneer, young Alexander probably found both the opportunity and the necessity for wage employment until his farm became productive. But within three years he was able to marry the young lady whom he had met en route from Glasgow. From then on, the young couple never looked back. Like so many of their ancestors, these Lairds were prolific parents. Janet bore nine children, six sons and three daughters. Mary died young, in 1856, probably in her early twenties, but the other eight survived both their parents. David, born in 1833, was the fourth child and the fourth son.

In view of their sponsorship, it was natural for both the Lairds and the Orrs to find their new homes in Lot No. 23, and for some at least of their descendants to remain there. An atlas of the Island shows that as late as 1880, Alexander's sons James, William, and Albert had land fronting on the Clyde, and Alexander was located near-by. Their total holdings amounted to 866 acres. The Orrs were also well represented, three of that name on waterfront property; another land-locked close by. The Mathiesons were relatively close neighbors, situated on Lot No. 33, the second one east of No. 23.

Alexander Laird was successful in other activities than that of paternity. On the occasion of his death in 1873, *The Patriot* noted his passing as follows:

Naturally, a whipping was anything but pleasant. Often it was followed by another at home, just on general principles. But a boy (not a girl) who was never so punished was scorned by his peers, somewhat as a sissy, a pantywaist, a teacher's pet.

Still and all, formal education was rather regarded as a sometime thing. For many reasons, schools could be closed for weeks or even months: inclement weather, inability to secure a teacher, lack of money to pay one. Even when the school was open, attendance was often erratic. Commonly during a whole term it might not reach or exceed fifty percent. Older boys especially were frequently required at home to help with the endless farm chores, especially during seed-time and harvest. Usually as soon as a farmer's son was able to do a man's work, about age fourteen at the latest, his schooling was finished.

If they had an unusually competent teacher, perhaps young Robert and David Laird were even introduced to Latin in their little country schoolhouse, but it seems more probable that their parents sent them to the Central Academy in Charlottetown for further education. This was the only secondary school on the Island open to Protestants.

But school was not the only educational influence to which young Islanders were exposed; equally important was the home, the family. In his delightful book, *The Scotch,* John Kenneth Galbraith writes about a settlement of Scottish-Canadian farmers distant in time and place from those of Prince Edward Island. Nevertheless, what he has to say applies equally to the Caledonian Islanders. Galbraith categorizes his Scotch (forgive the expression) as upright and downright, downright shiftless or spendthrifty, careless or ignorant, or even downright unlucky. He also classified them into two groups: those who drank and those who didn't.

In addition, Galbraith divides the society of which he writes into three socioeconomic classes, the uppermost of which he describes as Men of Standing;

> A Man of Standing was likely to have more than a hundred acres, although land in large amounts did a man no good . . . A Man of Standing had . . . to be strictly sober, a diligent worker and a competent farmer. Beyond these necessary but by no means sufficient conditions were . . . special factors.
>
> Regrettably, perhaps, family was one. No one would have dreamed of suggesting that one clan was inferior to another, and none would have conceded it. Yet it was tacitly agreed that some were better.
>
> Size was also an important crutch. The Men of Standing were usually, although not invariably, very large.
>
> The decisive source of esteem . . . was information and ability to put it to sensible use. This was, by all odds, the most admired trait. It was

partly a matter of education. . . . But education was only important if combined with good sense.

But neither was it sufficient merely to make good sense. The Scotch expected a man to prove his wisdom by putting it to useful purpose . . . not be confined to such areas of immediate or ultimate self-interest as his own farm or church . . . He should certainly serve on the Township Council.

The Man of Standing had, in short, to earn their esteem . . . it was a very good thing to be Man of Standing and a very good thing to have them in sufficient supply.[6]

There can be no doubt that the Lairds were Men of Standing. The hundred acres that were a *sine qua non* in Upper Canada were not necessarily the minimum on the Island, but whatever the minimum was, indubitably the Lairds met it. Strictly sober? David Laird never knowingly touched a drop of spirits in his life. As for family, the very name 'Laird' is aristocratic, meaning 'the lord of the manor.' Respecting size, typical of family, young David grew to be six feet four to six inches, depending on which authority one accepts.

Information and community service? As Frank MacKinnon has reported, Alexander Laird had

. . . become one of the most successful farmers in Queen's County. As an official of the Royal Agricultural Society of Prince Edward Island, he did much to further the development of agriculture. As a member of the local legislature, he gave sixteen years of service to active politics, during which he was a member of the government. He was one of the participants in the long struggle for responsible government in the province.[7]

There can be no doubt that Alexander Laird was a Man of Standing, as his son David was to become after him. But having a father of such exalted status did not make life any easier for young Davie as a boy; rather the contrary. If Alexander had become a successful farmer, it was as a result of hard work, his own, his wife's, his sturdy sons' and daughters'.

No doubt at an early age David Laird learned the essential skills of an early-nineteenth century farmer: to handle the shovel, the fork, the axe, the cradle, that sophisticated scythe, the plough and harrow, the hammer, saw, auger, and plane, to milk cows, butcher hogs, drive horses — in those long-ago days, horsepower was equine, not mechanical, and sometimes human, too — with minor assistance from wind and water. David was to receive much more formal education than most of his classmates, but even he was probably temporarily withdrawn from school during the busy seasons of seeding and harvest.

Staunch Presbyterians that the Lairds were, they inculcated in their progency such eminently Presbyterian virtues as thrift, hard work, punctuality, sobriety, generosity, particularly to the needy and afflicted, chastity, service to one's fellow man, piety. Especially piety. Surely Laird *paterfamilias* asked a blessing on every meal, held family prayers and read from the Good Book to wife, children and hired help every night, and attended kirk each Sunday without fail.

No doubt each of the Laird children was confirmed — accepted into full church membership — when he or she reached the age of understanding, accepted as being about thirteen years or so. But such status was conferred only after what must have been a rather frightening *viva voce* examination. One may imagine the nervousness of a young teen-ager facing a formidable array consisting of the minister and the elders, each of the latter in his 'Sunday-best' black serge suit, white, high-collared shirt, and stock, ancestor of today's four-in-hand tie. Perhaps for such a solemn occasion the minister even wore his Geneva gown. Nor were the questions easy. What is the nature of God? He is omnipotent, omniscient, and omnipresent — whatever those long words mean. What is the purpose of mankind? To glorify God and enjoy him forever. What is meant by predestination? redemption? salvation? grace? and so on. Obviously a mere knowledge of the Ten Commandments and the Lord's Prayer were not enough to make a Presbyterian.

Let it not be supposed, however, that such an austere home as the Laird's was an unhappy one. In an age when typhoid, cholera, small pox, appendicitis, puerpal fever, consumption exacted a yearly and sometimes fearful toll, the Angel of Death passed by the Laird family, at least until all the off-spring had left childhood.

D.C. Harvey, writing about young David, has affirmed, "As a boy he used to lie before the old-fashioned fireplace, his eyes glued to a book, pondering theproblems of life and duty, whilst the strict atmosphere of his Scottish home tended to develop in him a sensitive conscience and a somewhat narrow faith."[8] One may be excused for wondering whether Harvey's Lincolnesque portrayal is strictly factual or merely conjectural.

Certainly the pious atmosphere in the Laird home did not surfeit the off-spring with religion. The oldest, Robert, entered the Christian ministry, and it is from his daughter Bess that we are indebted for a rare glimpse of the young David. Writing to her brother, she stated that her father ". . . loved Uncle David with the real love of an older brother; was proud of him with the real pride of an elder brother thought him superior etc. helped him all possible."[9]

Robert was not the only one to consider a career in the ministry. When David had gone as far as the limited resources of the Island permitted, he enrolled in the Presbyterian Theological Seminary near Truro,

Nova Scotia. His still-extant lecture notes or revisions thereof show him to have been a most careful and conscientious student. The notebook bears the date Sept. 30, 1856, indicating that he was in attendance at that time, and his Ticket to the Humanity Class verifies his attendance from March to September, 1857. Family tradition has it that he spent only one year at the Seminary before 1859, although his residence may have been longer. Although he was never ordained, he gave long, perhaps life-long service to his church as an elder. Instead of the ministry, he turned to journalism and politics, and at the age of twenty-six a new chapter of his life opened before him.

But in the life of young David Laird there remains a mystery. If he began school at the age of seven or even nine years of age, and spent a dozen years in his education, there are several years between school and seminary that are unaccounted for. Did he stay home and help his father on the farm? With three older brothers, it hardly seems likely that his assistance was needed there. Did he, perchance, teach school, as many a young person has done to finance his further education? One family tradition so states. If so, where? Certainly not at New Glasgow. A letter from the Public Archivist, Prince Edward Island, states in part:

> I searched the Reports of the School Visitor for the years 1850-1859 but failed to note any reference to one David Laird. I did note a Robert Laird who taught school at New Glasgow 1851-1852. I imagine that it was with Robert that the suggestion arose.[10]

References

1. David H. Laird, "Family of Alexander Laird of New Glasgow, Prince Edward Island" (unpublished typescript), pp. 9-10.

2. Samuel Johnson in John Bartlett's *Familiar Quotations* (eleventh edition), p.234.

3. Lewis R. Fischer, "The Shipping Industry in Nineteenth Century Prince Edward Island: A Brief History," *The Island Magazine,* v.1, no. 4, p.17.

4. David L. Mathieson to John W. Chalmers, 8 July 1980.

5. Quoted by D.H. Laird, *op. cit.,* p.8.

6. John K. Galbraith, *The Scotch,* pp.52-56.

7. Frank MacKinnon, "David Laird of Prince Edward Island," *The Dalhousie Review,* v.26, no. 4, p.405.

8. D.C. Harvey, "David Laird The Man Whose Tongue is not Forked," *The Grain Growers' Guide,* 20 August 1919.

9. Bess Laird to David H. Laird, undated, c. 1917.

10. Nicolas de Jong, Provincial Archivist, P.E.I., to John W. Chalmers, 4 February 1980.

2

Publisher
of the Protestant

Upon graduation from the theological college at Truro, Nova Scotia (actually at near-by West River), Laird returned to the Island, but not to new Glasgow. Instead, he became editor and publisher in Charlottetown of the paper that was ultimately to become the *Patriot.* An unsigned and undated family record gives the origin of this newspaper as follows:

> On 20th July 1823 Jas. D. Haszard printed the "P.E. Island Registrar." In August 1830 he changed the name to "Royal Gazette" in 1851 he called it "The Gazette" this was continued by his son George T. Haszard in 1853 under the ownership of Haszard and Owen until it merged into the "Protestant Christian Witness" and afterwards called 'The Protestant Evangelical Witness." This last was published and edited by David Laird being the predecessor of the Weekly Patriot of today — 1864-1882 — made semi-weekly 1867-1882 then daily and Liberal organ to the present time.[1]

The source of this quotation is an old school scribbler, hand-written in pencil, probably during the first or second decade of this century. As the unknown author was no doubt drawing on his own memory and perhaps family tradition, sources notoriously fallible, one must regard this account with some scepticism. For example, this chronicler is not quite exact with respect to names. *The Gazette* was more properly called *Haszard's Gazette,* and it was the *Protector* (not *Protestant*) *and Christian Witness,* that name being adopted about the end of February, 1857.

In this late twentieth century era, metropolitan newspapers generally pride themselves as being independent in party politics, supporting now one party, now another on the basis of their current policies and personalities. They refuse to give unswerving and unquestioning loyalty to any, even if they may tend to lean in one direction or another. (Small weeklies, of course, are carefully neutral on all political issues.) But in the nineteenth century, papers were frankly and unavowedly Liberal or Conservative, in fair political times and foul, in prosperity and adversity. Indeed, many organs were established (or taken over) to serve as mouthpieces of political organizations. Although David Laird was never doctrinaire in his politics — he was an Islander before he was a Liberal — considering his new profession and his family background, it is unsurprising that he and his paper were soon involved in the public and controversial issues which exercised the Islanders during the 1850's and 1860's.

His father, Alexander Laird, that Man of Standing, had been elected on the Reform ticket to the Legislative Assembly as early as 1850. George Coles, the party leader, was his running mate in the two-member constituency of the First District of Queen's County. Coles was also successful in his candidature. Both men lost their seats with the defeat of the government in 1853, but were returned in the election of the following year. Until 1855 Alexander Laird was a loyal supporter of the Liberal government, by which time he was beginning to differ with his colleagues on the land question, of which more anon. By 1855 his alienation from his former colleagues was complete, and he campaigned in Queen's Second District. He was elected, as were enough other Tories to form the government, and the following year he entered the Cabinet. Although his tenure therein lasted only four years — perhaps even the Conservatives found him too independent-minded — he maintained his allegiance to them until his retirement from politics in 1866.

Nor was he the only Laird to be actively engaged in provincial politics.

> It may be noted that besides D. Laird Honorable Alexander Laird had another son who took an active interest in the public affairs of the Island.
>
> Hon. Alexander Laird represented Bedeque District in both the House of Assembly and Legislative Council for many years. His opinions were sought by the leading men on all important questions and were followed in many cases.
>
> Wm. Laird M.L.A. represented the 2nd District of Queen's County, was a powerful debater and did just love to have a political fight and besides being a fluent Speaker he had a good grip of events in the political field.[2]

Obviously not only was Alexander, Sr., a Man of Standing; his sons also had no trouble in reaching that exalted rank. Beside those mentioned above, another brother who did so was the Rev. Robert Laird, the oldest son, who became an ordained Presbyterian minister — to what more respectable position could one aspire?

As Canada stumbles and lurches towards the twenty-first century, the nation's political pundits seem primarily concerned with such issues as inflation, unemployment, and energy, although other issues are also important: separatism, immigration, railways, capital punishment, etc. On the Island in the 1850's and 1860's, the vital concerns were somewhat different: the land problem, the Bible question, and a little later, railways and confederation. And of course the struggle for responsible government. By the time David Laird returned to Prince Edward Island, that battle had been fought and won, a battle in which Alexander Laird, Sr., had played an honorable part. But the land question, to which summary reference has been made, was a very live issue.

It was really one which had its roots deep in Island history, and was really one of absentee landlordism.

The proprietorship of Prince Edward Island, one of the most productive portions of Canada, had passed through several proprietorial phases during the French regime under the name of "Ile St. Jean.". It had partially been colonized by the French and was granted as a seignory to Sieur Doublet, a French Naval officer. After the Peace of Utrecht in 1715 it was to some extent colonized by settlers from Cape Breton. It was, however, taken by the British in 1745 and afterwards restored to France. It was finally annexed to Britain in 1758. Its climate, milder than that of the mainland, and its remarkable fertility becoming known in Britain, it was disposed of piecemeal in a remarkable manner to British noblemen and others as political patronage.

These absentee landlords were supposed to do a certain amount of colonization but with only one exception they fell down on the job. The one exception was the Earl of Selkirk . . .

But even the difficulties inherent in absentee landlordism did not prevent settlement on the Island but the farmers soon found out that they were in bondage to the landlords in England, few of whom had ever seen the country. A great deal of the fruits of their toil went overseas and it was almost impossible for a farmer to acquire a clear title to his land.

When still a young man David Laird headed an agitation to get rid of this evil. Week in and week out he attacked the system in his newspaper and after several years agitation had the satisfaction of knowing that he had been chiefly responsible for striking the fetters of absentee land owners from the limbs of the farmers of the island. The system was changed and almost every farmer was placed in a position to become the owner in fee simple of his own acres.[3]

It must not be supposed, however, that David Laird was the leading figure in the struggle of the Island's farmers to obtain title to their holdings. That struggle had begun some years before he had returned from Truro, when in 1854 the Liberal government had passed a land purchase act.

When Laird came to Charlottetown in 1859, he found himself in confrontation with William Pope, Laird, son of a prominent Reformer (albeit eventually a sadly disillusioned one) and an agriculturalist, naturally sympathized with the debt-ridden tenant farmers. Pope, son of a shipbuilder, himself a lawyer, land agent, journalist, and politician, educated at Inner Temple, London, was a member of the local elite, the Island equivalent of Upper Canada's Family Compact. As such he was a defender of the property rights of the landlords, as well as agent of a number of them — something he had in common with both his father Joseph Pope and his father-in-law, Theophilus Des Brisay. But Des Brisay and his son-in-law, staunch though they may have been in their belief regarding the sacredness of property rights, were not above using their positions and influence for dubious private gain. Des Brisay, agent of one of the landlords named Charles Worrell, eager to dispose of his debt-encumbered and distant estate comprising five townships — 81,303 acres, sold it for £14,000 to Pope and his backers, who included the latter's father, Des Brisay himself, and one G.E. Morton. Pope immediately resold the property to the government for £24,100. In addition, Des Brisay allegedly received as commission or finder's fee an additional £1,700 from Worrell.

"The Liberals had been persuaded to pay what they knew to be an exorbitant price by Pope's thinly veiled threats to take the tenantry on his new estate to court for payment of arrears in rent . . . and such a proceeding would have caused riots." The memory of three deaths during the turbulent 1847 election was too fresh for the government to risk another such civil disturbance. "In fact, however, Worrell was only one of the absentee landlords, and their tenants' fight for ownership was to continue for many years. As late as 1865 the newly-formed Tenants' League, whose members were pledged to refuse payment of rents, created such a disturbance in Queen's County that the acting lieutenant-governor sent to Halifax for a force of soldiers, two companies, to restore order, action which gained the approval of the Imperial government and most of the Island's press.

Indeed, settlement of the land question was to remain a chronic problem for many years after the threatened up-rising of 1865, and refusal of Canada to consider it in discussions leading to Confederation was one reason why Prince Edward Island did not enter the union until 1873. The problem was not resolved by the purchase on the part of the Island government and its resale of the English-owned Island estates until Laird had left Island politics for the federal field.

For the citizens of British North America, the 1800's contained not just one *annus mirabilis* but many marvelous years. During the century they gained control of their own governments, fought off actual or threatened foreign invasions, cobbled together the new country of Canada. From 1867 to 1871, three and one-half million people expanded this country from a narrow domain along the St. Lawrence watershed, squeezed between the

United States to the south and Rupert's Land on the north and west, to a Dominion stretching *A mari usque ad mare* — from sea to sea — not only from the Atlantic to the Pacific but also to the Arctic. In four short years this tiny nation a-borning had become seised of half a continent. A like accomplishment, albeit under different circumstances, had taken the Americans almost a century.

But let it never be thought that these grand deeds were achieved without toil and agony, without mistrust and bitterness, without animosity and worse, without confrontations between whites and natives, between Protestants and Roman Catholics, between anglophones and francophones.

For the first thirty or forty years of the nineteenth century, an uneasy *modus operandi* prevailed, more or less, between the two great branches of the Christian church. But as the colonial governments gradually and reluctantly began to recognize their obligations to education, the rift between the two widened. To oversimplify, the Catholic view is that primary responsibility for the education of their children is that of their parents, their duty, if they are members of the Church of Rome, to have their off-spring educated in schools under the direction of that church, i.e. the hierarchy, if such schools are feasible. For the objective of the school is that of the church itself, to make children into good Christians and good Catholics. The opposed Protestant view, though less extreme, was that while the schools should follow the teachings of the Prince of Peace, all public schools, i.e. those publicly supported, should have as their primary objective the creation of good citizens, and therefore should be non-sectarian and under control of the government. However, on the Island in the 1850's the Roman Catholic Church stood strongly behind the principle of non-sectarian schools as the only one appropriate to a colony of diverse religious denominations.

The incident of active hostility between Protestants and Roman Catholics to which reference has already been made

> . . . occurred on 1 March 1847 at a byelection in Belfast, in southeastern Queen's County where a pitched battle took place between several hundred Scottish Protestants and Irish Roman Catholics armed with cudgels. At least three men died, scores were injured, the colony was shocked, and it never happened again.[5]

In 1859, when Laird returned to the Island, its population was between 71,496 (1855) and 80,857 (1861).

> In religion, the Island was approximately 55 percent Protestant, and among the Protestants . . . Presbyterians constituted a steady 58 percent . . . Among Island Protestants who were not Presbyterians . . . about another third were Anglican, another third were Wesleyan, and

the remaining third belonged to the Baptist or Bible Christian churches, the latter an off-shoot of the Wesleyan Church. Probably more than one-half the Roman Catholic population were Irish . . .[6]

In short, the Island's population would be:

	Per cent
Roman Catholic	45
Presbyterian	32
Anglican) Wesleyan) Baptist) or Bible Christian	23 one-third each
	100%

The "Bible question" was in the beginning really a non-issue.

"A serious and most unaccountable misunderstanding," was what Edward Whelan, the leading Roman Catholic Liberal, in early 1857 described as the root of the Bible question in Prince Edward Island. There was indeed a misunderstanding, but after it had been cleared up the conflict remained, and with the Bible question began a new era in the history of the colony. For the next two decades religion and politics would provide the primary motive power in Island politics.[7]

The Bible question began with the official opening of the province's Normal School on 1 October 1856, when John M. Stark, a Scottish educator whose recommendation was responsible for the establishment of the institution, urged that its program include daily reading and study of the Bible, excluding sectarian and controversial material. Recognizing an explosive political issue when they saw one, the province's Board of Education decreed that no books other than those on the approved list could be used at the Normal School. However, Roman Catholic Bishop Bernard D. MacDonald, reading a report of Stark's address and unaware of the Board's action, became alarmed that non-sectarian and uncontroversial religious material would in fact be Protestant propaganda and demanded that no religious teaching be permitted in the province's mixed, i.e., public and secular schools, adding that Catholics would be satisfied with nothing less.

The Protestants were equally alarmed. During the 1830's and later, when textbooks were scarce, the Bible and even the Shorter Catechism were frequently the only reading materials available in the schools. With growing abundance, or at least adequacy of supply of readers, these Good Books tended to be used less and less. Now the staunch Presbyterians and other Protestants saw the threat of their total removal from the common schools. What the Board of Education could ordain for the Normal Schools it could also do for other public educational institutions.

Protestant-Catholic animosities rapidly escalated from specifically educational to generally religious matters, and from there to politics. By and large, the Roman Catholics supported the Liberals, while the Conservatives drew their following from the Protestants. But religion was not the only political issue; another was the land question, which attracted many of the Non-Conformists to the Liberal banner.

David Laird, on his return to the Island, immediately entered the fray, with the *Protestant and Evangelical Witness* as his sword.

Strongly supported by the Presbyteries of the Island, the new paper assured that the Bible issue would not be forgotten. Its opening editorial promised "to give considerable space to articles . . . exposing the errors and noting the wiles and workings of popery."[8]

In 1859, the Legislature amended the *Education Act* to authorize (but not require) Bible reading in all schools, albeit without comment, thus meeting the wishes of the Protestants, but exempting the attendance during the exercise children of those parents who so wished, thus satisfying the Roman Catholics. As Laird's paper reported:

The introduction of the Bible, to be read . . . in all the public schools of this Island, of every grade, receiving support from the public Treasury, is hereby authorized, and the teachers are hereby required to open the school on each school-day, with the reading of the sacred Scriptures by those children whose parents or guardians desire it, without comment, explanation or remark thereupon by the Teacher; but no children shall be required to attend during such reading aforesaid, unless desired by their parents or guardians.[9]

Thus the Bible question was settled, but the religious controversy raged on. One aspect of it concerned the Prince of Wales College, secular and government-supported, which was founded in 1860, replacing the Central Academy. No provision was made for any kind of religious instruction in this new institution. However, it was not the only such post-elementary body on the Island; the Roman Catholics erected their own St. Dunstan's College (later University). Since through taxes they supported Prince of Wales, they felt that their college should also receive assistance from the public purse. But such a concession the Protestants adamantly refused to countenance. After all, the Roman Catholics were welcome to attend Prince of Wales.

From mid-July, 1861, for the next eighteen months, Catholic doctrines and "Catholic Ascendancy" became constant fare for the Protestant press. Ian Ross Robertson notes the role of Laird in the imbroglio.

> David Laird, editor of the *Protestant,* was not to be outdone. In the midst of the dispute over the temporal power of the Papacy, he had declared his belief that "the Rector of St. Dunstan's College venerates the Pope as God" . . . Laird had an obvious relish for controversies which provided him with the opportunity to make liberal use of terms like "Popery" and "Romanism." Many years later William Pope would describe him as being "very influential among the Scotch Presbyterians . . . narrow-minded . . . however a clever, hard-headed fellow, intellectually of the stamp of [Alexander] Mackenzie." But the complimentary part of this description did not fit Laird in the early 1860s, when his editorials were distinguished more by bombast than by logic or artistry . . . In any event, with characteristic verve he initiated a lengthy public dispute by his editorial of 30 November, concerning the *Index Prohibitory.* The article opened with the statement that "There is no charge more confidently preferred against the Roman Catholic Church than that she has exerted her influence to repress freedom of thought, and the expression of private opinion." Laird went on to discuss the history and contents of the Index Librorum Prohibitorum, and taunted Saint Dunstan's College and the Catholic Young Men's Literary Institute with the existence of these limitations upon their libraries . . . Through December 1861 and the first half of 1862, Laird continued to write editorials in support of his views, and accepted the assistance of abusive anonymous correspondents.[10]

So the battle raged until about 1865, when the fires of religious controversy tended to die down. But they were banked, not extinguished. Thereafter, Roman Catholics and Protestants tended to view each other with a rather vigilant wariness, and as Katherine Hughes notes, "After this period there were fewer places where Islanders of different religious persuasions could meet on a voluntary basis for common objectives.".[11] Perhaps to signify a change in editorial direction, Laird changed the name of his paper to *The Patriot.*

About a century later, rumor has it that a slight tremor shook the Island. It is reputed, but without confirmation, to have been caused by a mass turning over in their graves of Protestants and Roman Catholics when St. Dunstan's and Prince of Wales were united to form the University of Prince Edward Island.

Not all of David Laird's Island activities were devoted to journalism. It seems that no sooner had he settled in Charlottetown than he found himself an elder and a trustee of the kirk that later was to be known as Mount Zion Presbyterian Church; he also taught Sunday School there. Nor were his extra-vocational activities confined to the religious field. He was soon a member of the city council, of the Board of Education, and of the Board of Governors of Prince of Wales College.

But perhaps the most interesting and least documented phase of his life during this era was his courtship of a daughter of the Postmaster-General for the colony. Laird was thirty-one when he married, certainly more mature than more bridegrooms of that day or this. Still, he had not really begun his career as editor and publisher until he was twenty-six. And since his bride's parental home was in Charlottetown, he probably had not met her until he moved to that city. Rather more surprising is the fact that Louisa also was thirty-one. How had she managed to remain single in an age and place where marriageable females were in chronically short supply?

Family tradition has it that her father opposed her marriage to David Laird. Perhaps he regarded her suitor, although already or rapidly becoming a Man of Standing, as not quite high enough in status to be a suitable mate for a scion of the elite. Possible Owen was convinced that journalism was not quite respectable enough a vocation for the son-in-law of the Honorable Thomas. And it may be that family tradition is fallible in holding that Louisa would not go against her father's wishes, marrying David only after Owen had died, even though her mother approved of Louisa's choice. The family tradition is supported by an entry in a Laird family Bible which identifies Louisa as a daughter of the *late* Thomas Owen.

Katherine Hughes, writing in 1906 and probably not from first-hand knowledge, describes Mrs. Laird as

> . . . a charming young woman who had been a favourite in the gay colonial-English society of grey old Charlottetown. Petite, pretty, with the radiant charm of womanhood that is at once cheerful and sympathetic, offering a supplementing contrast of manner and appearance to the tall, serious-faced statesman. Mrs. Laird at Battleford dispensed Western hospitality in the same delightful manner that characterized her home life and social entertainments in later years.[12]

Hughes was surely exercising literary licence in describing Louisa as young, since she was well into her forties and had borne all of her six children. She died in 1895, nineteen years before her husband.

References

1. Family record in possession of Ms. Elizabeth Laird, grand-daughter of David Laird.

2. *Ibid.*

3. "Honorable David Laird," photocopy of unsigned, undated typescript in Saskatchewan Archives Board, Regina.

4. Ian Ross Robertson, "Pope, William Henry" in Marc La Terreur, *Dictionary of Canadian Biography,* v. X, pp. 593.

5. _____, "The Bible Question in Prince Edward Island from 1856 to 1860," *Acadiensis,* v. V, no. 2 (Spring 1976), p.4.

6. *Ibid.*

7. *Ibid.,* p.3.

8. *Ibid.,* p.21.

9. *Ibid.,* p.22.

10. _____, "Party Politics and Religious controversialism in Prince Edward Island from 1860 to 1863," *Acadiensis,* v. VII, no. 2 (Spring 1978), pp.41-2.

11. Katherine Hughes, "Canadian Celebrities: Honourable David Laird," *Canadian Magazine,* v. 27, no. 5 (September 1906), p.402.

3

Publisher and Politican

When David Laird married his Louisa in 1864, he no doubt realized that life would never again be the same, although, like other bridegrooms, he was to find that marriage held many surprises and some disappointments. That he also realized that the 1864-1865 period represented a definite if not abrupt turning point in his career is improbable. Yet such indeed was the case.

To a great extent, Laird was always a political creature. His father and one of his brothers had been or became members of the colony's House of Assembly, and David himself served on such public bodies as the Board of Education and the city council. Yet as a newspaper editor, to a large extent he stood on the sidelines, commenting on the important issues of the day, perhaps influencing their resolution, perhaps, at first unwittingly, serving as tool, cat's-paw, or mouthpiece of the elected politicians. At least, so Ian Ross Robertson suggests, in reference to William Henry Pope's anti-Catholic crusade, "Laird was something of a pawn in Pope's game, a fact which he later came to resent deeply."[1]

At length, perhaps slowly, realization must have come to Laird that though newspaper editors may have influence, politicians, at least elected ones, have power. It is they who are where the action is; it is in the realm of politics that the levers of power are manipulated.

When Laird first became editor of the *Protestant and Evangelical Witness,* the liveliest political confrontations were basically religious, and joyfully the young journalist waded into the fray. But by 1864 the Roman Catholic-Protestant battles were moderating into brief skirmishes which eventually gave way to a wary and (verbally) armed truce. As editor of a religious paper, Laird could look forward to reporting on foreign missions, Bible society activities, temperance crusades, and presbytery meetings, a prospect which he must have regarded unenthusiastically. Devoted to his church which he may have been (and was), secular politics promised more excitement. In 1864, Charlottetown was the locale of the historic Maritime

21

Conference, called to consider the organic union or confederation of New Brunswick, Nova Scotia, Prince Edward Island, and Newfoundland. To this gathering came uninvited guests from Canada. If they didn't filch the silverware, they stole the show with their proposal for a union of all of British North America. Here was a political issue on a grand scale. As the Bard might have written:

> To join, or not to join, that is the question.
> Whether 'tis nobler in the mind to suffer
> The slings and arrows of outrageous fortune,
> Or to take arms against a sea of troubles
> And by Confederation end them?

Nearly a decade was to pass before the Islanders gave their final answer to this question. Eagerly Laird girded his loins for the struggle and rode into battle. His paper became the *Patriot,* no longer primarily Protestant but, as his grand-daughter has indicated, a Liberal organ[2] — and for a number of reasons the Liberals were opposed to the Conservative dream of one nation from sea to sea, or at least to certain aspects of that vision.

Not that they were opposed in principle — agreement in principle is perhaps the biggest cop-out since the days of Machiavelli. Naturally, the Islanders wanted the best possible deal they could get. And of course their colony (like each of the others in its way) was unique, was beset by its own special problems. For one thing, there was the Island's physical isolation. How could it benefit from Confederation or contribute to the common weal, separated as it was from the mainland? What did the new federal organization intend to do about that? And what about absentee landlordism, that canker which had so long festered in the Garden of the Gulf? And, later, railroads? Surely Canada did not propose to tax Islanders to help pay for the Pacific railroad when not a tie or a rail would be laid on the Island's red soil!

If Laird's action in establishing the *Patriot* indicated a growing impatience with remaining on the sidelines of provincial politics, one may wonder why he waited until 1867 to enter the lists. No doubt he could have secured a nomination at the time of the 1863 election, in which the Conservatives (all Protestants) captured eighteen seats to the Libertals' (all Roman Catholics) twelve. Thus the Tories repeated their 1859 triumph, which had followed eight years of Liberal rule. Perhaps David Laird wished to avoid a legislative confrontation with his father, who was now arrayed with the Conservatives. In any event, only after Alexander Laird, Sr., retired from politics did David enter the arena, becoming a candidate in the 1867 election. However, he suffered defeat at the hands of the Honorable B. Davis, and the Conservatives remained victorious. Three years later, young Laird was again a contestant in a byelection, this time to lose to one

Donald Cameron — all Camerons name at least one son Donald — on a technicality. Some poll clerks had not signed their official declarations. Nevertheless, Laird's prospects were brightening, as he secured a majority of the votes.

Still, during those early and middle 1860's, the would-be politician had other interests. Mention has been made of his marriage to Louisa Owen, the ceremony taking place at Georgetown on 30 June 1864, with the Rev. David Fitzgerald, rector of St. Paul's, officiating. David and Louisa's first son arrived nine months and ten days later; five other children followed in the next nine and one-half years. The complete roster of the Laird family was:

> David Rennie, born 9 April 1865
> Mary Alice, born 7 February 1867
> Arthur Gordon, born 17 December 1868
> William Charles, born 8 November 1870
> James Harold, born 8 August 1872
> Fanny Louise, born 18 November 1874

David Laird, the Liberal, was not in the House of Assembly during 1870, but the Honourable Alexander, the Conservative, occupied a seat on the Government side. Incidentally, contrary to usual British parliamentary practice, the Government sat on Mr. Speaker's left, the Loyal Opposition on his right. The reason was that the fireplace which heated the small chamber was on the Speaker's left, and surely it was one of the perks of office for the incumbents to have their backsides properly warmed.

Family papers and available published sources alike are silent as to whether political differences affected family ties between the Laird brothers. Of course, the Lairds were always Islanders before they were doctrinaire party men. Certainly Alexander was active in support of the Government's policies (not all of which David opposed), as a few extracts from his speeches, summarized in the *Parliamentary Reporter,* indicate:

> He considered it was the duty of members of the Executive to ask the so-called all-powerful government of the Dominion what it could do to aid us in obtaining a redress of our grievances. It was admitted on all sides that we had been wronged by Britain with respect to our lands, and were this government, this noble government of Canada, to give some tangible proof that they had an irresistable influence with the Imperial authorities, it would go a great way to remove his objections to confederation.[3]
>
> Let the home government redress our grievances, and then we would be able to enter confederation on something like equal terms with the other Provinces. But even then, he would like to see our rights as a local gov-

ernment placed on a more substantial basis than the will of a parliamentary majority at Ottawa.[4]

He (Mr. L.) believed that it was wrong for the government to grant money for any denominational object, as long as the public funds were collected from people of various religious persuasion; and he contended that the state might just as properly be called to pay clergymen as to educate them. He might go further and say that, in his opinion, it was not right to vote money for any school, college, or institution of this kind, which was not under government control. If public money was granted to denominational colleges, it ought to be divided equally between the different churches, which was almost impossible. He, however, did not believe in granting money to any denominational institution; the main thing which government had to look to was to see that all within its bounds obtained a good common school education, so that they could read the Book of books and learn their duty for themselves.[5]

As to grants to colleges, he held to the principle that the Government was responsible for the expenditure of the public money, and to grant money otherwise than to institutions under their control would be a violation of the duty and functions of a government. The Prince of Wales College was a government institution, that of St. Dunstan's was, he believed, denominational. With respect to the Catholic schools in this City, he would only say that if parents preferred to send their children to private schools, they ought to be prepared, also, to enjoy the luxury of paying those who taught them. It would be utterly impossible for the state to support two distinct systems. One must give place to the other; and if the denominational was introduced it would soon destroy the other, and the result would be that the legislature would have to withhold the grant for education altogether. This he hoped would never happen, as he held it to be the duty of the Government to see that every child in the Colony had an opportunity to obtain a good education.[6]

The hon. member (Mr. Green) said the Dominion was sparsely populated, and they had to be heavily taxed to purchase the Red River territory, and he thought it a legitimate question to ask what benefit Red River territory would be to us. If it was the country it was represented to be, we should not be able to export anything to it. We were asked to join a country and submit to taxation to conquer a province that was united to them without their consent, and to be governed by men who were unfit to rule any country.[7]

He would ask was it any harm to request the Dominion Parliament to make the Land Question of this Island their own? And if they succeeded in settling it there would be great reaction in the feelings of the people of this Island towards them. They said they would settle the question, and the government told them to do so. It was agreed as an argument in favor of confederation that the Dominion Government had so much more power with the British Parliament than we had, and it was deemed advisable to test their power. The result proved that they had no more power than ourselves to settle this long existing grievance. He (Mr. L.)

would challenge any hon. member to put his finger on any passage in the Minute of Council to prove that the government pledged themselves to accept confederation, even had the Dominion Government settled the Land Question.[8]

Although in 1870 David Laird suffered his second defeat at the polls, the following year opportunity again knocked at his door. The Conservatives under Premier J.C. Pope had determined that the Island should have its own railway, and appointed James Duncan as commissioner (or minister). Until fifty years or so ago it was the law that an elected member of a Canadian legislative body appointed to a post carrying an emolument additional to his member's stipend had to resign his seat and seek a new mandate from his constituents. Therefore Duncan's appointment necessitated his resignation and a byelection. Often such a byelection was filled by acclamation, but not this time. Many citizens had serious doubts (well founded as later events were to demonstrate) about the Island's capacity to finance such an undertaking. On 6 July 1871 Laird contested the seat and won, joining the Opposition Liberals under R.P. Haythorne. Despite the defeat of his railway commissioner and growing opposition to the railway itself, Pope persisted in going ahead with the project. In the face of vociferous Opposition demands that the Government either resign or call a special session of the Legislature, Pope would do neither until the following 6 March. Immediately, charges of corruption were laid against his regime.

> It appeared that a "railway ring" had developed, composed of lobbyists and influential politicians who vied with one another in offering bribes to members in return for assurances that the recipients would exert their influence to have the railway pass through certain settlements. The affair became the subject of fierce debate in the legislature when William Hooper, member for Morell, asserted that he had been offered $1,000 by Caleb Carleton of Souris if he would vote for a branch line to the eastern end of the island. Carleton, when summoned to the bar of the house, freely admitted that he had offered the money to Hooper, for he knew "parties to the eastward that would subscribe liberally and help to shove along the branches." Though it was not proved that the government had been implicated in the "railway ring," Pope and his colleagues found that they had lost the confidence of the electors and were defeated by the Liberals under the Honourable R.P. Haythorne.[9]

Journalists are prone to decry the inappropriate behavior, the rudeness of shouting, even of profanities and obscenities which occasionally interrupt the proceedings of our esteemed legislators and mar the tranquility and dignity of their Houses. Yet in those legislative bodies modelled after the Mother of Parliaments at Westminster, such turbulence has a long if not honored history. Let it not be forgotten that the facing Government and Opposition front benches in the British Commons were placed more than two sword-lengths apart so that enraged parliamentarians could not readily have at each other before the Sergeant-at-Arms could intervene with the mace, symbolic relic of a once highly-functional weapon. That unseemly parliamentary conduct occurred during the "Six Day Session" is indicated by the following material from the Laird family papers:

> The first day the Government members pleaded for mercy while Laird Davies and Reilly simply castigated them. They could do nothing and as the Patriot said, "There they sat in their places, unable to carry a single motion or do anything but obstruct the business for which they had called the Legislature together." One member was given $1,000 to vote for the Government — he took it and laid it on the clerk's desk before all the members and then the fat was in the fire. Pope then gave up. Laird was the man they were after as the following extract will show.

<u>Police Court</u>

March 13th, 1872

> Before Mayor Desbrisey The Queen on the prosecution of David Laird vs. Pat R Bowers. Assault and Battery on the floor of the House of Assembly rooms on Monday last the 11th March last. David Laird sworn. Pat R Bowers addressed the Court. Convicted and fined $10 with costs, or in default of payment to be imprisoned one callendar (*sic*) month.

March 14th

> Before Councillors Dawson and Hooper. David Laird vs. Jacob Carvell. Assault and Battery — Spitting in the face an offensive substance. In the Policy Court the Defendant Convicted and fined $32.44 with costs or two months in the Common jail.

> Of the above Mr. Laird said in the Patriot "Elsewhere we publish two convictions in the Police Court. We do not wish to enter into the particulars further than to say there was no provocation on our part in either case. The assaults and attacks now made upon him by his friends and supporters of the Government show that they have much to lose and the people much to gain by a change of rulers."[10]

A few days after the police court action, Laird made his appeal to his constituents, all of them male, of course.

<u>To the Free and Independent Electors of the Fourth</u>

<u>District of Queen's County</u>

Gentlemen: — As a general election has been forced upon the

country, not on account of any dead-lock between political parties but at the will of a Government which forfeited the confidence of the people's representatives, you are now called upon to choose two representatives for the House of Assembly. You lately did me the high honor to elect me as one of your representatives; and fully believing that your principles are unchanged, I again offer myself as a candidate for your suffrage.

When last before you, I declared my uncompromising opposition to the present Government; and subsequent events have only confirmed me in the opinion that they are undeserving of the confidence of the people. Lobbying and bribery were unknown amongst us until the advent of the Coalition party to power; and as it has been proved that their supporters employed these unworthy means to secure them a majority at the late short session, it is to be hoped that the constituencies from East Point to West Cape will unmistakably set the seal of their disapprobation both upon the actors in and the abettors of such disgraceful attempts to influence Legislation in this Colony.

For discharging what I considered my duty to you and to my native country, vile abuse was heaped upon me, in common with other leading men of the Opposition, within the House, by members of the Government; and, since its prorogation gross Insult has been levelled at me by some of their outside supporters; but neither the one nor the other shall deter me from giving free expression of my opinions, and exposing favoritism, mismanagement, and fraud in the conduct of public affairs.

It shall be my constant effort, if you honor me with you confidence, to secure for your District a fair share of public moneys for local improvements. Other parts of the Island are being intersected by a Railway, and you are in justice entitled to some equivalent expediture of the funds to which you contribute equally with your fellow Colonists.

As the weather and the state of the roads at this season of the year are uncertain, I cannot promise myself the pleasure of meeting many of you before Nomination Day; but though I may not be able to overtake a complete canvass of the District, I yet feel confident that should you be called to the polls you will cheerfully extend me a still more liberal support than which you so nobly accorded me last summer.

I am, Gentlemen, yours &c.,

DAVID LAIRD

Ch'town, March 16, 1872 — sp.[11]

Laird was re-elected as one of the victorious Liberals, and became a member of Haythorne's Executive Council.

Politics, of course, is a serious business, but it does have its lighter moments, one of which is related by J.H. Fletcher, editor of *The Island Argus* from 1869 to 1882. It and the *Patriot* owned adjacent edifices, and a power press on which both papers were printed. As Fletcher relates:

I remember an episode that occurred when we were printing our papers on the same press from adjoining buildings. It was this: I was presenting the readers of The Argus with a series of political portraits, and in touching on Mr. Laird, who was then a member of the House of Assembly, I said that some people accused Mr. Laird of not being over-particular in the observance of the Seventh Commandment; I should have said the Ninth, which condemns the habit of bearing false witness against one's neighbour. But the paper went to press in that way. Mr. Laird, luckily, happened to be in the press room at the time, and picking up The Argus began to read his "portrait." "Why," he exclaimed, "What is this he has said about me?"

Then he rushed in to where I was, and demanded; "What do you mean by saying that I violate the Seventh Commandment?" I saw he was both excited and indignant, and replied; "Mr. Laird, they do say that you sometimes bear false witness against your political opponents." "Well," he said with a roar that came near to shaking down the plastering, "What has that got to do with it? You insinuate that I have been charged with adultery!"

The truth flashed across my mind in a second and I rushed into the press room and began taking out the type. I said to Mr. Laird, "What is the number of the Commandment I should have referred to?" and he thought for a moment and said, "the Eighth." Accepting his correction without question, I substituted the Eighth for the Seventh. but not more than a hundred copies were struck off when I heard Mr. Laird coming in a second time. "You've got that wrong again," he shouted. "I've turned the Commandments up, and I find you should have said the Ninth. The Eighth Commandment refers to stealing. You might as well say I'm a thief outright."

"Bless you, Mr. Laird; it's not my fault this time; it's your own," I said. "As an Elder you should have known better." "So ought you in the first place!" he retorted. "Change it again —change it quick — there's not time to be lost." So I ran in again, stopped the press and had it changed to the "Ninth."

· · ·

When I returned I found Mr. Laird sitting down in a deep study. Looking up, he said in the most mournful tone: "It was a miraculous escape!" When I got alone and thought the matter over, I had to laugh to think how that edition went forth — some of the papers insinuating that the good man was an adulterer, some that he was a thief and some that he was the bearer of false witness against his neighbour!

If Mr. Laird had been a vindictive man, he might have taken one of the first papers that came off the press, and had me arrested for libel. But he knew how it all came about, and he afterwards laughed over it as heartily as a man could.[12]

The new Liberal government soon found itself supporting the same railway policy which it had condemned when sitting on the Opposition side of the House, and proceeded to build expensive branch lines to Tignish and Souris. (The main line ran between the two principal Island centres of Charlottetown and Summerside.) Laird justified the policy on the ground that since all districts contributed to the cost of the Prince Edward Island Railway, all as far as possible should share in its benefits. However, not fairness but political expediency dictated the decision.

> When the Haythorne government took office, it found that the balance of power among its supporters was held by a group of members who were returned at the polls pledged to the construction of the branch lines. It seems evident that the government did not wish to build the branches, but if it refused, the pledged members would support Mr. Pope whose own party was so dependent on factional support that it would have to build the lines in order to form a government. In such circumstances the Haythorne administration embarked on what seemed to be the only course open to it.[13]

Political difficulties soon gave way to financial ones as costs escalated. The contractors were to receive approximately £5,000 per mile, but no limit had been placed on total mileage, so they were not slow to introduce curves and detours, adding to the project's length. Provincial debentures issued to provide funds in order to pay the contractors could not be sold, except at a substantial discount, and the whole economy of the Island's government seemed threatened with collapse. At this juncture, word was received from London, the money capital of the world, that if Prince Edward Island were to join Canada, its bonds could be sold at a good rate.

In January, 1873, Premier Haythorne and the now-Honorable David Laird made the perilous crossing of ice-choked Northumberland Strait, not by comfortable steam-powered ferry boat but by little ice boats that carried its passengers across open stretches of water from one floe to another, over which they were dragged to the next stretch of water.

In Ottawa the delegates obtained the "better terms" they sought, including the taking over of the railway by the federal government. Haythorne and Laird returned triumphant. Premier Haythorne immediately called a general election to secure ratification of the revised terms, and Laird entered the lists once again.

> Old timers tell of a good speech in market square, Charlottetown, on confederation, which he had first opposed, like most Islanders, but finally contended for with vehemence. Laird was defending the terms which he had secured for his province at Ottawa, and in illustration began: "Suppose that I was about to trade a horse with Mr. Davies, that

merchant yonder." "What has a horse to do with confederation?" asked a heckler. "Suppose," repeated Laird, "that I was going to trade a horse." "What has a horse to do with the question?" came the retort. "Well then," roared Laird, "we will say an ass, as you will be better able to see the point;" and he was allowed to continue his speech without further interruption from that source. But in spite of his able defence he was outwitted by J.C. Pope.[14]

Elections are seldom decided on single issues. The Conservatives under Pope claimed that not only could they secure even better terms, but they also promised the Roman Catholics to establish separate schools, a promise that remains unfilled to the present day. The Pope cohorts were successful. Laird retained his seat (parliamentary) but had to transfer his posterior (anatomical) to the unheated side of the House, where he was now Leader of the Opposition. In May, Pope and two colleagues travelled to Ottawa to renegotiate the terms of Confederation; they returned with a few minor concessions. The new terms were approved by both parties, and on 1 July 1873 the Island became Canada's seventh province.

When the Governor-General paid an official visit to the Island that summer, he passed under an arch of welcome which bore the slogan, "Long courted, won at last."

Prince Edward Island was now entitled to six Members of Parliament in the Commons at Ottawa, the number being determined by the ratio of its population to that of Quebec, which by the British North America Act was to have a constant representation of sixty-five. Subsequently this arrangement was altered and the Island guaranteed a minimum number of seats in the House of Commons equal to those it had in the Senate, i.e., four. Laird now resigned his seat in the provincial Legislature to seek one in Ottawa. He and three other Liberals were successful; the Conservatives elected two.

On the result of this election the *Patriot* of 20th Sept 1873 says, "Our opponents are given to boasting through the press. We are satisfied with the results of victory without a great flourish of trumpets. Mr. Laird is the best abused man in the Province but notwithstanding all the slander and malignity of his opponents, he today occupies the proudest position of any of the candidates who contested the election. He polled about 340 votes over the most popular man the local Government could bring out in Queen's County. Thus again the people's party have proved their strength. They always claimed that they were the larger part of the people of the Island. Their opponents only wished to allow them one candidate for Ottawa, when the talk was made about burying the hatchet. Mr. Laird and his friends were willing to accept three candidates for each party. Messrs. Pope and his friends would not consent, and now they have only two to represent their party views at Ottawa.

The people have triumphed, and the schemers and deceivers have been routed horse, foot and artillery.[15]

The new members from the Island found themselves in what was soon known as the "Pacific Scandal." Sir John A. Macdonald, chief architect of Confederation, was in no way content that Canada should remain a country sparsely populated and relatively small in area along the St. Lawrence watershed. He dreamed of a Dominion from sea to shining sea, embracing all of British North America north of the United States border. First brilliant step was the annexation of the Hudson's Bay Company's Rupert's Land and all that territory beyond, east of the Rockies, over which the Honorable Company's Red Ensign so proudly waved. This acquisition Macdonald accomplished within three years of Confederation. From it his government created the "postage-stamp" Province of Manitoba. Next step was to inveigle the Crown Colony of British Columbia into joining the union. This he did the following year, 1871, partly by promising the inhabitants of that lotus land a transcontinental railway within ten years.

Parenthetically it may be noted that the inclusion of Prince Edward Island in 1873 was followed by the addition of and international recognition of sovereignty over the Arctic Archepalego in 1880. But "Old Tomorrow" did not live to see his vision fully realized; Newfoundland and Labrador became Canadian only fifty-eight years after he had passed to his ultimate reward.

Macdonald soon found himself in tremendous difficulties over his promise of a railroad to the West Coast. He issued a charter to a company formed to build the road, but there was no way a private corporation could do so without federal assistance in the form of immense grants of land and money. The Liberal Opposition attacked the project, figuratively smiting the Old Chief hip and thigh. It was a foolhardy venture, they claimed, to build a railway across the uninhabited and impossible terrain of the Canadian Shield north of Lake Superior, across the almost equally uninhabited Great Plains farther west, and through the impenetrable Rockies. It would never pay for its axle grease; it would become two streaks of rust; it would bankrupt the country. If the Liberals were to win the 1872 election, they would repudiate the contract.

But the road *had* to be built, and for it to do so, the Conservatives had to win. As politicians well know, the sinews of politics, as of war, are money, a great deal of it, especially for close elections. Macdonald scraped the bottom of the barrel for funds, then turned to the very men who were to build the railway. Time after time he went to them, eventually extracting many thousands of dollars from those who hoped to make millions through the project. Was it extortion? blackmail? jiggerypokery? No matter, by the narrowest of margins the Conservatives were returned. But in those long-ago days, political party discipline was not as tight as it has since become, and as Macdonald's unethical machinations gradually came to light, he saw his majority begin to erode.

The arrival of six new M.P.'s, known to be Islanders before they were Liberals or Conservatives, the wily Macdonald saw as an opportunity to bolster his forces. He lavished his undoubted charm especially on Laird, the most influential of the newcomers, and paid the Islander the considerable compliment of himself introducing Laird to the House.

But Laird was not to be seduced by the charisma of the Tory leader. When Macdonald's pre-election manoevres became known, the Liberals moved a vote of non-confidence. Its support especially by two men, David Laird, Liberal, and Donald Smith (later Lord Strathcona), was crucial because of their influence on others. But both spoke against the Government; the Conservatives capitulated; Parliament was dissolved.

However, Macdonald was not yet willing to give up on the stiff-necked Presbyterian from the Island.

> On 20th Nov. 1873 when Mr. Laird came back for re-election he stated to a meeting in the Market Hall that Dr. Tupper asked him to support the Macdonald Government and to move the reply to the address — and that if he did a new Department would be opened for him. This Laird refused and said, "After having long and strenuously combatted what they believed to be corruption at home, it would not do for them (he and his associates) to become the supporters of avowed corruption in the Dominion.[16]

Macdonald would not forget Laird's rebuffs to his overtures.

David Laird now faced his fifth election in four years. But this was the easiest; on 2 December 1873 he was returned by acclamation for Queen's County and immediately accepted office as Minister of the Interior in the Liberal regime of Alexander Mackenzie. His jubilant supporters in the hundreds tendered him a complimentary banquet at the St. Lawrence Hotel, Charlottetown. Nor was this the only accolade hat he was to receive.

> In March 1874 L H Davies . . . who succeeded Mr. Laird as leader of the opposition said in the House of Assembly, "They (the hon. members) might congratulate themselves in having a gentleman — Hon. D. Laird — who lately occupied the high position he himself now held, to represent the interests of the people of the Province in the Dominion Cabinet. He was sure that even hon. members on the Government side of the house must be proud to see a man, who stood head and shoulders physically and mentally above nine-tenths of the hon. members of that house, occupy so proud a position. They could not but congratulate

themselves on the fact that the gentleman who represented them in the Privy Council of Canada, was a man they could trust with their most important interests and who would never sell or barter away their rights for his own aggrandizement. The position held by Hon. D. Laird was due to his talents and abilities, and the time spent in the service of his country.

"He was very much surprised that the leading members of the Government had not taken advantage of the opportunity now offered them to show some little political generosity in reference to the Minister of the Interior although they had many battles with him."

And the same session speaking of the defeat of Sir John A Macdonald he said, "Sir John fell, but it was not the hand of creeping thing or party that put him down. At first the men from the Island were disposed to support Sir John A Macdonald. But as honest men, they found they could not with honor, do so. No doubt, Sir John's friends imagined that their chief had come through many difficulties so successfully in the past, he would do so again. They found their mistake. Those whom the Liberal party sent to Canada were men they had every reason to feel proud of. They had every right to feel proud of their late Leader whom they had sent up to the dominion House of Commons. He was a man who would always support the party of purity. He (Mr. Laird) brought to the discussion on the floor of the House of Commons a calm and candid opinion. He was endowed with a mind which enabled him to form an honest judgement on any question it was brought to bear upon. He knew it had been in that great gentleman's power to attain honor by supporting Sir John. But he preferred his true honor to all such considerations. He came back for re-election, when not a man of them dared to oppose him. The men they had sent up to the Dominion Parliament, were Kings, not creeping things. When the Chief they had sent up from Queen's County came back again for re-election, they would be proud of what he had done, and only too glad to return him again." (Hear & Applause)[17]

From unsuccessful candidature for a seat in the Legislature of a small British colony to a cabinet post in Canada's Parliament, David Laird had come a far piece in four short years. The next seven were to be very different but quite as eventful.

References

1. Ian Ross Robertson, "Party Politics and Religious Controversialism in Prince Edward Island from 1860 to 1863," *Acadiensis*, v. VII, no. 2 (Spring 1978), p.41.

2. Elizabeth Laird, letter to this writer, 30 June 1978.

3. Prince Edward Island, *The Parliamentary Reporter! or Debates and Proceedings of the House of Assembly of Prince Edward Island for 1870*, p.26.

4. *Ibid.*, p.27.

5. *Ibid.*, p.55.

6. *Ibid.*, p.65.

7. *Ibid.*, pp.257-8.

8. *Ibid.*, p.258.

9. Frank McKinnon, "David Laird of Prince Edward Island," *The Dalhousie Review*, v. 26, no. 4 (January 1947), p.407.

10. Laird family papers in the possession of David Laird's grand-daughter, Elizabeth Laird. These include undated, unsigned memoranda, hand-written, and photocopied and original clippings from various publications, usually without date or source indicated. Hereafter referred to as "Laird papers."

11. *Ibid.*

12. *Ibid.* Photocopy of column from unidentified newspaper, "21 Dec. 48," but headed "Newspaper Recollections" under general title of "Old Charlottetown (and P.E.I.)," extracted from J.H. Fletcher, *Newspaper Life and Newspaper Men.*

13. McKinnon, *op. cit.*, p.408.

14. D.C. Harvey, "David Laird: The Man whose Tongue is not Forked," *The Grain Growers Guide,* Aug. 20, 1919.

15. Laird papers.

16. *Ibid.*

17. *Ibid.*

4
Treaty No. 4

The Governor and Company of Adventurers of England Trading into Hudson's Bay — probably no business corporation ever had so romantic a name as that under which the Hudson's Bay Company received its charter. But back in 1670, that such a designation was in any way unusual probably never occurred to the original adventurers. They were not the daring seamen who sailed the tiny *Nonsuch* through dangerous, ice-clogged Hudson Strait or navigated the *Beaver,* first steamer to enter Pacific waters, around the storm-cursed Horn to safe harbor at Fort Victoria. Nor were they the courageous traders and voyageurs who penetrated the hostile Canadian Shield and the boreal forest in search of furs. In the archaic seventeenth-century English, the adventurers were Prince Rupert and his affluent associates who (ad)ventured their capital in the risky fur trade.

The Company was unusual in more than its name. Its charter gave it not only a monopoly over the fur trade in its domains but full and complete ownership of all the land which drained into Hudson Bay — a full quarter of the North American continent. The fact that the good King Charles II knew neither the immensity of his grant nor did he really possess title to this tremendous piece of real estate did not deter him from effecting its transfer to the Honorable Company.

Of course, the Company was obligated to pay quitrent to the monarch for this largess: two elk and two black beaver whenever he, his successor, or the heir to the throne should visit Rupert's Land, as this realm was named. But this obligation was hardly onerous; for nearly two centuries neither the sovereign nor the Prince of Wales crossed the Atlantic until the future Edward VII came to Canada in 1860. The next such visitor was another Prince of Wales in 1919. No reigning monarch visited the Dominion, still so called, until George VI and Queen Elizabeth traversed Canada in 1939. However, since World War II his successor and other members of the royal family have made many trips to every part of the country.

On appropriate occasions, the Company has paid its rent, usually in the token form of mounted elks' heads and beaver pelts. But not always. In 1970, the beaver tendered to Queen Elizabeth II at the still-standing gate of Fort Garry in Winnipeg were very much alive. This ceremony was probably the last time the Company would pay such tribute, as in that year it received a new and Canadian charter, which makes no mention of elk or beaver. Perhaps it is just as well; Windsor or Buckingham Palace must be becoming rather cluttered with mounted elks' heads, which are a nuisance to keep dusted, and are rather susceptible to moths.

When David Laird became Minister of the Interior, he was immediately faced with responsibilities in Rupert's Land (and the territory beyond), except perhaps in the small area which had become the Province of Manitoba. Although for £300,000 Canada had purchased most of the HBC territory, except for sites around its posts and one-twentieth of the area in the so-called Fertile Belt, neither in 1670 nor in 1870 had the original occupants been consulted as to the change in ownership. Apparently the Canadian government had some doubts as to the validity of its title to its newly-acquired North-West Territories. Under international protocol, a nation may obtain sovereignty by conquest (as in New France in 1759 and 1760), by purchase (as in the United States' Louisiana Purchase of 1803), by treaty, or by discovery and occupation. The last applies only to uninhabited lands. But Rupert's Land and adjacent territories had never been conquered by force of arms, nor had Charles II purchased them from the Indians or Inuit. Nor could his claim to ownership be defended on the basis of discovery and occupation; these lands were not uninhabited and had already been discovered and occupied by these same aboriginal peoples. It therefore behooved the federal government to validate its title by extinguishing their claims.

Regardless of these circumstances, the Hudson's Bay Company had transferred ownership in fee simple to Lord Selkirk most of what was to become the infant Province of Manitoba, and the drainage basin of the Red River in what has since become United States territory. Selkirk named his grant Assiniboia. Here he was to establish his colony of displaced Scottish tenants and some others. In 1836, some years after his death, his heirs transferred Assiniboia back to the Honorable Company.

Before Confederation the responsibility of coping with the aboriginal population had gradually devolved from the Imperial to the Colonial (provincial) governments, and one or the others had concluded a great many surrenders of Indian lands. Only two of these agreements, negotiated by the pre-confederation Province of Canada, have been designated as treaties, the Robinson Huron and the Robinson Superior, embracing those parts of Upper Canada (Canada West) north of the lakes to which they refer. These date back to 1850, when they were signed by the government under Premier Robinson.

By the British North America Act, which designated the respective areas of responsibility for the provincial and federal governments, the latter became responsible for all Indian Affairs. This section of the Act was tacitly assumed to include Indian education, although another section of the Act gave jurisdiction over education, without restriction, to the provinces.

After the tremendous geographical expansion of the new Dominion west and north, the federal government moved promptly to validate its title to the new lands by effecting treaties with the original inhabitants. However, it did not then try, nor has it ever done so, to reach an agreement with *all* the natives in the plains, parklands, forest, and tundra of this "last best West." Through the years the federal government, Liberal or Conservative, dealt with the natives only as fast as actual or imminent white settlement or penetration of their lands required it to do so. Thus the first two of these "Great Treaties," covering the area, approximately, of the infant Province of Manitoba, were concluded as early as 1871, when this was the only part of Rupert's Land that had a permanent white population. There were, of course, many Métis, but legally they had white, not Indian status. In 1873 the area between Treaty No. 1 and the Robinson Superior Treaty — present-day south-eastern Manitoba and south-western Ontario — came under Treaty No. 3.

Interestingly enough, Treaty No. 1 was not the first to cover the Red River Settlement, the third and last of Lord Selkirk's Colonies. For this treaty, Selkirk himself conducted the negotiations with the Indians. To his surprise, he found that the resident Indians, the Assiniboines, did not consider the land as their own. They regarded it as the property of the Crees, even though they had driven the latter from their ancestral homes. In the end, Selkirk decided to deal with both groups, as described by this writer elsewhere:

> On July 18, 1817 the treaty was signed. On that day as many as possible the bands of natives were assembled to meet Selkirk and an imposing retinue of followers, including his own settlers. The powwow began. First, Selkirk assured the Indians of his peaceful intentions, spoke at length of the great services they had performed for his people, and especially thanked Peguis, the old Saulteaux chief, who had persuaded the reluctant Crees to attend the ceremony. Then Selkirk explained that he wanted for his colonists a strip of land along each side of the Red River from its mouth to the Grand Forks (at the mouth of Red Lake River), and from the mouth of the Assiniboine along each side of the river as far as Muskrat Creek. This strip of land was to be as far from side to side as one could see under the belly of a horse on a clear day (about two miles). In addition, he wanted all the land within six miles of Fort Douglas, Fort Daer, and the Grand Forks.

> Peguis was the first to reply. He reviewed the troubles which the settlers had experienced, modestly bragged of the way the Saulteaux had helped them, and took time to reject the claims of the half-breed Bois Brûlés.

"We do not acknowledge these men as an independent tribe," he concluded.

Kayajieskabinoa, called *L'Homme Noir,* or Black Man, a chief of the Assiniboines, was the next to speak. He reminded the others that when the Nor'Westers had sought their aid against the colonists, the Assiniboines had stayed aloof, uncertain which side to trust.

"We have often been told you were our enemy," he said, " but we hear from your own mouth the words of a true friend."

Mechkadewibonaie, known also as Black Robe or *Robe Noir,* of the Chippeways, also expressed his own previous uncertainty.

"Clouds have overwhelmed me," he declared. "I was a long time in doubt, but now I begin to see clearly."

By the terms of the treaty, Selkirk agreed to pay to the Saulteaux a hundred pounds of good merchantable tobacco each year on or before October 10 at the Forks of the Assiniboine. The Crees were to receive a like rent, payable at Portage La Prairie.

Selkirk placed his signature at the foot of the document. The five Indian chiefs signed the accompanying map by drawing crude pictures of their totem animals on the areas over which they claimed control.[1]

Perhaps it should be made clear that the Saulteaux are a branch of the Chippeways or Ojibwas.

By the time that David Laird assumed his portfolio as Minister of the Interior, the Province of Manitoba was off and running, but the federal government had scarcely begun to assume its responsibilities to the land and peoples beyond. The North-West Territories did not even have a government of its own; the Lieutenant-Governor and Council of Manitoba doubled in brass, so to speak, serving the same functions for the Territories. And although the Manitoba Act had been passed in 1870, there was no similar legislation for the Territories. Nor was there an Indian Act, although Indian Affairs had been established as a Branch of the Department of the Interior in 1873, and was therefore part of David Laird's responsibilities.

Despite their criticisms of the Conservatives with respect to the "Pacific Scandal," in power the Liberals did not repudiate the agreement with British Columbia to build a railway to that distant province. But the ten-year deadline they regarded as visionary and impossible to meet, and the severe economic depression which was gripping the country made it fantastic to believe that the Pacific railway could be built by private enterprise. The federal government would undertake the project itself, but with due care and caution, doing the easy sections first and in gentle stages. Thus the line would be constructed across the Prairies, but for the time being the rugged terrain north of Lake Superior would be by-passed. Perhaps that section would be replaced by a water line across Lakes Huron and Superior, or at least the latter. Possibly it would be wiser to divert the railway by the relatively easy route south of Superior through the United States, although such an expedient would be a blow to Canadian pride. In the meantime, treaties must be concluded with the western Indians to allow access through their traditional tribal territories. Treaty No. 3 had already been negotiated primarily for this purpose, to allow the line to be built between Fort William (now Thunder Bay) and Selkirk or Winnipeg.

It was, of course, right and reasonable for the government to satisfy the Indians respecting their claims to the lands which they saw being rapidly pre-empted by others. But governments seldom do anything, and never in a hurry, for reasons of abstract justice; witness the interminable delays of the present day in settling aboriginal rights of both the Inuits and West Coast Indians. Another example of such unexcelled dilatoriness and procrastination is shown in connection with Treaty No. 11, covering a large part of the Mackenzie Basin, which promised Indians their reserves. Over fifty years were to pass before even the first one was granted to them.

Even before Laird became Minister of the Interior, pressure was on his Department to establish reserves beyond the first three treaty areas. However, it came about, not from the Indians, but indirectly. Various individuals and organizations were pressing for title to the lands they were occupying. By its Deed of Surrender the Hudson's Bay Company was to retain around its various posts land varying from ten to five hundred acres, plus one-twentieth of the so-called Fertile Belt, that vast stretch between Palliser's Triangle and the North Saskatchewan River. The various churches wished to have confirmed their ownership of their mission sites and farms around them. Many Métis, some of whom had fled from Red River when the Province of Manitoba was formed, desired to be secure on their narrow little holdings, their fronts on the river, near Prince Albert, St. Laurent, in the Qu'Appelle Valley, and elsewhere. The Canadian Pacific Railway had been promised title to its right-of-way and every alternate section, each of six hundred and forty acres, for twenty-four miles on each side of its main line, or the equivalent elsewhere. And since much of such land in the East was already pre-empted, its deficiency was to be made up from unoccupied land in the West. Moreover, already immigrants were seeking free land in the Company's former holdings. In 1874 alone, over eleven hundred Mennonites entered Manitoba, and Icelanders were expected in the very near future.

But before these various suppliants could be granted titles to their acres, desired or occupied, the land had to be surveyed and the natives granted their reserves on which, it was assumed, they would be sequestered. Even in the early 1870's it was apparent that that staff of Indian life, the buffalo, was a vanishing resource. If the Plains Cree and Saulteaux, the Assiniboines and the Blackfoot-speakers were not to follow that noble beast, through starvation, into the dustbin of history, immediate action was required. Once on their reserves, they could be persuaded (or coerced) to abandon their nomadic life-style and adopt a more secure livelihood, i.e., farming. To this end they were to be given every encouragement, once on their reserves, to engage in agriculture. That these Plains Indians had neither interest in nor tradition of farming seemed to be beside the point; it was their only hope for survival.

The federal government was responsible for both sides of the Indian-farming equation: the people and the land. By the B.N.A. Act, Indian Affairs were a federal responsibility, and when HBC transferred its territory to Canada, natural resources, including unalienated lands, were retained by the Crown in the right of the Dominion in both the Territories and Manitoba. Although the four original provinces kept possession of their natural resources, it was felt that those of Manitoba and the other provinces subsequently formed from the North-West Territories should be retained by the Dominion and revenues therefrom be used to compensate the federal government for expenses in developing the West, for example, subsidies to railways. Not until 1930, when the British North America Act was amended, with the consent of the other provinces, were these resources surrendered to Manitoba, Saskatchewan, and Alberta.

But these developments were far in the future. In 1874 the time seemed ripe to persuade the Indians west of "the postage-stamp province" to enter into an agreement similar to the three Great Treaties already negotiated. In summer, Laird left Ottawa for that purpose.

Through the years, many articles have been written on the life and career of David Laird; none seems to detail this his first visit to the West. However, it appears reasonable to suppose that he would travel by the most comfortable and expeditious route possible. If so, he would follow that pursued earlier the same summer by the second contingent of the North-West Mounted Police. From Ottawa he would proceed to Toronto, not his first visit to that city, where he had been a delegate to a Presbyterian conference in 1870. The train trip from Toronto to Sarnia, on Lake Huron at the head of the St. Clair River, lasted several hours. A ferry crossing brought Laird into the State of Michigan. Jean D'Artigue, NWMP, gives his impression of the American landscape in the early summer of 1874.

> The progress made by this state, during the last thirty years, is certainly wonderful. Passing rapidly over the country, and catching hurried views of the rich fields of wheat, the neat and comfortable cottages, surrounded by large orchards of various kinds of fruit, my mind went back to the time when that region was covered with dense forests, and the possession of which by the white man was obtained after many bloody battles with the Indians, the original and lawful owners. The wigwams are no longer to be seen, and the plough, which carries civilis-

ation with it, has taken the place of the tomahawk and the scalping knife of the savage.[2]

After many hours more, the train arrived at Chicago, even in 1874 Carl Sandburg's

> Hog Butcher for the World,
> Tool Maker, Stacker of Wheat,
> Player of Railroads and the Nation's Freight Handler;
> Stormy, husky, brawling,
> City of Big Shoulders.[3]

For D'Artigue and his fellow-Mounties the journey from Chicago to St. Paul required two nights and a day; for Laird it was probably equally as long. Incidentally, it was at St. Paul that the local residents tried to dissuade the policeman and his colleagues from continuing their safari because of the danger from hostile Indians. D'Artigue "replied that we were not afraid, and that they must not forget, that a Canadian fighting under a British flag, considers himself equal to three or four Yankees."[3]

For the NWMP and no doubt for Laird also, St. Paul was not the end of their transportation in "the cars," as trains were then called; it continued to Fargo, Dakota Territory, via the Northern Pacific, an all-night run for the Mounties. From Fargo the police travelled north on their own mounts, which they had brought all the way from Toronto, but the usual conveyance for others at least relatively affluent was by paddle-wheel steamer. By 1874 there was a large number of such vessels running between Fargo and the infant and muddy metropolis of Winnipeg, a mile or so north of Fort Garry. Most of these monarchs of the waters were stern-wheelers, a hundred or more feet in length. The lower deck contained the boilers near the bow, the engine towards the stern, and cargo space between. The upper deck was for passengers; its main feature was the saloon, so called, off of which and over-looking the water were a number of tiny cabins. The saloon served as dining-room, drawing room, card room, and bar (but not this last for David Laird). One level higher, accessible by a narrow stairway — excuse it, please, a ladder — was the bridge, over-looking the bow, where the captain, or sometimes a river pilot, held sway, with perhaps a crew member at the six-feet-high wheel by means of which the vessel was more or less steered. Near-by was the brass telegraph by which signals were transmitted to the engineer for full-speed or half-speed ahead or astern, or, at the end of a voyage, "Finished with engines." High above the bridge towered the twin stacks from the boiler fires. Most impressive from the Indians' point of view was the shrill steam whistle which they claimed frightened the game animals and disturbed the spirits of the Indian dead, for which their descendants demanded adequate compensation.

Because the Red and other rivers into which such craft ventured were shallow and plagued with shifting sand and gravel bars, they were of shallow draft, perhaps eighteen to to thirty-six inches light (unloaded) and bit more when full of cargo and passengers. It was claimed that an experienced captain could manoeuvre his ship on a heavy dew, but probably this was pure hyperbole. In shipwrecks, of which there were some, the water usually did not reach the passenger deck, and so the loss of life was not even minimal.

Typical of these river steamboats was the *Selkirk,* built in the winter of 1870-1871.

> Her tonnage was 108 and with her flat bottom she was able to move in 18 inches of water travelling light, although she drew four or five feet when loaded, which was often the case. Mr. John Kelly, who was employed as a clerk in the early 80's, gives a description which shows that it compared favourably with the Mississippi steamboats of an earlier period: "The boat was handsomely finished inside and out and there were two decks with the usual row of cabins on the upper deck. The engineroom was on the lower deck and it was there the freight was carried. The pilot house was above the upper deck. A list of the personnel in 1881 follows:
>
> "Captain, Alexander Griggs; two pilots, two mates, two engineers, two firemen, two clerks, a steward, a cook and even two maids and two cabin boys; seventeen altogether. Besides these there were required from ten to fifteen roustabouts to handle the freight."[4]

Vessels such as the *Selkirk* could carry up to two hundred passengers. Of course, few of these could enjoy the comfort of staterooms. Every luxury, including wine and spirits, was available on the more pretentious steamers, not that Laird would be interested in such libations. But Red River voyages were not exactly holiday outings, as the Countess of Dufferin, wife of the Governor-General, noted in 1877 in her diary:

> I can only tell you that we go from one back to the other, crushing and crashing against the trees, which grow down to the water-side; the branches sweep over the deck, and fly in our faces, and leave pieces behind them. I had just written this when I gave a shriek as I saw my ink-bottle on the point of being swept over-board by an intrusive tree . . .
>
> The consequence of this curious navigation is that we never really go on for more than three minutes at a time; we run against one bank, our steam is cut off, and in some mysterious manner we swing round till our bow is into the other; then we rebound, and go on for a few yards, till the sharp curve brings us up against the other side. Our stern wheel is very often ashore, and our captain and pilot must require the patience of

saints . . .

This exceedingly twisty river is the 'Red Lake River'; it is forty miles to travel through the distance of only twelve from point to point. When we reached the Red River itself, we found the stream wide enough for us to go straight down it, less sinuous, but quite as muddy and uninteresting. Trees come down to the water's edge, and one can see nothing beyond them; behind them stretches out the prairie, and every now and then we were just able to see how thin the screen of trees really is between the river and the plains.[5]

Although the river wound through the celebrated Red River Valley, what the ship's passengers occasionally saw through the trees which lined each bank appeared to be a plain as level as soup on a plate — after all, this was the bed of ancient, shallow Lake Aggisez. Now, and in the nineteenth century, when the snow is melting and running off along the river's upper reaches to the south, the lower stretches farther north may still be clogged with ice. When the water rises above the river's low banks, it rapidly spreads for miles in every direction, inundating fields, roads, houses, and other building. In 1897, for instance, the stern-wheeler *Assiniboine* docked on the Main Street of Emerson, Manitoba, a town almost on the Forty-Ninth Parallel. Fortunately, such floods occur only every quarter-century or so, the latest being 1950 and 1979. None of such proportions is recorded for 1874, and in any event, Laird was in the West in September, long after the early summer's high-water crest.

Perhaps — probably — as Laird's ship approached the Forks of the Red and the Assiniboine, he was greeted by the sound of St. Boniface's Cathedral bells, which inspired John Greenleaf Whittier's "The Red River Voyageur," written about 1851:

> The voyageur smiles as he listens
> To the sound that grows apace,
> Well he knows the vesper ringing
> Of the bells of St. Boniface,
>
> The bells of the Roman mission
> That call from their turrets twain
> To the boatman on the river
> To the hunter on the plain.[6]

The "turrets twain" that Laird would have seen, however, were not those of which Whittier wrote, and which Paul Kane depicted nearly twenty years before. In 1860 the "Roman mission" was destroyed by fire and the three bells reduced to a shapeless mass of broken, half-melted and congealed bronze. Nevertheless, by 1864 they had been recast and were again reminding the faithful of their religious duties.

As Laird approached the Forks, on the starboard side he would see the Cathedral, epitomizing the society and culture of the francophone, largely Métis, Roman Catholic population, the church spires pointing to Heaven, man's eternal home. Directly across the river, at the mouth of the Assiniboine, stood Fort Garry, solid, four-square, somewhat forbidding in appearance, typical of the Scots Presbyterian fur traders who had toiled therein during the previous thirty years for the greater glory and profit of the Governor and Company of Adventurers of England.

Beyond the Fort a mile or so, and also on the left bank of the Red, lay Winnipeg. When the British and Canadian forces had arrived there four years previously, to establish the Canadian presence in the newly-acquired Territories, it had been a muddy little village. By 1874 it was a thriving town of two thousand people. Its Main Street paralleled the Red River north of Fort Garry. Portage Avenue, branching off it to the west, followed the course of the Assiniboine, although half a mile to the north. It led eventually to Portage La Prairie, from whence it took its name. Effete Easterners found these streets incredibly wide, and city planners have been given much credit for so designing them that they could adequately handle urban traffic a century later. No such foresight, however, was responsible for their generous width. Both were originally trails worn by Red River carts, which scoured ruts through the prairie sod into the glutinous gumbo soil, ruts which turned into tenacious mud in wet weather. Then the drovers would simply start a new trail beside the old one, and so the roadways became wider and wider.

The corner of Portage and Main soon gained the reputation, not wholly undeserved, of being in winter the coldest spot in Canada. Fortunately, David Laird's visit was in August.

No Journals, diaries, or letters, if any, which Laird wrote about his visit to the Red River Colony seem to have survived. One yearns to known whom he met on this his first visit to the West. Bishop Tache? Probably not; Laird's attitude towards Roman Catholics was hardly ecumencial. Charles Mair, the bumptious government agent, journalist, poet, promoter, merchant and adventurer? If so, it would have been the beginning of a friendship that would endure for half a century.

At Winnipeg or Fort Garry the treaty commissioners assembled. Chief commissioner, or at least the one whose signature was to be the first appended to Treaty No. 4, was Alexander Morris, Lieutenant-Governor of Manitoba and therefore also of the North-West Territories *ex officio*. The third member of the trio was William J. Christie, a former Chief Factor of the Hudson's Bay Company in charge of its Saskatchewan district, retired and a resident of Brockville, Ontario. It is probable that he had come west with Laird.

The first treaty rendezvous with the Indians was scheduled for Fort Qu'Appelle, in what is now Southern Saskatchewan. The fort was located on the Qu'Appelle River, thus the unofficial designation of "Qu'Appelle Treaty."

The route to this first meeting-place was via Portage La Prairie and Fort Ellice, the latter, the half-way point, being located just below the junction of the Qu'Appelle and the Assiniboine. For the first half of their journey, the travellers had two choices: overland by the Carleton Trail, which led to Fort Edmonton, or by water. The latter, although less expensive for freight, was much longer. The Carleton Trail paralleled the steamer route to Portage La Prairie, then struck almost straight west to Fort Ellcie. On the other hand, the river from this point angled south-west, then west, then north-west. Especially in its upper reaches, it had more bends, if less regular, than a sine curve, thus greatly increasing the distance between any two points. And like most prairie streams, the Assiniboine is a shallow river. In the fall — Treaty No. 4 was finally signed on 15 September — its low water made for very erratic steamer schedules. So the commissioners travelled overland. They were accompanied by a contingent from the Provisional Battalion of Infantry located at Winnipeg, under the command of Lieut.-Col. Osborne Smith. The military were not for protection but to add dignity and impressiveness to the occasion. The officers rode, but the enlisted men had to march on foot all the four hundred miles to Fort Qu'Appelle, and the same distance back to their base.

For subsequent treaties, the escort was to be supplied by the Mounted Police, but on the day that Treaty No. 4 was signed, the bulk of the Force was far to the West, near the Sweetgrass Hills. Thither they had been sent by Prime Minister Mackenzie to chase the ruthless whiskey traders back to Montana, and were nearing the end of their great trek west to find and capture notorious Fort Whoop-Up. On that historic 15 September they were temporarily ensconced at aply-named Cripple Camp, men and horses weary, sick, under-nourished, suffering from bad water. Their harness and other equipment to a great extent had been lost, damaged, or worn out. The men's clothing was in rags. Even their foot-wear was falling apart, as they had walked many weary miles to spare their suffering mounts.

As the treaty party slowly made its way westward, they left the sporadically forested parklands of Manitoba to emerge on the level and monotonous plains of the Territories. Many reasons have been advanced for its then-threeless character: the depradations of the great buffalo herds, already vanishing, the winter onslaughts of bark-eating rabbits whose numbers waxed and waned, prairie fires set by lightning or by Indians to encourage the succulent spring grass that would lure the buffalo to the natives' hunting grounds. But the valley of the Qu'Appelle, at the Fort perhaps a mile wide and two hundred feet deep, did provide shelter and moisture for poplar, scrub oak, Manitoba maple, willow, and other such timber. Indeed, it was the presence of wood for building and fuel, together with water transportation provided by the river, which determined the location of the Fort, at the head of the narrow little lakes through which it flows.

The 1874 Fort, not the first of its name, had been built only ten years previously. Facing the bare northern hills of the valley, it was enclosed in a stockade about one hundred and fifty feet square. Reflecting the Company's decreasing apprehension from Indian attack, its defensive walls were only about eight feet high, as compared to the eighteen or twenty of the palisades of earlier-built Fort Edmonton. And unlike the latter, Qu'Appelle was not protected by the bastions at opposite corners.

The buildings of the fur posts, like the forest themselves, were sometime things. They were erected, altered, abandoned, demolished, rebuilt. Nonetheless, Qu'Appellle in 1874 was probably little different from what it was in 1867, as described by Apprentice Clerk Isaac Cowie

> "At the rear of the square," he tells us, ". . . stood the master's house . . . thickly thatched with beautiful yellow straw . . . This and the interpreter's house were the only buildings which had glass windows . . . All the other windows in the establishment being of buffalo parchment. The west end of this building was used as an office and hall for the reception of Indians . . . the east end contained the mess room and the master's apartments . . . behind was another building divided into a kitchen and cook's bedroom and into a nursery for Mr. McDonald's children and their nurse . . . On the west side of the square was a long and connected row of dwelling houses . . . each with an open chimney of its own for cooking and heating . . . Directly opposite the row of men's houses was a row used as fur, trading and provision stores, with, at the south end, a room for the dairy, and at the north end a large one for dog, horse, and ox harness . . . To the right of the front gate stood the flagstaff . . . and in the middle of the square was the fur packing press." Outside the stockade was a large kitchen garden, and a ten-acre field containing potatoes and barley; there was also a hay-yard, stables for horses and cattle and a long ice-house with a deep storage cellar. About a hundred feet from the fort was the ford of the Qu'Appelle.[7]

By 1877, as a contemporary drawing indicates, some changes had already been made.

W. J. McLean, officer in charge of the Fort in 1874, welcomed the commissioners and provided them with quarters inside the stockade. The troops camped near-by, on the edge of the lake.

At first, negotiations with the Indians proceeded slowly. One reason was that the previous year, a party under Dr. Robert Bell had come to the valley to begin a geological survey, action which puzzled and frightened the then-treatyless Indians, as they regarded such action as the first step to the appropriation of their lands. According to Clifford Wilson:

> This was the most difficult of all the seven treaties, largely owing to the intractability of the Saulteaux or Ojibwas. First they demanded that the conference should be held in their own camp, not in the HBC reserve. Then, on being refused, they tried to prevent the Crees from going to the treaty tent, and for a time succeeded. Next, they cut down a Cree chief's teepee on top of him, with the result that the Crees armed themselves with knives. And finally, they went to the length of placing six of their "soldiers" in the treaty tent for intimidation purposes — a move which Governor Morris at once checkmated by calling in six of his own soldiers from Fort Garry.
>
> For several days it was touch-and-go, with most of the arguing being done by the Saulteaux orator, Otakaonan, "The Gambler." His demands were hopelessly exorbitant, and had to do mostly with the Company, which he seemed to think was still the governing power in the country. He had learned from Mr. McDonald of Fort Ellice that Canada had given £300,000 to the Company, as well as much land, to recompense them for the rescinding of their rights. And he demanded that his people, not the HBC, should be given the money. Moreover, he wanted the Company to trade only at its own forts, and nowhere else. But even he admitted that the Indians would be lost without it. "Supposing you wanted to take them away," he said, "I would not let them go. We always trade with them, and would die if they were not here."
>
> With infinite patience, the commissioners listened to their demands, pointing it out time and again that the Company had nothing to do with the government, but simply had the same rights as any private trader. Gradually the Indians saw the light, and after six days of argument, the treaty was signed.[8]

The three commissioners affixed their signatures; thirteen chiefs and headmen made their marks. Also inscribed on the document were the signatures or marks of the witnesses: Charles Pratt, interpreter; M. G. Dickieson, private secretary to the Minister of the Interior; Lieut.-Col. Smith and other officers of the military battalion; Hudson's Bay Company people, and others, including Helen M. McLean. And there was one other woman, Flora Garrioch. In 1874, females may not have been persons eligible for appointment to Canada's Senate, but they were acceptable as witnesses to men's signatures on an Indian treaty.

Treaty No. 4 is so similar to all the others concluded in the 1870's that one cannot avoid the conclusion that they were imposed rather than negotiated. In return for surrendering their territory in what is now part of southern Saskatchewan and western Manitoba, the Crees and Saulteaux were to receive reserves at the rate of one square mile for each family of five — in effect, one hundred and twenty-eight acres per Indian — plus an annuity in perpetuity — the so-called "treaty money" — of five dollars per head. Chiefs went at twenty-five dollars; headmen at fifteen. Yet even for this land, title was not transferred to the Indians, either as bands or as individuals. It remained with the federal government, which would hold it in trust for the natives — and sometimes persuade them to surrender all or part of their reserves.

There were other provisions — initial gifts of twelve dollars per Indian, fifteen dollars and a coat per headman, twenty-five dollars, a coat and a medal, plus for all, "powder, shot, blankets, calicoes, strouds, and other articles."[9] The treaty also called for agricultural equipment and supplies, and carpenter's tools — farming was the destiny planned for the natives — "a school in the reserve allotted to each band as soon as they settle on said reserve and are prepared for a teacher."[10] But they were to get schools whether they were prepared or not.

> Her Majesty also agrees that each Chief and each Headman, not to exceed four in each band, once in every three years during their term of their offices shall receive a suitable suit of clothing, and that yearly and every year She will cause to be distributed among the different bands included in the limits of this treaty powder, shot, ball and twine, in all to the value of seven hundred and fifty dollars; and each Chief shall receive hereafter, in recognition of the closing of the treaty, a suitable flag.[11]

The flag, of course, was to be the Union Jack, as Canada was not to possess such a national emblem for another ninety-plus years. Nearly a century after the signing of Treaty No. 4, one band in its area refused to accept its treaty money until the maple leaf flag flying over the encampment was hurriedly replaced with the traditional Union Jack.

"And further, Her Majesty agrees that Her said Indians shall have the right to pursue their avocations of hunting, trapping, and fishing throughout the tract surrendered,"[12] subject to certain provisions. Many years later, Indians were to find that such promises made on behalf of the Great White Mother were of little import when they conflicted with provincial game laws.

Treaty No. 4 was only the first of five in which David Laird was to be more or less intimately concerned, the next two as Minister of the Interior, No. 7 as Lieutenant-Governor of the North-West Territories, and No. 8 as Indian Commissioner.

But with No. 4, Laird's duties were not yet concluded. Next stop was back at Fort Ellice, where the first adhesions were signed with two chiefs, Man Proud of Standing Upright, and The Man Who Stands on the Earth. One of the witnesses was Chief Factor Archibald McDonald, formerly of

Fort Qu'Appelle, in charge of the Company's Swan River District with headquarters at Fort Ellice. There he dispensed to the visitors the hospitality for which HBC had long been renowned.

Fort Ellice's palisade was even less impressive than that of Fort Qu'Appelle; it was hardly more than a fence, a mere vestigal token of a stockade. But the HBC Red Ensign flew as high and as proudly there as over any of the Company's other posts. A contemporary account describes Fort Ellice as "composed of the Hudson's Bay Company's buildings and a few wigwams of Sioux, Saulteaux, and Crees."[13]

Business concluded, David Laird began the long, slow journey back to Ottawa, bearing a gift from the Indians. It was a new name — Meywasin Kitche Ogemow, meaning Good Big Chief. Thus he was known thereafter by the native peoples of the Western Plains.

During the next three years, additional adhesions to Treaty No. 4 were to be secured at Qu'Appelle Lakes, Swan Lakes, Fort Pelly, and Fort Walsh, but Laird was not destined to be present on any of these occasions.

References

1. John W. Chalmers, *Red River Adventure*, pp. 134-5.

2. Jean D'Artigue, *Six Years in the Canadian North-West*, p. 21.

3. *Ibid.*, pp. 24-5.

4. Molly McFadden, "Steamboating on the Red," Historical Society of Manitoba, *Transactions*, Series 3, No. 7, pp. 24-5.

5. _____, "Steamboats on the Red," *The Beaver*, September, 1950, p.26.

6. Harry Shave, "The Bells of the Turrets Twain," *The Beaver*, September, 1953, p. 43.

7. Margaret Complin, "Calling Valley of the Crees," *The Beaver*, March 1935, p. 22.

8. Clifford Wilson, "Indian Treaties," *The Beaver*, March 1939, p. 39.

9. Canada, Queen's Printer, *Treaty No. 4 between Her Majesty the Queen and the Cree and Saulteaux Tribes of Indians at Qu'Appelle and Fort Ellice*, p. 4.

10. *Ibid.*, p. 5.

11. *Ibid.*

12. *Ibid.*

13. R. C. Fetherstonhaugh, "March of the Mounties," *The Beaver*, June 1940, p. 24.

5

Minister of the Interior

Historians and biographers have given little attention to David Laird's incumbency as Minister of the Interior, 1873 to 1876, except to note his expedition to Fort Qu'Appelle for the signing of Indian Treaty No. 4. Yet this was a period of climactic importance for the West. When Laird assumed his portfolio, only three years had passed since the Hudson's Bay Company, by Deed of Surrender, had transferred to the infant Dominion of Canada one-quarter of the North American continent. Suddenly the fledgling federal government found itself responsible for the administration of a vast territory comparable in size with all of Europe, for the disposition of its countless square miles of prairie and parkland, forest and tundra. And even more important, for the maintenance of peace and order and good government generally. And for the protection and welfare of its peoples, white and Métis, Indian and Inuit, bands and tribes and communities who suddenly found themselves nationals of a far-off country which most of them had probably never heard of. And all this without even so much as a by-your-leave.

To establish all the legislative and administrative machinery for control of Canada's newly-acquired domains was not to be achieved in an instant. Nevertheless, the Conservative government under John A. Macdonald had made a good start, before being forced out of office in 1873. In 1870 it had created the postage-stamp Province of Manitoba and three years later the North West Mounted Police. By that same year it had also negotiated the first three of the Indian Great Treaties and established Indian Affairs as a branch of the federal government. And it had made a start on surveying the Prairies, in anticipation of an expected flood of homesteaders. But when David Laird became Minister of the Interior, much still remained to be done.

Although Indian Affairs Branch was established in 1873, the federal government still had no legislation to regulate its relations with these native peoples, other than the Imperial Parliament's British North America Act of 1867. That statute simply decreed that Indian affairs were to be the exclusive responsibility of the federal authorities. But the North-West did not even have a territorial government to call its own, the Lieutenant-Governor-in-Council of Manitoba serving *ex officio* in that capacity for the Territories.

Nor when Laird became Minister of the Interior had more than a start been made towards extinguishing aboriginal land claims. The first three of the Great Treaties, concluded in 1871 and 1873, covered only what is now the southern portion of Manitoba and adjacent corners of Ontario and Saskatchewan. And even they, or at least the first two, were in need of immediate overhaul. For these there were "outside Promises," i.e., verbal commitments by the government outside the written treaties, and they had to be honored. One of them was more symbolic than anything else. From time immemorial, agreements made with Indian chiefs on behalf of the British sovereign had been sealed by the bestowal of silver medals on the former. But those distributed by the parsimonious, newly-created Canadian government were of base metal, perhaps pewter. As the Hudson's Bay Company had long ago learned, the Indians were always sharp judges of quality, demanding (if not always receiving) only the best. And of one thing they were sure; the tin (?) medals being foisted on them were not the best. Nor was the "treaty money," the so-called annuity of $3 per individual Indian in any way adequate. Laird's measures in dealing with the Indians' dissatisfaction are recounted later in this chapter.

Land tenure and property rights demanded Laird's immediate attention. Some scions of the fur trade held titles issued by the Hudson's Bay Company before the Deed of Surrender. Others, Selkirk Settlers who had arrived between 1811 and about 1825, or their descendants, traced their proprietorship to grants or sales made by Lord Selkirk himself or his heirs. Still others had no official documentation to support their title to the little farms on which they or their forefathers had lived for half a century. They were, in effect, simply squatters, but relied on the old adage that possession is nine points of the law. But it wasn't simply a matter of issuing patents or confirming title to the land they occupied. Their lands followed the old French-Canadian system of ownership, and consisted of narrow farms fronting the Red or Assiniboine River, or other body of water, and running back therefrom a distance of two miles or so, with pasturage rights for a farther two miles. But the federal government had adopted, with slight modifications, the United States system of land survey, based on the section or square mile. These sections, organized into townships six miles square, would eventually form a grid blanketing all the arable land west to the Rocky Mountains, with the exception of small and isolated areas, where the French-Canadian system had preceded it. In these places the two systems had to be reconciled, a difficult task in surveying.

In October, 1874, when Laird departed for Ottawa from Winnipeg, which had leapt from village to city status only the previous December, most of his ministerial problems were still before him. His return to the capital was the same route as his outward journey, through St. Paul, Chicago, and Toronto. There is some evidence that he began his journey by steamboat, but a letter of his indicates that he travelled by stagecoach. Possibly he used both methods. In any event, it was not wholly an enjoyable journey. For one thing, the jolting of the coach over the primitive roads was a physical ordeal, particularly hard on his knees. For another, not all of his fellow-travellers were such as this austere and abstentious Presbyterian would have chosen of his own free will. Writing to Governor Morris in Winnipeg, he reported, "At Pembina we took on four or five *roughs* who had been laborers on the Boundary Survey. Their oaths were awful, and as they kept drinking, the swearing also continued."[1] However, after they reached the railhead at Moorhead, Minnesota, Laird was presumably free of these unpleasant companions.

Today, a Minister of the Crown is buttressed by a tremendous support staff: deputy-minister, executive assistants, branch directors, secretaries, clerks, a whole phalanx of bureaucrats. Apparently things were different in 1874. In the same letter of Morris, penned in his own crabbed handwriting, Laird stated, "Mr. McBeth is not here — he had not yet returned from New Brunswick where his wife had been ill for some time at St. Andrew's. He telegraphs he will be home this week. Colonel Dennis is some better, but he is yet very feeble. With my principal men thus missing, my work will be slower than I would like."[2]

Despite his exalted status, the Hon. David Laird had to deal with problems which today would probably be the responsibility of a junior civil servant. One of these concerned a mentally-deranged Mrs. Urquhart, whose husband, an official of the Privy Council, had died suddenly in Manitoba, leaving a twelve-year-old son as well as his widow. Governor Morris felt that since the Urquharts were not residents of Manitoba, but merely wayfarers, that the province should not be responsible for the poor woman and her boy. Furthermore, Manitoba had no "Lunatic Asylum" to which she could be commited, nor was there any institution to take care of her son. In the end, despite the fact that she was not a Roman Catholic, two Sisters and Charity accompanied her, without compensation, to Kingston, whence eventually she (and presumably the boy) were returned to relatives in England.

As a politician, by 1874 Laird was accustomed to attacks by the press, more personal and libelous in the nineteenth than in the twentieth century. He refers to one such attack in his letter to Morris: "I see the correspondent of the Montreal *Witness* has been venting some of his spleen upon me for refusing to take him to Qu'Appelle. *You* did everything, he says, and I was only an old woman looking on. I will survive such a selfish, spiteful attack.

He goes so clearly out of his way to make the remark, that it is easily seen something is the matter with himself."[3]

But if Laird found no favor with the anonymous journalist, his relations with Governor Morris were clearly cordial. Not only is the whole letter couched in friendly terms, but he concludes with "My kind regards to Mrs. Morris and all the Misses Morris,"[4] and his regret that he was unable to say good-bye to the latter.

During the two years after Laird's return to Ottawa, there occurred many changes that were to affect the Department of the Interior, its Minister, and the North-West Territories. For one thing, having chased the American whiskey traders back across the United States border, the North West Mounted Police established the rule of law across the vast reaches between Hudson Bay and the Rocky Mountains.

Laird's duties as Minister of the Interior were manifold. An example of his involvement with Indian Affairs is indicated by a letter to Alexander Morris in the latter's capacity as Lieutenant-Governor of the North-West Territories. Since Laird is communicating as one government functionary to another, the tone is formal and official, contrasting sharply with the informal and unofficial style of the epistle written to Morris shortly after Laird's return to Ottawa. The latter is from friend to friend, not from official to official, and is inscribed in the author's own crabbed handwriting. The other, the original (except for the signature), in beautiful copperplate penmanship of a civil servant, follows in full:

No 476711B

Ottawa, 7th July 1875

His Honor
    The Lieut Governor of the
        North West Territories
            Fort Garry
                Manitoba

Sir,
    I have the honour to enclose printed copies of the Order of the Governor General in Council passed on the 30th April last, on the subject of the so called "Outside Promises" in connection with the Indian Treaties Nos 1 and 2. The substance of which was at the time unofficially communicated to you.

2. It is important that the decision of the Government on this subject, which has been from the first a source of misunderstanding and dissatisfaction among the Indians affected by the Treaties in question, should be communicated to them in the most formal and authoritative way.

3. In this view I am glad to learn from you that I can avail myself of your valuable services in the conduct of the necessary negotitations with the Indians, feeling assured that your Official position as Lt Governor

of the North West as well as your experience in such matters and your personal influence with the Indians, will enable you to explain to them satisfactorily, the action of the Council in this matter, and to secure their willing acceptance of the liberal terms now offered them by the Dominion Government.

4. It is left entirely to your discretion to determine as to the best mode of securing the formal acceptance by the Chiefs of the terms offered by the Order in Council, but, assuming that you will think it desirable to obtain such acceptance over their own signatures, a copy of the Order is sent herewith specially intended to be signed by them.

5. In any case it will probably be well to hand each Chief for himself a printed copy of the Order.

6. You are at liberty to associate with you in this duty (in addition of course to the Indian Commissioner or his Assistant) any gentleman whom from his knowledge of the Indians or of their language you may think likely to be of use to you in the proposed negotiations.

7. It has not been thought necessary to print with the order in Council the Memorandum therein referred to as having been attached to the Copy of Treaty No 1, as the promises embodied in that Memorandum have, for the most part been already carried out. A Copy of the Memorandum, is however, enclosed for your information, and for such further use as may be required.

8. The suits of clothing for the Chiefs and Headmen allowed by the Order in Council have been forwarded to the Indian Commissioner Mr Provencher for distribution, if possible, at the time of the interview with each Band.

9. In connection with the proposed negotiations, I am to state, that the Surveyor General reports that a doubt has arisen as to whether the Islands in the vicinity of Grind Stone Point and generally in the Southern part of Lake Winnipeg were surrendered by the Indians when Treaties 1 and 2 were concluded. It is important that this question should be finally and authoritatively set at rest and it is thought that the present negotiations afford a favorable opportunity of so doing. I have therefore to request that you will bring the matter under thenotice of the Indians interested and obtain from them, as in view of the liberal concessions which the Government is now making. I trust you will have no difficulty in doing a formal surrender of these Islands.

10. In your interviews with the Indians I should be glad if you would explain to them that, on assuming the office of Minister of the Interior my attention was called by repeated representations from yourself and from the Indian Commissioners to the discontent among them, arising out of the "Outside Promises" and that when at Winnipeg last year, I gladly availed myself of that opportunity to ascertain the views of the Indians on this question. For that purpose, as the Indians will no doubt remember, I had interviews with several of the Bands and promised them on my return to the Seat of Government to bring the whole subject

under the notice of the Governor General, the representative of their great Mother the Queen, and the Queen's Councillors generally.

11. The promise which I then made has been faithfully kept and the result is found in the Order in Council which you are to formally communicate to the Indians.

12. The terms of the Order in Council of the 30th April last, speak of the Indian Commissioner as the person to carry out the instructions therein contained. It appears to me, however, that no technical objection to you acting in this matter can arise from the wording of the Order in Council, in as much as your original Commission as a Member of the Indian Board has never been formally superseded.

13. Forty seven (47) Silver Medals were on the 6th Instant, sent to your address by Express. Some of them are intended to replace those of base metal originally issued to the Indian Chiefs interested in Treaties 1 and 2. You will have the goodness to Obtain the Medals of base metal from the parties who received them, giving each Chief one of the new Medals instead and returning the others to the Department. You will also give a new Medal to each Chief who had previously not received one.

14. You will please retain in your own possession the Medals intended to be used when negotiating the Treaty (No 5) this season with the Indians on either side of Lake Winnipeg, and hand those intended for Treaty No 3 to Mr Commissioner Provencher.

15. Each Medal has engraved on it the number and year of the Treaty to which it relates.

16. A Copy of this letter will be forwarded to Mr Indian Commissioner Provencher who will be instructed, either personally or by his Assistant, as you may desire, to co-operate with you in carrying out the wishes of the Government as contained in this letter.

I have the honor to be,

Sir,

Your Obedt Servant,

David Laird

Minister of the Interior

P.S. As the printed Copies of the Order in Council are not yet ready I enclose, in the meantime, a Certified Copy in manuscript.

D.L.

COPY of a Report of a Committee of the Honorable the
    PRIVY COUNCIL, approved by His Excellency the
    GOVERNOR GENERAL in Council, on the 30th April 1875.

On a Memo: dated 27 April 1875, from the Hon. the Minister of the Interior, bringing under consideration the very unsatisfactory state of affairs arising out of the So-called "outside promises" in connection with

the Indian Treaties, No. 1 and 2, — Manitoba and North West Territories, — concluded, the former on the 3rd August 1871 and the latter on the 20th of the same month, and recommending for the reasons stated:
—

To the Honorable
  The Minister of the Interior,
     &c.,&c.,&c.

1st That the written Memorandum attached to Treaty No. 1 be considered as part of that Treaty, and of Treaty No. 2, and that the Indian Commissioner be instructed to carry out the promises therein contained in so far as they have not yet been carried out, and that the Commissioner be advised to inform the Indians that he had been authorized so to do.

2nd That the Indian Commissioner be instructed to inform the Indians, parties to Treaties No. 1 and 2, that, while the Government cannot admit their claim to anything which is not set forth in the Treaty and in the Memo: attached thereto, which Treaty is binding alike upon the Govt and upon the Indians, yet, as there seems to have been some misunderstanding between the Indian Commissioner and the Indians in the matter of Treaties 1 and 2, the Government out of good feeling to the Indians and as a matter of benevolence, is willing to raise the annual payments to each Indian under Treaties 1 and 2, from $3.00 to $5.00 per annum, and make payment over and above such sum of $5.00, of $20.00 each and every year to each Chief and a Suit of Clothing every three years to each Chief and each Headman, allowing two Headmen to each Band, on the express understanding, however, that each Chief or other Indian who shall receive such increased annuity on annual payment shall be held to abandon all claim whatever against the Government in connection with the so-called "outside promises" other than those contained in the Memo: attached to the Treaty.

The Committee submit the foregoing recommendation for Your Excellency's approval.

Certified

(Signature
illegible)[5]

In 1875, the federal government negotiated Treaty No. 5, its area corresponding approximately with the present-day Northern Manitoba. The following year saw the completion of Treaty No. 6, covering the South Central portions of what is now Saskatchewan and Alberta. At about the same time the Canadian Parliament got around to passing the first Indian Act, introduced by David Laird, legislation which was to undergo many revisions over the next eighty years.

But these revisions were not to change its essential nature. Implicit in the Act was (and is) the concept that the Indians were basically children

— they were denied both federal and provincial franchise for many decades — incapable of making wise decisions respecting their own welfare, unable to manage their own affairs. They were not given title even to their own reserves nor control of their own band funds; both were held in trust for them by beneficent Indian Affairs. Having surrendered vast tracts of their traditional hunting and trapping grounds, they were not even owners of the pitifully-small reserves left to them. They were scarcely even tenants, although subject to, and often being dispossessed through persuasion, coercion, and chicanery of the white man. The reserves became, indeed, almost prisons, for the Indians for long years were forbidden to leave them without passes from the Indian Agents. Should they be found off their reserves after the expiry of their passes, they were in the same position as soldiers absent without leave, subject to arrest and punishment.

Even the most personal aspects of their lives were eventually subject to regulation. The sun dance, that most sacred ceremony of the Plains Indians, became illegal, and indeed their whole religion was destroyed, almost if not completely. Matrilineal tribes were required to trace individual descent from the paternal rather than the maternal line. Thus in such a tribe, the child of an Indian mother would not have Indian status if the father were not Indian, despite tribal custom. Indians also had to assume surnames, although for untold generations they had got along quite comfortably without them — just as had the patriarchs of the Old Testament.

The privilege of getting drunk, or even of buying, owning, or drinking alcoholic beverages was denied to our brown-skinned brothers for scores of years. Not too long ago a North-West Territories Indian was arrested and convicted of being drunk off the reserve, despite the fact that in the Territories there was no reserve that he could be drunk off of. Fortunately for Drybones — such was his singularly appropriate name — his conviction was reversed on appeal.

Indians had to send their children to school, even though the first seven treaties seem to leave optional such a splendid gift of civilization. Thus Treaty No. 4 provides for Indian education only as soon as the Indians "settle on said reserve and are prepared for a teacher."[6] Treaty No. 6 provides for schooling "whenever the Indians of the reserve shall desire it."[7] Surely the inference is clear: if the Indians were not prepared for a school or did not desire it, they needn't have it, white opinion as to its desirability to the contrary notwithstanding. But the Indian Act requires Indian children to be educated regardless of their parents' wishes.

Even an Indian's last will and testament is not inviolate, legal as it might be by the white man's criteria. If, in the opinion of the Minister, i.e., in practice the Indian Agent (whatever his present title might be), the testator has dealt unjustly with his off-spring, or for other reasons, the will can be set aside and other disposition made of the estate.

Generally the treaties state that "the said Indians shall have the right to pursue their avocations of hunting and fishing throughout the tract surrendered,"[8] some also include trapping. But in 1962, Michel Sikyea, a treaty Indian of the Yellowknife district and resident in Treaty No. 8 area, found out that the government didn't really mean it. While out hunting for food to support his family, he shot a duck out of season and was convicted of a violation of the Migratory Birds Convention Act. The Convention or treaty was negotiated with the United States in 1916; the treaty with the northern Indians in 1920. Mr. Justice Jack Sissons reversed the magistrate's decision, but the Crown appealed that of Sissons, ultimately all th e way to the Supreme Court of Canada, which re-instated the original verdict. The final effect was to negate the affirmation in the Order in Council quoted above respecting an earlier Indian treaty, "which Treaty is binding alike upon the Govt and upon the Indians.[9] In short, a treaty with a foreign power reduced an Indian treaty to the status of a mere agreement between Indians and the government, which the latter could unilaterally abrogate at its pleasure. And if, as a Saskatchewan Indian found to his cost, he kills a moose in Alberta, he is subject to Alberta game laws, even though he be a Treaty No. 6 Indian hunting in the the tract encompassed in his treaty.

In retrospect, it appears that Canadian society — government, church, schools,— has done terrible things to the Indians of the Plains, ironically with the best of intentions. Unlike the policy of the American republic to the south of us, where government policy has often seemed to be one of extermination — the only good Indian is a dead Indian — in Canada church and state have consistently endeavored, according to their rather dim lights, to civilize the so-called savage, to make him self-supporting, usually as a farmer, that he might have the means of surviving when the West would be completely settled and the old hunting economy and way of life no longer possible. The fact that, in Western Canada at least, he had neither tradition nor desire in that direction was seen as irrelevant. But it is easy to be wise after the event. Hindsight is always 20/20.

Since the Great Treaties and the Indian Act (and Regulations thereto) are often at odds with each other, for more than a century the Indians of the Great Plains, and others as well, have eaten the bitter bread of disappointment and frustration. For a "treaty" Indian, his treaty is his Decalogue, his Habeas Corpus Act, and his Bill of Rights rolled into one. In any confrontation with a bureaucrat, he always argues from his treaty (even though he may never had read it). The bureaucrat, however, like a good civil servant, governs his actions by the legislation under which his Department operates, and under regulations made pursuant to it. And when two parties argue from different premises, agreement is difficult and usually impossible.

As mentioned, the Indian Act became legislation in 1876, but the previous year saw passage of another statute which was to be equally significant, if not more so, to the West. This was the North-West Territories Act, which provided for the government of the immense area between Hudson Bay and the Rocky Mountains, between the white man's Medicine Line (Latitude 49°) and the Arctic Coast. It replaced the improvised and *ad hoc* arrangement by which the Lieutenant-Governor-in-Council for Manitoba performed gubernatorial functions for the Territories. Instead, the latter was to have its own lieutenant-governor and appointed council.

But the Territorial lieutenant-governor of the 1870's was a far different person from his provincial equivalent of a century and more latter. Today, the latter fills a purely formal and decorative function, often very well, analogous to that of the sovereign, who reigns but does not rule. Today the office is held through political largess or patronage, usually as a reward for long and faithful service to the party in power at Ottawa. A hundred years ago, although it was a political appointment, that it was no sinecure is evidenced by the fact that Prime Minister Mackenzie's first appointment cost him a valued cabinet minister. The man who was first to assume that office in the 1870's was in a very real sense the governor of the Territories, advised, it is true, by a council but by no means obliged to accept its advice. The only real restraints to his power were to be the Act, the far-distant federal government which appointed him, and the financial resources with which it provided him.

The scope of his activities was immense. He would be concerned with the maintenance of law and order, land tenure, exploitation (and protection) of natural resources, education, public health — as recently as 1870 a small-pox epidemic had devastated the West —land and water transportation and communication, regulation of trade and commerce and of the professions, administration of justice, municipal government, and a host of other concerns. Very importantly, since the first incumbent was also to be Indian Commissioner, he would also be responsible for all matters affecting the native population. Obviously this was not a post for a political hack; it called for a robust and vigorous man of known sagacity, integrity, and relevant experience. It called for David Laird.

After the Liberal government was defeated in 1878, according to Laird family papers quoting *The Life of Alexander Mackenzie,* by William Buckingham and George W. Ross, Mackenzie wrote to Laird, giving the reason for the appointment. "I was very sorry to lose you when you went to the North West, but it was essential to the public welfare to have a fast friend and an upright man in a position of such vast importance, that I felt compelled to submit to the sacrifice."[10]

The sacrifice was not all on one side, as Laird's reply indicates:

> I appreciate your assurance that you were sorry to lose me as a colleague. Well the truth is I did not want to leave the Government at that

time. My friends too on the Island were opposed to my accepting the new post, and I was loth to desert those with whom I had fought so many hard battles. But you urged me to accept, and, like a loyal supporter, I yielded, supposing that you somehow thought it would be in the interests of the country.[11]

It was November before David Laird found himself once more in the West, although his appointment as Lieutenant-Governor and Indian Commissioner had been announced as early as February, 1876, when it met with almost unanimous approval. About the only dissenters were his friends back in Queen's County, who were losing their Member of Parliament. But in Ottawa, even the Leader of the Opposition, the Rt. Hon. John A. Macdonald, was generous in his commendation of a man who had been largely instrumental in forcing the resignation of the Conservative government. According to the Parliamentary Reporter (as quoted in the Laird paper), on February 12, 1878:

He regretted that his Hon friend the Leader of the Government had felt it his duty to send Mr. Laird to the North West, for that Hon. member had just begun to understand the very complicated duties of the Minister of the Interior, and last session when he had a very difficult measure to carry through this House. Although he was put to a little trouble occasionally in the course of the discussion of the details, the Minister of the Interior showed that he had really grasped the details, and understood the questions involved in the clauses of the Indian Bill. He had therefore hoped that as long as the present Government lasted, the country would have the benefit of the experience that the Minister had gained as the head of that department. It was of the greatest importance that the Minister at the head of Indian Affairs should fully understand his subject.[12]

Mackenzie, speaking after J. C. Pope, naturally was complimentary to the man whom he himself had chosen to be Laird of the West. He stated:

The Honorable member's own leader had spoken five minutes before of Mr. Laird's supreme ability and even went so far as to imply that his successor would scarcely be worthy to fill his place for a long time to come. Mr. Laird, however, was chosen for his ability. He had proved his ability by the manner in which he had discharged his duties here, and he would prove it in the discharge of his duties in the North West.[13]

If Mackenzie was commendatory, there is no reason to doubt his sincerity.

References

1. David Laird to Alexander Morris, 19 October 1874 (Provincial Archives of Manitoba).

2. *Ibid.*

3. *Ibid.*

4. *Ibid.*

5. David Laird, Minister of the Interior, to His Honor the Lieutenant-Governor of the North-West Territories, 7 July 1875 (Provincial Archives of Manitoba).

6. Canada, *Treaty No. 4 between Her Majesty the Queen and the Cree and Saulteaux Tribes of Indians at Qu'Appelle and Fort Ellice,* p.5.

7. Canada, *Copy of Treaty No. 6 between Her Majesty the Queen and the Plain and Wood Cree Indians and Other Tribes of Indians at Fort Carlton, Fort Pitt and Battle River with Adhesions,* p. 3.

8. Canada, *Treaty No. 4,* p. 5.

9. Laird to His Honor, *op. cit.*

10. Wm. Buckingham and Geo. W. Ross, *The Life of Alexander Mackenzie,* quoted in Laird family papers.

11. *Ibid.*

12. Canada, *Parliamentary* Papers, quoted in Laird family papers.

13. *Ibid.*

6

The Lairds Move West

FORT LIVINGSTONE, First Capital of the Northwest Territories, 1876-77. Here Lieutenant-Governor Laird and his Council were sworn into office on Nov. 27, 1876, and here, on March 8, 1877, was held the first session of the Northwest Council.

So reads the inscription on a cairn located a mile or so north-west of Pelly, Saskatchewan. For about a year, as the inscription indicates, the Fort — that designation appears to have been strictly honorary — was the seat not only of the Territorial government but also of the North West Mounted Police.

Every astute civil servant soon learns the wisdom of any decision varies inversely according to the distance between where it is made and where it is to be put into effect. So it was with the choice of the North-West Territories' first capital.

The site of Fort Livingstone was a high hill covered with large boulders embedded in the ground. Only with immense difficulties did the sweating Mounties remove enough of them to form a parade ground. Furthermore, half the area's hay, essential for their horses, had been destroyed by prairie fires. The Police were not pleased. Hardly had their barracks been completed then Ottawa gave orders to the Force to saddle up and ride out — permanently.

What. . . prompted a federal government order to abandon the newly constructed police barracks and other buildings in favor of the site near the crossing of the Battle River?

It appears that contractor John Oliver and his construction party were resting from their labors after completion of the barracks when their attention was called to an unusual circumstance some 400 yards distant.

Investigating, they noticed that the earth in three depressions over an area some 30 feet long and four feet wide was literally moving.

Soon the truth became clear — the government buildings had been constructed almost on top of a snake den. With the coming of the warm weather, the men had only to move a stone or boulder in the vicinity to uncover snakes by the hundreds, many interwoven into a mass, like yarns in a ball.

Mr. Oliver divided his men into teams, 10 to a side and offered a prize of $10 to the team that caught the greatest number of live snakes in 20 minutes. The highest score was 1,136, not counting some small ones!

Whether the thought of so many snakes was too much for the government officials is not known, but the next mail packet from Ottawa brought instructions for Mr. Oliver to proceed to South Battleford to build new barracks for the police, in addition to the buildings for the territorial government.[1]

Over eleven hundred snakes, "not counting some small ones?" Too often, second and third-hand accounts, such as this, of events long past have proven incorrect, even wildly erroneous, but the above story is corroborated by S. B. Steele, NWMP. In July, 1875, Steele was posted to Fort Livingstone — Swan River, as it was always known by the Police — as chief constable, i.e., sergeant-major. Steele was not impressed with the site. He writes:

At the end of the barrack reserve an extraordinary spectacle might be seen in the autumn or the early spring. There were several beds of stone about 25 feet square, on which lay a huge mass of garter snakes basking in the sun. The reptiles took refuge there when the nights became cool, and for the most part paid no attention to intruders. When summer came these snakes left their beds, and were found in every direction for miles round, and some of them were even found in the barrack-rooms. Fortunately they were quite harmless, if unpleasant, and the children gathered boxes full of them, or amused themselves chasing their playmates with a snake in each hand. These beds gave the creek its name and had been the resort of snakes from time immemorial.[2]

Whether because of the snakes or for other reasons, before the new lieutenant-governor even arrived at his new capital, Oliver and his men were busy erecting new barracks for the Police and a building for the government officials in Battleford. Probably the new location was chosen at least partly because it was anticipated that it would be on the route of the Pacific railway, which was to go through Fort Edmonton and the Yellowhead Pass on its way to the West Coast. Of course, when the Conservatives regain power in 1878, the route was changed to one much farther south.

Meanwhile, on October 6, 1876, the Hon. David Laird received his long-awaited appointment as lieutenant-governor of the North-West Territories. Almost immediately he set out to take up his new assignment, leaving his family behind until he could be assured of adequate accommo-

dation for them. However, he did not travel alone. His staff included
Amedée E. Forget, his private secretary, who was also to serve as clerk of
the Territorial Council. No doubt Forget's fluency in French, his mother
tongue, was most useful to the fledgling government of the Territories,
where about half of the white and Métis population were francophones.
Forget was destined to become the last lieutenant-governor of the North-
West and, in 1905, first of the new Province of Saskatchewan. Another
member of the official party was M. G. Dickieson, who was to act as Indian
secretary — Laird was also Superintendent for Indian Affairs in the
North-West. The previous year, Dickieson had acquired relevant experience by acting as agent in the payment of treaty money to the Indians. A
fourth dignitary was William J. Scott, who had been appointed Registrar
for the Territories.

Travelling the last stretch by stagecoach, by October 25 the Laird
party had reached Winnipeg. Five days later they set out for Fort Livingstone. For transporting the party and their baggage, Contractor W. F. Al-
loway charged $501.20. This amount covered teams, teamsters' wages,
even nineteen bushels of oats at a cost of $5.70. The first half of the over-
land safari was to Fort Ellice, a route that Laird had traversed in 1874, but
from there on the trail was over *terra nova* for the new governor. As on the
expedition two years previously, Laird had an escort, but this time of
Mounted Police rather than of soldiers. Progress was considerably ham-
pered by a heavy and early snowstorm, but on November 10, according to
his nephew David, the gubernatorial party reached Fort Livingstone and
Laird took up residence in the quarters of departed Commissioner French
of the NWMP.

On October 18, 1931, David Henry Laird and his daughter, nephew
and grand-niece of the Honorable David, visited the site of Fort Livingstone, leaving Winnipeg the previous day and spending the night at Dauphin, Manitoba. As David Henry notes, his journey was somewhat faster
than that of his uncle. "In 1876, 55 years ago, the Honourable David Laird
left Winnipeg on 30th October, and reached Fort Livingstone on 10th November, while we made the trip in a little over a day."[3]

The new governor spent some days getting himself and his staff established in the rather cramped quarters built for the Mounted Police, with no
thought that they would also have to accommodate the personnel of the
civilian government. Nor were any arrangements under way for the newcomers; as already mentioned, the move to Battleford had already been
decided upon. But soon Laird was involved in official business. On November 21 he was writing to Ottawa for copies of the Dominion and Ontario
statutes, and Orders-in-Council. He was also concerned about mail service
to Fort Livingstone.

Four days later he wrote to his friend, Lieutenant-Governor Morris of
Manitoba, reporting his safe arrival and that his health had been good all

the way. Laird added that his new quarters were "tolerably comfortable," but somewhat lonely — a natural feeling for a man so far removed from his family. He also mentioned that he had heard from a priest at Qu'Appelle to the effect that conditions on the Indian reserve were not in a healthy state, and that the reverend father was requesting agricultural implements for his flock. Apparently the federal government had not yet honored its commitment in Treaty No. 4 that:

> . . . the following articles shall be supplied to any band thereof who are not actually cultivating the soil, or who shall hereafter settle on their reserves and commence to break up the land, that is to say: two hoes, one spade, one scythe an one axe for every family so actually cultivating, and enough seed wheat, barley, oats and potatoes to plant such land as they have broken up; also one plough and two harrows for every ten families so cultivating as aforesaid, and also to each chief for the use of his band as aforesaid, one yoke of oxen, one bull, four cows, a chest of ordinary carpenter's tools, five hand-saws, five augers, one cross-cut saw, one pit-saw, the necessary files and one grindstone, all the aforesaid articles to be given, once for all, for the encouragement of the practice of agriculture among the Indians.[4]

This was probably the first problem which Laird encountered in his role of Indian Superintendent.

November 27 was an important date for the North-West. On that day the Hon. David Laird and three members of his council took their oaths of office. Thus the Territorial government formally came into existence. One of these advisors was Matthew Ryan, from Montreal, a stipendiary magistrate who had accompanied Laird to the North-West. Another such magistrate was Lieut.-Col. Hugh Richardson, who later became a judge in Regina. It was these two, acting as commissioner *"per Dedemus Potestatem"* who administered the oath to the new governor. The third councillor was Commissioner James F. Macleod, NWMP.

The following spring, but not until after the first meeting of the council, its fourth member was appointed. He was Paschal Breland, a Cypress Falls storekeeper, the only one who had been a permanent resident of the North West before his appointment and the only representative of the French-speaking Roman Catholic Métis who constituted about half of the territorial population.

Such condescension towards a constituency of such size — one representative among four, or five if the governor is counted — would be called sheer tokenism, a move to eliminate the appearance but not the reality of outright, even outrageous discrimination. One cannot avoid the impression that the federal government (regardless of party affiliation) and the East generally felt that they knew what was best for the West; therefore there was no need to consult its denizens. Yet the North-West Territories Act to some extent provided an automatic corrective to the situation. As soon as any area of one thousand square miles — a territory which could be approximately thirty-three miles square, say, or forty by twenty-five — could claim an adult population of one thousand, it could elect its own member to the council. And when the members so chosen reached a total of twenty-one, the council would be abolished, being replaced by a legislative assembly composed of elected members only. Before Laird ended his term in 1881, he had scheduled one such election.

The establishment of a legislative assembly did not, however, mean that political power automatically passed from the governor to the assembly. The struggle for responsible government — power to the people — which had convulsed Eastern politics in the 1830's and '40's was to be repeated in the West during the 1880's, but the Hon. David Laird was to have no part in it.

Although the council was formally constituted in November, it did not meet until the end of the winter, which was well under way. In the meantime, Laird was the government. An example of his activity as such is indicated in his letter, dated March 15, 1877, to the Minister of the Interior; which reads in part:

> As some doubts existed respecting the position of Justices of the Peace in the Territories, since the coming into operation of "The North-West Territories Act of 1875," I, on the 12th December last, reappointed the following gentlemen Justices of the Peace for the North-West Territories: —
>
> Richard Hardisty of Edmonton,
> Lawrence Clarke of Carlton,
> Roderic McFarlane of Athabasca,
> Horace Belanger of Cumberland,
> William Lucas McKenzie of McKenzie River,
> Alexander Matheson of the Pas,
> Ewen McDonald of Ile a la Crosse,
> Julian Onion of McKenzie River,
> William McKay of Fort Pitt,
> Archibald McDonald of Fort Ellice,
> Isaac Cowie of Manitoba House.
>
> On the same day I appointed William I. McLean of Qu'Appelle a Justice of the Peace, also Henry Stewart Moore, of Prince Albert, to the same office, on the 19th January last.

The worthy gentlemen mentioned in the first paragraph quoted above were senior officers of the Hudson's Bay Company, which before 1870 had been the government, *de jure* and *de facto,* of Rupert's Land and the Indian country to its north and west. It is to such men that Canada owes a largely-unacknowledged debt. Their wise, firm, and honest dealings with the natives were largely what made it possible for Canada to assume sovereignity over the West without inter-racial warfare. Their presence also inhibited the northern expansion of the United States, many of whose politicians felt that their country had a manifest destiny to occupy the North American continent from the Rio Grande to the Arctic Ocean.

At the end of the 1876-77 winter, the lieutenant-governor caused the following notice to be issued:

> Livingstone, Swan River, N. W. T.
> Government House,
> 7th day of March, 1877
>
> Sir, — The members of the council of the Northwest Territories are summoned to meet in legislative session tomorrow (Thursday) at Government House, at the hour of three o'clock p.m.
>
> By command of His Honor the Lieutenant-Governor,
>
> (Signed) A. E. Forget,
>
> Clerk of the Council[5]

An anonymous columnist gives the following account of that memorable meeting:

> We have no special record of that most significant and historic event, nothing but the minutes of the proceedings, and the statement of one who was present:
>
> "It was a cold day — terribly cold. We all gathered around the fire and waited for the governor, who came into the room and took his seat on the 'throne' — the throne on that occasion being a comfortable house chair, the council met in the 'best' room in the gubernatorial mansion, a very ordinary looking building indeed, which today might be called a 'shack.' There was no military escort — guard of honor — no Windsor uniform nor was his honor crowned by a cock hat. He wore a tweed suit, took the chair, and read the Speech from the Throne in a friendly if dignified tone. He carried the speech in his own hand and there was no attempt at formality. After the session was over we partook of the hospitality of his honor and then went our various ways."
>
> The first session of the Northwest Council held brought in a "Bill for the Preservation of the Buffalo." There was little need for debate on this matter, for already the west was feeling that some prohibitory measures were necessary along this line.[6]

Mr. Breland, not yet having received his appointment to the council, was not present, but all the other members were. Not all meetings were as well attended. On one occasion, the only member on hand, aside from the lieutenant-governor, was Mr. Ryan, who by himself hardly constituted a quorum.

In addition to passing an ordinance to protect the fast-vanishing buffalo from extermination, a measure rescinded the following year, the tiny legislature in 1877 passed bills respecting masters and servants, short forms of indentures, ferries, licences, gambling, and the administration of justice.

In this era when even provincial budgets run into billions of dollars, it is interesting to note that total government revenue raised in the Territories was rather more modest. Specifically, for the period May, 1877, to July, 1878, it was:

Fines under Prairie Fire Ordinance	$37.50
Breaches of Masters & Servants Act	16.00
Ordinance for Prevention of Gambling	302.00
Buffalo Ordinance	7.50
Miscellaneous fines	20.00
	$526.00

Of course, most of the Territories' revenue came in the way of grants from Ottawa, which, holding the purse-strings as well as the power to appoint the governor and council, really controlled the government of the North-West.

Both before and after the council meeting, Laird was busy with a multiplicity of duties. January 11 found him writing to the Hon. D. Mills, Department of the Interior, respecting ordinances to govern bridges and ferries, and concerning surveys for the former. In February, letters to the same honorable gentleman dealt with confirmation of appointment of stipendiary magistrates, and requesting funds to be placed at his disposal, plus a recommendation that witnesses in criminal proceedings have their expenses paid. On March 16, the governor was in correspondence with a Dr. Douglas of Battleford respecting an outbreak of small pox at that centre. This was no doubt most alarming, as only seven years had elapsed since an epidemic of that dread disease had devastated the West, and the memory of it was still vivid in the minds of all inhabitants. On March 27, Laird approved the issuance of vaccine for all Indians in the Territories, no doubt acting in his capacity of Indian Superintendent. And in April he was concerned about the issuance of marriage licences, a matter for which there was no territorial legislation. However, Laird was resolved that this deficiency would be corrected at the next session of the council.

During the summer, the lietenant-governor was much occupied, both officially and personally, with the imminent move of the capital to Battleford. There was, for example, the matter of transporting 1,792 pounds of freight, at a cost of $125.44, from Winnipeg to the new seat of government. The contractor was the same F. W. Alloway who had brought the gubernatorial party to Fort Livingstone the previous year. The bill of lading listed the following items:

1	Case no. 4	Furniture
1	Case no. 3	"
1	"	Cooking Stove
2	"	Solar Stoves
1	"	Pipes and Boiler
1	"	Pots and Kettles

September saw the arrival of a large quantity of furniture for the lieutenant-governor, "chairs to sit on and desks for the elbows of thought," imported form the United States by Gerry and Co., Winnipeg, and by them shipped to Battleford. Did this furniture, one may wonder, include the council's heavy table that now reposes in the Battleford Historic National Park's museum? At one time this table was thought to be the "Confederation table" at which the Fathers of Confederation worked when they met in Charlottetown in 1864. However, careful research by two Saskatchewan historians, Allan Turner and J. D. Herbert, has shown that the Charlottetown table has been confused with another used by the Fathers at their Quebec conference, whence it was probably shipped to Ottawa and subsequently to Regina, the Territories' third capital. That happened after Laird's term had expired. As to the one which still remains at Battleford, "Nobody seems to know where it came from."[7]

With plans well under way for the transfer of the seat of government from the provisional capital of Fort Livingstone to its permanent venue at Battleford, David Laird decided to bring his family from the Island to a new home in the West. He was not able to go for them himself, since he was busy with preparations for the signing of Indian Treaty No. 7, to which the next chapters will be devoted. However, his Louisa and the children would not be without their protectors on their long journey. Col. Richardson was making a trip to Ontario to bring out his family, and both Forget and Scott were eastward-bound to be married. They and the Laird family were to travel west together.

Nevertheless, for the leg of the journey from Charlottetown to Montreal, Louisa Laird bore the responsibility, with the assistance of an unmarried sister, Martha. Certainly, travelling with six young children was no picnic, although there is evidence that they youngsters thought so. In the summer of 1877 the Laird off-spring were: David Rennie, twelve years of age; Mary Alice, ten; Arthur Gordon, eight; William Charles, six; James

Harold, five; and Fanny Louise, two. About 1930, Mary Alice committed to writing her memoirs (now in Laird family papers) of their long journey:

At Montreal we met Mr. Forget and his bride. He was the Governor's secretary and a delightful French gentlemen full of kindness and honour. His wife was also very charming and they adopted me at once as a special pet — I was ten years old — and as they had no family I remained in favour as long as I stayed there. Mr. William Scott (brother of Sir Richard Scott) and his bride from Ottawa were also of the party. He was "Registrar" and she a beautiful girl, gay and with a charming voice. They travelled the rest of the way with us and did much to add to the pleasure as well as shouldering much of the responsibility.

At that time there was not a continuous railway line. We travelled by rail to Sarnia; to Duluth across the Great Lakes by steamer. From there, on an American line to Glyndon on the Red River, then on boats up that narrow winding river, where one had to be watchful not to be brushed off by the overhanging trees. At last we arrived in Winnipeg and there our real difficulties began.

Winnipeg at that time was a long narrow street with at one end "Fort Garry" (within whose walls was the residence of Lieutenant-Governor Morris of Manitoba and the Hudson's Bay store). At the other, the Post Office and on and on — a great trail across the Prairie leading over the Rocky Mountains, the longest street in the world, now known as "Portage Avenue." We remained there for three weeks, stopping at the Canadian Pacific Hotel, not much like hotels of today.

I also remember my mother, aunt, and myself being entertained at Government House (within the Fort) and playing with Governor Morris' daughter, about my own age.

Our delay in Winnipeg was caused by the Guides, Horses and supplies being got ready for our long Prairie trip. After repeated delays (very harassing to my mother) we at last got started. I wish I had a snapshot of that long train of carriages and vehicles of all descriptions. There were waggons for the ladies and children driven by Guide Grant or some of his sons. Others for the servants, provisions and tents. The Forgets had a buckboard and a pair of mules, and many a conflict they had along the way, much to the amusement of the younger members of the party.

The first night we spent at Silver Heights, not far from Winnipeg. Then began our long trail across the Prairie, stopping for meals, and camping where the Guides knew there was water. This went on for a month and during that time, we only slept once under a roof, that at Fort Qu'Appelle. It was beautiful weather as it often is in the early fall in the West.

During that month on the Prairie camping out each night we had only one wet day, and that a most miserable one, huddled in our tents on the shores of the South Saskatchewan. Our family had a large Bell tent, most comfortable when the weather was fine. It was all of interest to us, more like a grand picnic; stopping for dinner, watching the cooking and the women baking bread before the fires, seeing the tents put up, animals cared for, etc. There was not a dull moment for the children.

After we left Manitoba, for days we would not see a living being, but we had such a jolly party with us we did not mind. There was a winding trail over the Prairies, scarcely a tree, but often low brush. No land cultivated, except near the Hudson Bay Fort or some few settlers near there. The only living things we met were some Indians or Half-breeds on horseback, prairie wolves which kept their distance by day but had to be watched by night. There was no buffalo in that part of the country.

At last we reached "Battleford" in October and greatly to the disappointment of my mother, my father was away at a "Treaty" with the "Blackfeet" Indians and did not arrive home for sometime. Another disappointment, the houses were not finished though they were hurrying along with "Government House." We were able to occupy some of the rooms while the carpenters were busy with the rest.

The Forgets and Scotts also had to stay with us as their houses were not nearly ready, but I think it helped them all from being lonesome — so far from home and in a strange land. I can see the picture of our arrival yet. It was after dark and we were not expected so soon. Great was the consternation of the servants and workmen when we drove up. Mr. George Dickieson, of New Glagow, P.E.I. (who was my father's secretary when he was Minister of the Interior) had been sent out to Battleford (on account of his knowledge of Indian affairs) was there to welcome us, and took charge of arrangements. With the assistance of the women, we were soon made comfortable and a tired band we were.

Owing to the lateness of the season, our furniture did not arrive until next spring, and many were the make-shifts that winter.

Moving supplies over the long road in "Red River Carts" was a slow process as well as most expensive. Everything was brought from Winnipeg in this way, so that living expenses were very high, for instance $1.00 had to be paid for freighting 100 lbs. for 100 miles. This made $6.50 for hauling a sack of flour costing $4.00 in Winnipeg, making $10.50 per bag, $21.00 per barrel. This made salt cost almost as much as sugar and there was no change during my father's residence there.

The furniture sent by the Government of Canada arrived in the Spring. Very good walnut furniture, and an ample supply of glass, china and silver.[8]

What with the Richardsons and their three daughters, the Forgets, Lairds, Scotts, Miss Owen, a maid and a cook, the official party would total about twenty, plus of course the guide and all those in the business of provinding transportation and other services en route. But even without the last, who presumably would be returning to Winnipeg, the arrival of the official party would be a substantial increase to Battleford's meagre population.

Today's visitor to Battleford will find it a quiet but thriving town on top of the north bank of the valley of the Battle River. Now it is quite overshadowned by the up-start North Battleford, a few miles distant across the North Saskatchewan. The younger centre, largest between Saskatoon and Lloydminster., owes its existence to the fact that the Canadian Northern Railway (now Canadian National) was built on the north side of the Saskatchewan River. But, unlike many other towns when bypassed by the railroad, Battleford refused to die. However, it has greatly changed since the days of David Laird. Then, Government House stood on the southern edge; the town occupied the valley of the Battle, and the Mounted Police post guarded the northern extremity. Today that NWMP fort is a Historic National Park on the southern limit of the town, while a mile across the southern limit of the town, while a mile across the valley, empty of edifices, stands Government House in solitary splendor. Nor is it the same building in which Mary Alice and the other Lairds resided. Many wings have been added to it, and, after numerous metamorphoses, it has become a seminary of the Roman Catholic Oblate order.

But we can still envisage life at Battleford in the 1870's, partly from Mary Alice's story, which continues:

> Thus began our life in the far West. As there were no schools (except for Indians and half-breeds) a Presbyterian minister, Rev. Peter Straith lived with us and was our tutor. He also took part in the Presbyterian service in the church. There was one Protestant church in which one service was taken by an Anglican clergyman, Rev. Mr. MacKay, and a joint choir and Sunday School. My aunt played the organ and there was a very good choir made up of the wives and daughters of English residents and men of the Mounted Polce. Mr. MacKay had a wife and three daughters. There was also a Mr. Clarke, an English curate, who did missionary work among the Indians and half-breeds. In the Catholic Church the priests were French and besides looking after their English flock, did much missionary work among the Indians. I recall thenames of Pere Andre and Pere Lestang. In spite of the fact that we were so far removed form the centre of civilization, we had a wonderful life there. There was a mail only once a month, but one can imagine what an event that was. Letters were hungrily read, then the papers and magazines (of which we took many) were pored over from page to page for it was not easy to procure news. My father had a fine library, and we there got a knowledge of Dickens and Scott. Our friends supplied us with books so we fared very well.

> The social life was quite varied and a nice little circle soon formed with Government House as the centre.

I remember reading an article written by an early writer:

> The coming of the wife of Lieutenant Governor Laird gave a new and finer perspective to the land of Buffalo. A lady of the old school, kind, generous,

aimiable, and sensible of her responsibilities, she at once set about forming what proved to be the social life of the West. A warm welcome for every sojourner and a "place" for every visitor, and that subtle something which took the place of the rougher life of the Lone Land. To her "The little Lady Blessing" this passing tribute is paid.

Among those closely associated with our life there were Mrs. Forget, a gay little French woman, and Mrs. Scott with a lovely personality and charming trained voice which was a great asset in the choir, at concerts or in social life. Mrs. Richardson, wife of Judge Richardson, with three beautiful daughters. Mrs. Richardson died while we were there.

Major Walker was head of the Mounted Police at the Fort at Battleford — a tall imposing man — he brought his bride there soon after our arrival. They had one son.

Captain French of the R.C.M.P. (*sic*) and his wife were also among our greatest friends. He was a handsome dashing Irishman and his wife delightful. He was killed in the Rebellion of 1885. His last words were, "Remember, boys, I led you." Dr. Miller of the Mounted Police, a fine man and endeared to my memory as he was so good to me, always bringing me good books that my mother could approve. Besides these, Col. Macleod of Fort Macleod, Lawrence Clarke of Fort Carlton, and Charles Mair of Prince Albert, a poet who wrote "Tecumseh," were frequent visitors. There were also many travellers, Englishmen on their way to the Rockies seeking Big Game. There were also engineering parties surveying the country for the proposed railway. Many called at Battleford as the capital, and it was a resting place after their long journey over the plains.

There were many stately dinner parties, and other functions made dazzling to childish eyes by the gold lace and red coats of the officers and the gay dresses of the ladies.

I think some of the happiest years of my childhood were spent in that country, careless and free, riding across the prairies and learning to skate on the Battle River, little realizing the heavy burden of care and anxiety soon to be laid on my parents. There was coming the dark side of the picture. While councils were meeting and treaties made, over the vast domain, troublesome times were looming.[9]

Nor are we wholly dependent, for a description of Battleford in its infancy, on the memoirs of Mary Alice (Mrs. J. A.) Mathieson, as she became, wife of Prince Edward Island's premier. Drawing on the files of Patrick G. Laurie's *Saskatchewan Herald,* Mrs. A. N. Wetton has given us a vivid picture of the new capital one short year after Mary Alice arrived there, although by Christmas, 1878, three of the Laird children were away, presumably to attend school.

High on the south bank of the Battle River, west of its junction with the North Saskatchewan River, stood Government House, the judge's house, the registrar's house, and the Land Titles office, while on the plain between the rivers stood the spacious building of the North West Mounted Police post. . . all of them shining and new.

Scattered around were the log shacks of its first settlers, "big enough to hold a bed, a packing case or two, each with its mud fireplace and floor; with cotton sacking filling a small square hole at the side of each shack that served as a window; and a larger hole, framed with rawhide, that did duty for a door."

Nearby were three crudely-built stores, and the printing office in which Laurie prepared his first Christmas number for The Saskatchewan Herald.

Between Battleford and Portage la Prairie, the nearest settlement to the southeast, stretched a near-untrodden wilderness of snow. West, some 250 miles distannt, stood the lonely trading post of Edmonton; while northeast, with not even a habitation between, was Prince Albert.

The elite of Battleford's society, remote, but not unfriendly, lived in the government buildings that Frank Oliver built two years before.

At Government House, the Hon. David Laird, a stickler for propriety, lived in isolated splendor, with Mrs. Laird, three of their children; Rev. Peter Straith, the tutor, Miss Owen, the governess; A. E. Forget, the lieutenant-governor's secretary, and their servants.

Colonel Richardson, the Stipendiary Magistrate, and his wife, occupied the judge's house; while nearby, in the registrar's house, lived Mr. and Mrs. W. J. Scott. Across the river, in the barracks, lived Major Walker, officer commanding the post, and Dr. Millar, the police surgeon. Here and there were the homes of the early missionaries: Rev. A. J. MacKay, Mrs. MacKay and their family at the Anglican Mission; and at the Catholic Mission, the newly-arrived Father Hert and Father Merer.[10]

The writer mentions the modest homes, scattered about the settlement, of a number of other and more humble residents: construction workers, teamsters, a bronco-buster, veterans of the fur trade. Then she continues:

For food, they still relied on pemmican, and game, which were everywhere to be found. Flour, which had to be brought in, was dear, even at the recently reduced price of six dollars a sack. Potatoes were scarce, and butter a luxury that few could afford.

Big fat deer, shot near the bluffs a mile away from the settlement, found their way onto many a Christmas table 80 years ago; and fresh buffalo meat, "plenty of it," that hunters brought in from 50 miles distant on the plains. There was fresh fish to be had, too, from Turtle and Jackfish Lakes.

Officially, because of the recent death of Princess Alice, Christmas Day was observed quietly. Mrs. MacKay and Miss Owen decorated the

Anglican school house with evergreens and mottoes for the Christmas Day service, which was conducted by Mr. MacKay and Mr. Straith. Midnight Mass on Christmas Day was celebrated in a blaze of light and evergreens in the Catholic Church, which was filled to overflowing.

The little Indian children in the nearby Eagle Hills mission were remembered by Mrs. Laird, who provided them with "a feast of cakes, and other good things."[11]

Such was Battleford, the Hon. David Laird's home for some four years. But before he could settle into enjoy it, there was the matter of Indian Treaty No. 7 to be negotiated. This was accomplished in the fall of 1877.

References

1. Anon., "Snakes Moved the Capital," *Winnipeg Free Press,* 26 April 1969.

2. S. B. Steele, *Forty Years in Canada,* p. 96.

3. D. H. Laird, "Fort Livingstone, Saskatchewan," unpublished typescript dated 22 October 1931 in Laird family papers.

4. Canada, *Treaty No. 4 between Her Majesty the Queen and the Cree and Saulteaux Indians. . .,* p. 5.

5. Anon., "The Prairie Parliament," *The Colonist,* 1905 (exact date undetermined).

6. *Ibid.*

7. Bob Bowman, "Confederation Table Still at Charlottetown," *Winnipeg Free Press,* 26 November 1967.

8. Mary Alice (Laird) Mathieson, "Early Days in the North West Territories," Unpublished typescript (c. 1930) in Laird family papers.

9. *Ibid.*

10. Mrs. A. N. Wetton, "Christmastide in Old Battleford," *Saskatoon Star-Phoenix,* 24 December 1958.

11. *Ibid.*

7

Treaty No. 7:
Overture

No episode in the Hon. David Laird's career is as well documented as is the negotiation of Indian Treaty No. 7. At least seven first-hand accounts of that memorable event are readily available. Including Laird's own official report to Ottawa, three members of the North West Mounted Police, S. B. Steele, C. E. Denny, and William Parker, have described the drama from the point of view of actors who had "walk-on" parts. Other accounts ere provided by Frank Oliver, founder of the *Edmonton Bulletin* and subsequently a member of Wilfrid Laurier's cabinet, and by Richard Hardisty, son of Chief Factor (later Senator) Richard Hardisty of Edmonton. Finally, an anonymous journalist for the Toronto *Globe* provided lengthy despatches for his paper. Like Laird's, his story was written immediately after the event, while most of the others were not prepared until many years later.

Whether these chroniclers were police or civilian, participants or observors, they — and most subsequent historians of Treaty No. 7 — have this in common: that they have written from the viewpoint of the dominant society, that of the white newcomers to the ancient hunting grounds of the Plains Indians. But of course, as has been wisely observed, history has always been written by the victors, not the vanquished. And if the Indian tribes who accepted the treaty were not defeated in battle, they were as effectively overwhelmed by white technology and other gifts from Euro-American culture, such as liquor, small pox, and venereal diseases. Furthermore, they were a pre-literate race, often with an educational system highly relevant to their life styles, but their literature and history were oral, not written. Yet one writer, albeit he is white, has managed to understand and express the native viewpoint with respect to Treaty No. 7 and many other aspects of Indian-white relationships. He is Hugh A. Dempsey, married to a Blackfoot wife, son-in-law of the late James Gladstone, Canada's first Indian senator. From Dempsey's work as well as from first-hand accounts the material in this and the next chapter has been synthesized.

With the signing of Treaty No. 6 in 1876, native land rights in almost all of the arable areas of the Territories were extinguished. One exception was the Peace River country, the potentialities of which were unrecognized in the 1870's. The other was the south-west corner of the Great Canadian Plains, a territory approximately equivalent to present-day Alberta south of Red Deer.

This was the homeland of five different tribes of Indians, each of which consisted of a number of bands. Most numerous were the Blackfoot-speakers: the Blackfoot (or Blackfeet) proper, east of Calgary, the Peigans, west of Fort Macleod, and the Bloods, south of Fort Macleod and Lethbridge. The last group was and still is divided by the International Boundary, the white man's Medicine Line. Together with their allies, the Sarcees, these all formed the Blackfoot Confederacy, a very loose association without, however, any federal structure, one that tended to atrophy in times of peace, become more viable during the Indian wars. The Sarcees, on the south edge of today's Calgary, spoke a language which they shared with the Beavers, hundreds of miles north, and the Navaho, even farther south, lingiustic evidence that their long-ago ancestors came to North America by way of the Mackenzie Basin.

In contrast to the Sarcees, the Mountain Stoneys, or Assiniboines, were comparative newcomers. Inhabiting mostly the foothills country west of Calgary, by language they appear to be a Siouan people, although traditionally no friends of the American Sioux. Originally their home was far to the east, but as early as the 1600's the arrival of the Europeans with their relatively high technology had created a pressure wave that eventually set Indian bands moving westward clear to and beyond the Rockies. Thus, a century or more after the Stoneys crossed the Great Plains, the original denizens regarded them as interlopers — and acted accordingly towards them.

By the mid-1870's, to prevent conflict between the Stoneys and the Blackfoot-speakers, between the latter and their hereditary enemies the Crees, and for reasons even more urgent, at least to the government, it was becoming expedient for the Blackfoot, their allies, and their enemies to be brought under treaty. Already Mennonites, Icelanders and others were moving into the West; already prospective ranchers and farmers from Upper Canada, as it was still called, and others were avariciously eyeing the treeless and fertile prairies between the Cypress Hills and the Rocky Mountains, already the buffalo, the Plains Indians' staff of life, were diminishing with alarming rapidity. Both to protect and to succor those wards of the Canadian Government, the Indians — and to keep them from harassing the white settlers — it was expedient that federal authorities extend the treaty system over these last free natives of the North-West.

A further disturbing factor was the arrival during the winter of 1876-77 of hundreds, then thousands of Sioux refugees, fugitives from the United

States. In 1876 under Chief Sitting Bull, goaded beyond endurance by the injustices under which they suffered, at the Battle (or Massacre) of the Little Big Horn the Sioux had wiped out to the last man a force of the U.S. Seventh Cavalry. Incidentally, a massacre is a battle that "our side" loses. After this one, the Sioux, rightly fearing reprisals from the United States Army, had fled to Canada. This was one time, and not the only one, when Canada did not welcome political fugitives from a foreign land. The Canadian Indians resented the newcomers, and not only because they were hereditary enemies of even their cousins, the Stoneys. They also regarded the Sioux as competitors for the diminishing resources of buffalo and other game. The presence of the fugitives also made the Government very nervous, jeopardizing as it did the often-fragile Canadian-United States relationships, and threatening to give Americans an excuse, which many politicians and others sought, to take over the whole North-West.

Accordingly, the Federal Government sent missionaries such as the Rev. John McDougall and Father Albert Lacombe among the Indians to prepare them for the shape of things to come. It also appointed two commissioners to negotiate what was to be known as Treaty No. 7, the Blackfoot Treaty. For once, political patronage seems to have been set aside, and the two best men possible were chosen. These were Commissioner (Lieut.-Col.) J. F. Macleod, of the highly respected Mounted Police, known to the Indians as a man of complete integrity, and Lieut.-Gov. David Laird, who had represented the government in the Qu'Appelle Treaty negotiations. As Minister of the Interior he had also been involved in Treaties No. 5 and No. 6. To the Indians he was known as "the man whose tongue is not forked."

On 4 August 1877 Laird received a telegram (dated three days before), informing him that he and Macleod had been appointed commissioners for the proposed treaty. His commission and other relevant documents were being forwarded to Fort Macleod. The governor immediately began preparations for his impending journey. These took a full week, as he also had to make arrangements for transfer of the Territorial capital to Battleford, to which he would return on completion of the negotiations. On 11 August he left Fort Livingstone for Battleford, where his arrival would complete the first stage of his journey. At the Elbow of the South Saskatchewan he met Inspector James Walker, NWMP, en route to Carlton, to meet Treaty No. 6 Indians for distribution of promised articles which had not arrived when they received their treaty money earlier in the month. Laird reported:

> Some of the Indians had not dispersed since they received their payments, and interested parties were causing dissatisfaction among them by reporting that the provisions intended for them, while assembled to receive their annuities, having now arrived, should be distributed to

them, as well as the agricultural implements and other articles promised.

I advised Inspector Walker to distribute to those Indians still around Carlton their share of the presents, and to give them a small quantity of provisions from the Government supplies, to enable them to proceed without delay to their hunting grounds.[1]

Laird continued on to Battleford, which he reached on 24 August. There he found Inspector A. G. Irvine, NWMP, who had arrived only a few hours before. Irvine brought a message from Commissioner Macleod to the effect that he had changed the treaty venue from Fort Macleod to Blackfoot Crossing, on the Bow River. This ford, the Indian name of which means "the ridge under the water," was a place of special and religious significance to those who spoke the Blackfoot tongue.

Laird's own report to the government contains some ambiguity. He states that he arrived on Monday, 28 August, and continued his journey the following day, but he also says, "On Friday I had interviews with several parties on business, among whom were 'Red Pheasant,' the Chief of the Battle River Crees, and a portion of his Band."[2] Again it was a matter of the non-delivery of supplies as promised, unusually heavy rains having made freighting from Winnipeg very slow. The Indians seemed quite content with Laird's explanation.

Whatever the day of the week, he states that on 25 August he left for Fort Macleod, escorted by Inspector Irvine and four policemen. Also in the party were Laird's personal servant, unnamed, and a guide. With no immediate official responsibilities, the governor apparently found the cross-country trek pleasant and interesting.

On the third day out we first sighted buffalo, and every day subsequently that we travelled, except the last, we saw herds of the animals. Most of the herds, however, were small, and we remarked with regret that very few calves of this season were to be seen. We observed portions of many buffalo carcasses on our route, from not a few of which the peltries had not been removed. From this circumstance, as well as from the fact that many of the skins are made into parchments and coverings for lodges, and are used for other purposes, I concluded that the export of buffalo robes from the territories does not indicate even one-half the number of these valuable animals slaughtered annually in our country.

Antelope, though not very abundant, are widely scattered over the plains. The numerous lakelets abound with water fowl. Some of the pools contain alkali, but we experienced no inconvenience on the journey from scarcity of fresh water.

The grass in many places is short and thin, but in the hollows feed for horses is easily obtained. Altogether, though the plains are perfectly treeless, not even a fine shrub being visible, a journey across them in fine weather, such as we experienced, when the "buffalo chips" are sufficiently dry to make a good camp fire, is not disagreeable.[3]

On 29 August the governor and his party reached the Red Deer River, where they had considerable difficulty in finding a suitable ford, but eventually were successful in reaching the other side. Two days later they were at the Blackfoot Crossing of the Bow, which unites with the Old Man River to form the South Saskatchewan. Laird was much impressed with this location, where the treaty was to be signed some days later. He describes the river itself as being bordered with a narrow fringe of cottonwoods and other trees which provided fuel and shelter for visitors. A ridge under the river's clear waters facilitated movement back and forth between its banks, while on the south side a beautiful "bottom" stretched back a mile from the water's edge and three miles along the stream. This area afforded not only excellent campsites but also fine grazing for the hundreds of horses which would soon be assembled there.

On arrival at the Crossing, and the following day, a Sunday, Laird met a number of Indians, including Sotenah (Rainy Chief), head chief of the North Bloods, also Jean L'Heureux, a white man who had spent twenty years among the Blackfoot speakers and was confidential advisor to Chief Crowfoot. The governor found this unexpected encounter most fortunate, as L'Heureux provided him with

> . . . much valuable information respecting the numbers and wishes of the Indians, together with an elaborate list of the different Chiefs and minor Chiefs of the Blackfeet, Bloods, Piegans, and Sarcees, with the principal families of their respective tribes and clans or divisions. This list the Commissioners found very useful in enabling them to understand the relative influence of the several Chiefs and the strength of their bands.[4]

Resuming their safari on Monday, the party reached Fort Macleod on the morrow, 4 September. Three miles from the Fort, Governor Laird was met by some officers and a large party of the Mounted Police, and escorted into town. The pomp and circumstance with which the Governor was greeted was in marked contrast to the informality which had marked the first meeting of the Territorial Council. As the party approached their destination, the Mounted Police's artillery, the field pieces which in 1874 they had hauled all the way from Red River, boomed out a thirteen-gun salute. On their arrival at the village, the police band burst into a lively musical greeting. The entire population, white and native, had turned out to welcome the Honorable the Lieutenant-Governor. Laird's carriage was halted in the centre of the settlement, and John C. Bell, a prominent local citizen, read the following address:

TO THE HONORABLE DAVID LAIRD,
Lieutenant-Governor, N.W.T.

We, the citizens of Fort Macleod, beg to welcome you to this little village, one of the pioneer settlements of this great North-West.

To have so distinguished a visitor in our midst is an honor we all appreciate, as in that visit we feel an assurance of your interest in our welfare and prosperity, which had its dawn with the advent of the Mounted Police in the North-West, and which, through their care and vigilance, has continued to this time.

We trust that your visit here will be as pleasant to you as it will be long remembered by us.

> CHAS. E CONRAD,
> THOMAS J. BOGY,
> DANIEL SAMPLE,
> LIONEL E. MANNING,
> JOHN C. BELL.

To which the Governor replied:

Gentlemen,

I thank you for your kind address, and for the hearty welcome you have extended to me on my first visit to this pioneer settlement of the Canadian North-West. After roughing it for the last twenty-four days on the broad unsettled prairies, you have surprised me by a reception which betokens all the elements of civilization.

It affords me unfeigned pleasure to learn that the advent of the Mounted Police in this country has been fraught with such advantages to you as a community.

Permit me to express the conviction that in return for that diligence and care on the part of the Police Force which you so highly and justly value, you will always be found conducting yourselves as becomes worthy subjects of that illustrious Sovereign whom I have the distinguished honor to represent in these territories.

In conclusion, I would remark that you have taken me so unexpectedly by your address that I feel unequal to making an appropriate reply; but the agreeableness of the surprise will tend to heighten the pleasure of my visit, as well as to render abiding the interest which I undoubtedly feel in your welfare and prosperity.[5]

Nor was this welcome the end of ceremonial. During his stay at the Fort, Laird reviewed the Police garrison, Troops C and D, and the artillery. The *Globe* correspondent relates, "They deployed at a walk, trot, and gallop, and His Honor expressed his unqualified admiration at the splendid form of the men. He was especially pleased with the artillery, whose horses and equipment were in beautiful condition, and requested Commissioner Macleod to convey to the officers and men his surprise and pleasure at finding the force at this post so perfectly drilled and acquainted with their duties."[6]

To twentieth-century minds, the thought of a police force possessing artillery may seem startling. But one must remember that the NWMP, that semi-military body, was organized on a military model, that of a cavalry unit (hence the RCMP's still-continuing yellow stripe on their trousers). The Police began their great trek west with a battery of nine-pounders, to reduce the hostile forts of Montana whiskey traders. Fortunately, in its history, these guns have never had to be fired, as they say, in anger.

One may well imagine that Regimental Sergeant-Major Sam Steele had drilled the constables within an inch of their collective lives. When the NWMP had spent the winter of 1873-74 at Lower Fort Garry, Steele, then a troop sergeant-major, had been the Force's riding and drill instructor. He had had the recruits out-doors, in the saddle and on the parade ground every day that the temperature did not fall below -36° F. Because of his harsh demands on the newly-inducted Mounties, he was called (but not to his face) Smoothbore Steele.

> The story was told of how a bronco threw a rider in the Lower Fort Garry corral, then proceeded to stamp on him: "Someone catch and look after that poor horse," Steele is supposed to have shouted. "And a couple of you carry that awkward lout off the square!" The awkward lout in question was one of Steele's brothers.[7]

Subsequently, Steele rose to the rank of superintendent in the Mounted Police and major-general in the Canadian Army, and served in the North-West Rebellion, the Boer War, and World War I. Thirty years after the signing of Treaty No. 7, both Steele and Laird found themselves holding important positions in Winnipeg. Since Winnipeg was then a small if rapidly growing city, it is probable that two such prominent citizens would meet from time to time, although there seems to be no record of such encounters.

At Fort Macleod, formalities and ceremonial out of the way, Laird mixed business and relaxation. He had interviews with several Blood chiefs, who wished to negotiate their adherence to the proposed treaty at Fort Macleod rather than at Blackfoot Crossing. The governor promised that in the future, annuities would be paid to the Bloods wherever was most convenient to them, but for the initial negotiations it would be well for all chiefs and their head men to meet together, so that all might feel that they had been consulted. The Bloods departed, quite satisfied with Laird's diplomatic explanation.

Laird had been directed — of course, in the most courteous language — to use the services of Father Lacombe in conducting his negotiations with the Indians. For some months that celebrated priest and his Methodist counterpart, the Rev. John McDougall, had been busy preparing their respective adherents for the treaty. Unfortunately, en route to Fort Macleod, Lacombe had fallen ill. His place was taken by his fellow-Oblate, Father Constantine Scollen, whom Laird interviewed at the Fort.

With some time on his hands, the governor did a bit of sight-seeing. After the fiasco of Fort Livingstone and the crudeness of nascent Battleford, he was surprised at the amenities in Fort Macleod. He found it supplied with excellent stores well stocked with dry goods, hardware, and groceries, and with a quite good blacksmith shop using coal obtained from the Pelly River, some twenty miles away.

There is an old adage that one may take a boy off the farm, but one can never take the farm out of the boy. So it seems to have been with David Laird, who examined the countryside with an astute agricultural eye. In his report to Ottawa he noted:

> The land around the fort, and indeed for almost the whole distance between the Bow and Old Man's Rivers, is well adapted for grazing; and where cultivation has been fairly attempted this season, grain and vegetables have been a success. In short, I have very little doubt that this portion of the territories, before many years, will abound in herds of cattle, and be dotted with not a few considerable homesteads.[8]

On 12 September, Commissioner Macleod rode out for Blackfoot Crossing, accompanied by the two troops stationed at Fort Macleod and the artillery from that post. Two days later, Inspector C. E. Denny left Fort Calgary for the same destination with a detachment of F Troop. Also on 14 September, a Friday, Laird departed from Fort Macleod. He reached the Crossing the following Sunday.

Probably never in the history of the North-West Territories had so many people assembled in one place at the same time. They included not only the 4,392 Indians who were to come under Treaty No. 7 but another 432 Crees who had arrived to indicate their adhesion to Treaty No. 6. Some half-breeds — that word not yet a pejorative term — were on hand to seek assistance from the governor. Representatives of such influential American trading companies as T. C. Power & Bro. and J. G. Baker & Co. were there, eager to exchange their goods for the Indians' treaty money, as were the Hudson's Bay Company and a number of independent traders. These businessmen requested permission of the governor to cut sufficient timber to erect secure storehouses for their stocks-in-trade. Since the Indian chiefs objected to the trees along the river being destroyed for such a purpose, Laird ". . . deemed it prudent, to prevent complications, to ask the traders to erect only temporary stanchions sufficient to support canvas coverings. They complied with our wishes, and the Indians gave us not further trouble on the subject."[9]

Others were at the Crossing for diverse reasons; the missionaries and the Mounties because duty required their presence — but probably neither group would willingly have been absent. Nor would such journalists as the anonymous correspondent of the Toronto *Globe* or twenty-four-year-old Frank Oliver, recently of the *Winnipeg Free Press* and soon to establish the *Edmonton Bulletin*. Eventually he would join Wilfrid Laurier's cabinet. When he was seventy-eight years old, his story of the treaty would appear in *Maclean's Magazine*.

There are few occasions when witnesses of great historic events, other than the principals, are present by their own choice. Usually they are on hand either through chance or because duty has required them to attend.

Before the Battle of Agincourt, Shakespeare has Henry V inspiring his soldiers by telling them of the momentous and climactic significance of the coming engagement:

> This day is called the feast of Crispian.
> He that outlives this day and comes safe home
> Will stand a tip-toe when this day is nam'd,
> And rouse him at the name of Crispian
>
>   . . .
>
> And Crispin Crispian shall ne'er go by,
> From this day to the ending of the world
> But we in it shall be remembered;
> We few, we happy few, we band of brothers.
>
>   . . .
>
> And gentlemen in England, now a-bed,
> Shall think themselves accurs'd they were not here,
> And hold their manhood cheap whiles any speaks
> That fought with us upon Saint Crispin's day.
>
>   (Henry V, Act iv, Sc. 3)

Shakespeare, of course, was knowledgable after the event. It can be doubted that the conscripts in Henry's army heard any such stirring call to arms, or that they realized, then or later, that they were makers of history. One can well imagine that for them the impending battle was merely the latest in a long series of engagements, and would be followed by still others. In the end, each of those who lived to return home might brag about how he won the war, but at the moment, survival and not glory was his immediate and personal goal. Great historical moments usually slip by unrecognized.

But not always. Somehow, in 1877, throughout the whole North-West there was a recognition that with Treat No. 7, history was being made. Yet it was neither the first nor the last of the Great Treaties, nor in comparison with several others did it encompass a large area. A hundred years after its signing it is hard to understand why it has attracted so much attention, then and now. Yet such was and is the case. Perhaps it is because so many first-hand accounts of that treaty have been published and republished.

That September of more than a century ago saw the greatest assembly the North-West Territories have ever witnessed. In addition to the approximately five thousand Indians who converged on Blackfoot Crossing and those whites who had business there — police, traders, missionaries — other whites and Métis travelled many weary miles to be present. Practically the entire able-bodied population of Fort Macleod followed the treaty commissioners to the site. Others came from tiny Fort Calgary, sixty-odd miles west, and still others trekked some two hundred and fifty miles from Fort Edmonton.

Among the latter was that Fort's Chief Factor (later Senator) Richard R. Hardisty. Keeping an eye on his Company's business was only part of the reason for his presence, as he brought his whole family along. The youngest member was his six-year-old namesake, Richard C. Hardisty, whose account of the great event would appear in the *Calgary Herald* almost sixty years later, and in the *Alberta Historical Review* in 1957.

The other Great Treaties are forgotten and neglected, except by historians and those most intimately concerned with them, i.e., the Indians and the bureaucrats in Indian Affairs. But not Treaty No. 7. On the centenary of its signing, descendents of original signatories, Indian and white, and Mounties, and even — especially — Charles, Prince of Wales, gathered at the Crossing to mark the anniversary. "Chief Leo Pretty Young Man of the Blackfoot tribe says the treaty carries deep spiritual significance to the Blackfoot nation, but he views it more as a commemorative event than a celebration."[10]

The landscape at the Crossing in July, 1977, when the commemorative ceremonies took place, was little changed from what it had been a century before. No town or village stood on the banks of the Bow; no highway or railway passed within four miles of it. But as the appointed 17 September 1877 approached, the scene changed; the wilderness became a great camp.

As Treaty Day came closer, during that beautiful September of 1877, more and more people, native and white, gathered at the Crossing and on the flat expanses on either side of the river. Young Richard Hardisty's remembrance of the scene was rather different from Laird's almost-contemporaneous description:

> On the north side of the river at Blackfoot Crossing there was a large flat; on the south side of the river the flat was small, with a semi-circle of high hills to the river's edge.[11]

The Hardistys and the McDougalls, somewhat apprehensive about the temper of the Blackfoot and their allies, camped on the north side of the river.

> On the south side of the river were the imposing group of white tents of the Treaty Commission; the tents and freight wagons of the traders from Macleod, ready to gather in the flood of Canadian dollars that would be let loose by the signing of the treaty. On the north side were camped the Mountain Stoneys from the Upper Bow, and Chief Bob-Tail's band of Crees from Battle River. Their tents were of buffalo leather, like those of the Blackfeet, and were of the style and pattern universal among the Indians of the plains.

> There was, besides, a numerous and miscellaneous assortment of unattached Indians, half-breeds and whites from the more Northerly plains and the Edmonton settlements on the North Saskatchewan and other Northern points, who were without any special reason for their presence except a desire to see what was to be seen and to tread hitherto forbidden ground. Of these I was one.[12]

So wrote Frank Oliver. His account continues:

> Eastward from the camp, the valley for miles was full of horses which seemed to be unguarded. But if the herd were approached, a Blackfeet head promptly popped up from among them. This was accepted as notice to move in another direction. Horses were wealth, power, prestige, quick transport that made Indian life on the buffalo plains most pleasant and desirable. They were the most valued possession of both Indians and whites, and were guarded accordingly.[13]

As the day and hour appointed for the commencement of negotiations approached, tension mounted. Mounted Policeman William Parker has told of activities on the day preceding the opening formalities:

> Early the next morning we noticed there was quite a stir in the Indian camp. Women were working on horses which were tied up here and there at their teepees, and parties of two and three warriors kept riding up the hill to the prairie bench above. Then we heard shouting and fierce Indian yells. We all turned out and lined the south side of the camp as Indians galloped from the coulee in twos and threes, mounted on their

painted horses. The riders were all naked except for breechcloths and were painted in the most hideous colors from head to foot. Some had yellow and black spots all over; others, white spots; still others, the body was half black and half white. As they passed us at full gallop, they woud lie alongside their horses on the opposite side with just their foreheads showing over the horse's mane. They would shoot off their rifles under the horse's necks right over our heads and after firing they would come to an upright position on the horse. Then, as they galloped off, with hand to mouth they would yell out their shrill war cries. They circled the entire valley and finally wound up at their own camp.[14]

Inspector Denny was equally impressed by the constantly shifting panorama by these last free Indians of the Plains.

There must have been as least a thousand lodges in camps on both sides of the river. . . Their horses, herded day and night, covered the uplands to the north and south of the camp in thousands. It was a stirring and picturesque scene; great bands of grazing horses, the mounted warriors threading their way among them, and, as far as the eye could reach the white Indian lodges glimmering among the trees along the river bottom. By night the valley echoed to the dismal howling of the camp's curs, and from sun to sun drums boomed from the tents. Dancing, feasting, conjuring, incantations over the sick, prayers for success in the hunt or in war, all went to form a panorama of wild life vastly novel and entertaining, and seen but once. Never before had such a concourse of Indians assembled on Canada's western plains; never had the tribes appeared so contented and prosperous.[15]

On the appointed morning, as young Richard remembered, the Hardistys, along with hundreds of on-lookers, began to make their way towards the treaty tent.

Boylike, I took in everything that was taking place. The police were busy putting the camp in order, folding blankets and rolling tent sides. One only was carrying on sentry, marching the length of the front of the camp. The sun was bright with a slight chill in the air. The commissioners were standing about enjoying an after breakfast pipe. The meeting with the chiefs was o take place at 10 a.m.[16]

About 8:30 a.m., without warning, not even the bark of a dog, the piercing war cries of some 3,000 braves led by their war chief rang out, followed by a deafening roar of the firing of hundreds of muzzle-loading guns and pistols. There appeared on the skyline the naked warriors in war paint mounted on ponies bareback, one line in their ponies' mouths, many carrying two braves, yelling their war cry and firing their guns. They made a mad dash down the hill, the leaders only drawing their horses to their haunches when their noses almost touched the first row of tents. Then, from somewhere unnoticed till that moment, a dignified and stately figure walked to the centre in front of the commissioners' tents (the commissioners already being seated) followed by two other figures. One spread a robe on the ground. A stone pipe was filled and lighted. Crowfoot took one puff and the pipe was then passed to Governor Laird who also took a puff. The conference was now open . . .[17]

References

1. David Laird, "Special Appendix C" in Canada, *Sessional Paper (No. 10)*, 1878, pp. xxxiv-xxxv.

2. *Ibid.*, p. xxxv.

3. *Ibid.*

4. *Ibid.*

5. Anon., Toronto *Globe*, despatch dated 4 October 1877.

6. *Ibid.*

7. Robert Stewart, *Sam Steele Lion of the Frontier*, p. 21.

8. Laird, *op. cit.*, p. xxxvii.

9. *Ibid.*, p. xxxviii.

10. Reg Vickers, "Cluny treaty ceremonies," Toronto *Globe and Mail*, 12 July 1977.

11. Richard Hardisty, "The Blackfoot Treaty an eye witness account," *Alberta Historical Review*, v. 5, no. 3 (Spring 1957), p. 20.

12. Frank Oliver, "The Blackfoot Indian Treaty," *Maclean's Magazine*, 15 March 1931, p. 32.

13. *Ibid.*

14. H. A. Dempsey, editor, *William Parker Mounted Policeman*, pp. 40-41.

15. Hardisty, *op. cit.*, p. 20.

17. *Ibid.*

8

Treaty No. 7:
Drama

As is well known to lawyers, police, historians, psychologists and others who from time to time are required to weigh and evaluate evidence, eye-witness accounts of the same even may vary widely, especially if one account is related long after the event itself and long after another. Fur-

Painting by A. Bruce Stapleton, original owned by J.B. Cross. At left standing is Major Irvine, next to him in buckskin is interpreter Jean L'Heureux. Seated: Col. Macleod and Lt. Gov. Laird. At right is Crowfoot, with an interpreter beside him. (Glenbow Institute, Calgary)

thermore, interpretations of the same occurrence may differ, depending on the observors' mental and emotional baggage, their social and cultural background which they bring to the *mise-en-scene*. Thus Richard Hardisty indicates that only Crowfoot and two other Indians met the treaty commissioners early on the morning of 17 September 1877. But David Laird's own account is somewhat different. He reported:

> The Commissioners were visited by Crowfoot, the principal Chief of the Blackfeet, shortly after their arrival. He desired to know when he and his people might meet us. We ascertained that most of the Indians on the ground were Blackfeet and Assiniboines or Stonies, from the upper part of the Bow River. But as the 17th was the day named, the Commissioners determined to adhere to the appointment, and sent a messenger early in the morning to invite the Indians camped around to meet them at the council tent at two o'clock, p.m.
>
> Half an hour before the time appointed a gun was fired as a signal for the Indians to assemble. The meeting was well attended. The Chiefs came forward first and were introduced to the Commissioners, and their followers, on being invited, sat up close to the tent.
>
> I addressed them, stating that the Queen's Government had last year promised that they would this year be visited by Commissioners to invite them to make a treaty. That months ago I had named this very day to meet them, and that in accordance with the promises made, the Commissioners were now here to discuss the terms of a treaty. Yet as we had learned that very few of the Bloods, Sarcees or Piegans had arrived, we would not unduly press forward the negotiations, but wait until Wednesday to give the others time to arrive.[1]

Today it little matters whether only three Indians or several turned up for that first session. What is significant is that on that occasion the Bloods, Peigans (Piegans), and Sarcees were virtually unrepresented.

The Toronto *Globe* correspondent who was present on that occasion has provided a full text of Laird's address:

> Last year a message was sent to you by the Councillors of the Great Mother that they would meet you at an early date, and as her councillors always keep their promise, they have appointed Col. Macleod and myself to meet you here now. We appointed this day, and I have come a very long distance to keep my promise, and have called you together to discover if you all have responded to my summons, and if any Chiefs are now absent, to learn when they shall arrive. You say that some of the Blood Chiefs are absent, and as it is our wish to speak to them as well as to you, and as they have a very long way to come to reach this place, we shall give them until next Wednesday to come in. On that day I will deliver to you the Queen's message, but if any of the Chiefs would desire

to speak now, we will be glad to listen to them. I would tell you now that while you remain provisions will be issued or the use of those who wish to accept them.[2]

Of course, the governor's speech was delivered through an interpreter. It was the function of the Police guide and interpreter, the celebrated (or notorious) Jerry Potts, to render the address into Blackfoot, and so after a few sentences Laird stopped, to give him an opportunity to do so. But on this occasion Potts proved a broken reed. Fluent as he was in Blackfoot, he understood not a syllable of Laird's formal language, and even if he had, the Blackfoot tongue did not have the words to permit a literal translation.

Potts was the son of an American trader of Scottish origin and an American Blackfoot woman. After his father was murdered, Potts identified with his mother's people. Unimpressive in appearance and stature, he grew up to be the terror of the Blackfoot-speakers' enemies. Probably he himself did not know how many had killed in battle or in self-defence. For his unquenchable thirst also, he was a legend in his time. He was married, probably informally 'according to the custom of the country,' four times, simultaneously to his second and third wives, who were sisters.

With the coming of the Police to the North-West Territories in 1874, he crossed the Medicine Line to spend the rest of his life with them. As a tracker and guide he was unexcelled. As an interpreter, his translations were, to say the least, laconic. Dempsey has given two examples of his masterly summaries of verbose orations:

> On one occasion a party of starving Indians visited Fort Macleod and the police listened patiently to the chief, who kept up a constant tirade for several minutes. Potts, sitting quietly, made no attempt to translate. Finally Col. Macleod tapped his interpreter on the shoulder. "What is he saying, Potts?" he asked.
>
> "He wants grub!" was the summation of the chief's entire speech.
>
> The situation was much the same when several prominent chiefs were in attendance. Col. Macleod, who had learned a few words of Blackfoot, recognized "napi-okee" as "whiskey" and "napi-kwan" for "white man" and rightly guessed that the chiefs were expressing their gratitude to the Mounted Police for ridding their hunting grounds of the whiskey traders. Potts said nothing but upon being asked, he shrugged his shoulders and commented simply:
>
> "Dey damn glad you're here."[3]

That Potts was also literal-minded is indicated by an incident, related by William Parker, which occurred during the treaty negotiations:

All Indians, before addressing the commissioner, had to have their names interpreted into English. An Indian stepped up to make a speech and Lavallee interpreted his name as Horse's Tail. Jerry Potts got very mad and yelled out, "you son of a bitch, you lie. I tell you it is Horse's Ass." I saw the governor hold up his hands in horror. He was a very religious man and probably had not heard such choice prairie language before.[4]

Because the Blackfoot-speakers, unlike the Cree-speakers, had hitherto been relatively untouched by the white man's culture — they were buffalo-hunters, not trappers — there were few who knew both Blackfoot and English. Jean L'Heureux, Crowfoot's confidential advisor, was one, but as such he was not a disinterested party to the negotiations, and therefore was not acceptable to the treaty commissioners. About fifty years old, he had been a seminarian in Quebec but, involved in some criminal activity, he had been expelled and made his way to Montana. There he passed himself off as a priest, convincing both American Jesuits and, later, Oblates at St. Albert. Despite exposure and overt homosexuality, an orientation more acceptable to Indians than whites, he gained and kept many friends among the Blackfoot nation. Among these was Crowfoot, to whom he was for many years scribe, interpreter, and advisor. During this period he performed many priestly functions, such as baptizing children and solemnizing marriages. But in white eyes he was a renegade, despised and distrusted, and it is most probable that the commissioners in no way wanted to be under any obligation to him. He died in 1919 in the Lacombe Home near Calgary, presumably in the order of sanctity.

Eventually a suitable interpreter was found in a man known throughout the West as Jimmy Jock. According to Frank Oliver:

This man had lived with the Indians for over half a century, and now was blind as well as old. His real name was James Bird, member of a numerous family connection of that name in the Red River settlement. His father had been an important Hudson's Bay Company officer who had sent his brightest son to England to be educated. After his return to the Red River and before he had reached manhood, he had the misfortune, while using a bow and arrow, to cause the death of a companion and relative. Although the tragedy was accidental, it laid a cloud on his life among his own people. When the buffalo hunters next went to the plains he went with them — and did not return. He had been with the Blackfeet ever since. He was of middle height, well featured, with greying wavy hair which he wore long and well kept, falling to his shoulders. He carried a staff which he used to support his hands while standing between the curved lines of Indians and whites who faced each other. The two commissioners were the central point of the line of whites, as

Crowfoot and the other head chiefs were the centre of the Indian line. He was a striking, and as it seemed to me an almost uncanny, figure. With sightless eyes he faced those who spoke while they were speaking, and then, turning without a moment's delay delivered the message to the line of listeners opposite. His speech was distinct and clear. He never hesitated for a word nor asked the meaning of a phrase. His English was perfect, and no doubt his Indian was quite as good. The fact that, under widely changing and in many cases trying circumstances, no question was ever raised by the Indians as to an interpretation of the terms of the treaty must be credited in great measure to the clear and definite understanding received by them through old and blind, but reliable and efficient, "Jimmy Jock."[5]

Potts, L'Heureux, and "Jimmy Jock" were 'bit' players in the drama that was unfolding on the banks of the Bow. Principals were the commissioners on one side; the Indian chiefs on the other. Among the latter the star was undoubtedly Crowfoot.

Perhaps no other Indian leader has been so little understood, both in his own time and subsequently, by members of the white superordinate society. Some had regarded him as virtually the sovereign of the Blackfoot nation, despite the fact that Blackfoot-speakers were divided into four tribes: The Canadian and American Bloods (the latter sometimes known as Blackfeet or as Piegans), the Peigans, and the Blackfoot proper. Further, each tribe was divided into two or more bands, each of which was self-governing. So far was Crowfoot from being a supreme ruler that when his mark was affixed to the treaty document, it was a head chief of the South Blackfoot only. Others signed for the North and Middle Blackfoot; still others for different bands of the Peigans and Bloods. Those who thought Crowfoot almost a monarch have been misled on two counts. Accustomed to think of government in terms of white models, systems with power-wielding kings, vice-roys, governors, they simply could not understand government by consensus, one in which those who disagree with a group's decision are not bound by it, one in which a leader may have influence but not power, one in which, far from imposing levies on his followers, it is his moral duty to meet their material needs before looking to his own welfare. And since Crowfoot was the most prominent of the Blackfoot nation in its contacts with the whites, the latter considered him the most powerful, indeed, almost omnipotent, among his own people.

To some starry-eyed romantics, Crowfoot was the perfect exemplar of a dark-skinned British subject, as loyal to the British crown and British institutions as was, for example, Sam Steele, who spent half a century in the uniform of his sovereign. To others, Crowfoot was a puppet in the hands of the Mounted Police, a cat's paw that they used to pull their chestnuts out of fires, a stooge who cajoled other Indians into signing away their birthright for a mess of pottage. But as Hug Dempsey has pointed out in *Crow-*

foot Chief of the Blackfeet, his loyalty was always first and foremost to his people — his adopted people, for he was born a Blood. When he advised co-operation — submission — to the white government, it was because in his judgment any other action in the long run would be disastrous.

Others have denigrated Crowfoot not as a 'war' but as a mere 'camp' chief. These also have misread the man and misunderstood the nature of Indian society. In the first place, Crowfoot had shown himself to be both a brave warrior and a hunter of unlimited skill and courage. On one occasion, for example, he had single-handed attacked and killed an enraged grizzly bear. Secondly, being a war chief, self-appointed, was a sometime thing, a rank which existed only during war and only as long as such a chief could persuade his followers that he could lead them to wealth or glory. They were free to resign from his army at any time. And when the war was won or lost, the war chief became simply another member of the band, perhaps not even a councillor or headman. But a so-called 'camp' chieftainship was a permanent position. Among Amerindians, such a chief was chosen by traditional practice, at least north of the Rio Grande. This practice varied from one band to another; in some, only the women participated. Three qualities were requisite for such a leader: courage, generosity, and wisdom, the last including the verbal ability to persuade others of the soundness of one's views. Thus oratory too was important to a chief, and legend has it there was many a Demosthenes among Indian leaders. Courage, of course, was self-evident. Generosity on a chiefly scale required wealth, but that was its principal advantage. Otherwise, the richer a Plains Indian was in material possessions, except for horses, the more encumbered he was and the less mobile in a mobile and nomadic society.

Contrary to the impressions of many, Great Plains chieftainships were not and are not hereditary. Perhaps the son of a chieftain had an inside track when the office became vacant through the death or retirement of the incumbent. For one thing, his father could have left him with the material resources to be as generous as a chief was expected to be. Perhaps more important, since more was expected of chief's child, he tended to try harder and achieve more than his peers. As any psychologist is aware, high expectations are very effective motivators.

Laird may have been annoyed but was hardly disturbed that few Peigans and Sarcees and almost no Bloods were present for the formal opening of negotiations. Perhaps he should have been. The Police had originally announced that the treaty would be negotiated at Fort Macleod; Crowfoot stated that he would not attend a meeting in a white man's fort. Because of Crowfoot's prestige in white men's eyes, the location was altered to Blackfoot Crossing. This change angered the Blood chiefs, nor did Laird's soothing words alleviate their feelings, although he may have thought so. Nor, according to Dempsey, was Crowfoot entirely blameless.

Crowfoot was aware of this misunderstanding and, although he usually saw that his fellow chiefs were consulted, there were times when the robe of supreme commander did not feel uncomfortable on his shoulders.[6]

Accepting Laird's offer of supplies, one Blood and the Stoneys applied for flour, tea, sugar, and tobacco. Crowfoot and some of his followers would accept no rations until they heard the terms of the proposed treaty, feeling that acceptance of supplies would commit them to the commissioners' proposals. "Though I feared this refusal did not augur well for the final success of the negotiations," Laird reported, "yet I could not help wishing that other Indians whom I have seen, had a little of the spirit in regard to dependence upon the Government exhibited on this occasion by the great Chief of the Blackfeet."[7]

Adjourning the conference from Monday to Wednesday did not provide a holiday for the treaty commissioners. On Monday evening Laird received a message from Bob-tail, chief of a Cree band encamped on the north side of the Bow, a prudent distance from their hereditary enemies on the south bank. Bob-tail wished to bring his band into a treaty, but had not appeared with Crowfoot and the others because he was unsure that the commissioners would welcome him with the Stoneys and those from the Blackfoot nation. Laird asked Bob-tail to meet the commissioners the following day, separately from the other Indians.

Accordingly, the next day Chief Bob-tail and his followers conferred with the commissioners at 2 p.m. It appeared that this Cree band, who dwelt near the Upper Bow headwaters, were within the geographical bounds of the proposed treaty, but wished a reserve in the Pigeon Lake area, within the limits of Treaty No. 6. In view of the long-time animosity between the Cree and their neighbors to the south, Laird agreed that the Crees should be separated from the others as widely as possible, and Bob-tail's band should receive their annuities with other Crees north of the Red Deer River. Bob-tail consented to this arrangement. Laird then stated that his people could not be paid until after the Blackfoot and other groups had received their money and gifts; otherwise jealousy and dissention might arise. In the meantime, the Crees could receive rations. Bob-tail accepted Laird's plan and agreed to sign an adhesion to Treaty No. 6 any time the lieutenant-governor was prepared to receive him.

Tuesday must have been a rather anxious waiting period for the commissioners. Would the Blood and other missing chiefs appear or not? In fact, a number of bands did arrive, but few of the Blood chiefs. Nevertheless, the commissioners decided against any further postponements beyond Wednesday. On that day, presumably in the morning, they renewed the offer of rations to the Indians, telling them that acceptance of such supplies did not commit them to the terms of the proposed treaty. Most chiefs, even

Crowfoot, asked for flour, tea, sugar and tobacco, and within a day or two, for meat also. Thereafter, the supply of beef cattle began to decrease rapidly.

Early Wednesday afternoon saw what was really the formal opening of the treaty negotiations. Laird reported that the proceedings began at 2 p.m., and surely he would have known. The *Globe* correspondent differed slightly on this detail:

> On Wednesday the Commissioners met the Chiefs at the great Council House. A guard of honor of fifty mounted men accompanied them, commanded by Major Irvine. The Police band received them, and at one o'clock the guns fired a salute as the Governor and Col Macleod took their seats. There were present at the opening of the treaty a number of ladies and gentlemen who had come long distances to witness this novel spectacle. Mrs. Macleod, Mrs. Winder, Mrs. Shurtleff, and a number of other ladies from Morleyville and Edmonton, also the Rev. Messrs. Scollen and McDougall, Mr. De L'Hereux, Mr. Conrad, Mr. Bogy, and the whole white population of Fort Macleod. Nearly all of the Chiefs and minor Chiefs of the Blackfeet, Blood, Piegan, Stony, and Sarcee tribes were seated directly in front of the Council House; and forming a semi-circle of about one-third of a mile beyond the Chief, about four thousand men, women, and children were squatted on the grass, watching with keen interest the commencement of the proceedings.[8]

The journalist was incorrect in stating that most of the chiefs of the five tribes were present. Certainly there were few of the Blood leaders on hand, and indeed, only the Blackfoot and the Stoneys were well represented. It is highly probable that he also over-estimated the number of onlookers.

The same correspondent also despatched a verbatim transcript to his paper of Laird's address to the Indians. This version, the only one extant, Steele used in its entirety in his *Forty Years in Canada*. These, according to this version, were Laird's words:

> The Great Spirit has made all things, the sun, the moon, and the stars, the earth, the forests, and the swift running rivers. It is by the Great Spirit that the Queen rules over this great country and other great countries. The Great Spirit has made the white man and the red man brothers, and we should take each other by the hand. The Great Mother loves all her children, white man and red man alike; she wishes to do them all good. The bad white man and the bad Indian alone she does not love, and them she punishes for their wickedness. The good Indian has nothing to fear from the Queen or her officers. You Indians know this to be true. When bad white men brought you whiskey, robbed you, and made you poor, and through whiskey made you quarrel amongst yourselves,

she sent the police to put an end to it. You know how they stopped this and punished the offenders, and how much good this has done. I have to tell you how much pleased the Queen is that you have taken the Police by the hands and helped them, and obeyed her laws since the arrival of the Police. She hopes that you will continue to do so, and you will always find the Police on your side if you keep the Queen's laws. The Great Mother heard that the buffalo were being killed very fast, and to prevent them from being destroyed her Councillors have made a law to protect them. This law is for your good. It says that the calves are not to be killed, so that they may grow up and increase; that the cows are not to be killed in winter or spring, excepting by the Indians when they are in need of them as food. This will save the buffalo, and provide you with food for many years yet, and it shows you that the Queen and her Councillors wish you well.

Many years ago our Great Mother made a treaty with the Indians far away by the great waters in the east. A few years ago she made a treaty with those beyond the Touchwood Hills and the Woody Mountains. Last year a treaty was made with the Crees along the Saskatchewan, and now the Queen has sent Col. Macleod and myself to ask you to make a treaty. But in a very few years the buffalo will probably be all destroyed, and for this reason the Queen wishes to help you to live in the future in some other way. She wishes you to allow her white children to come and live on your land and raise cattle, and should you agree to this, she will assist you to raise cattle and grain, and thus give you the means of living when the buffalo are no more. She will also pay you and your children money every year, which you can spend as you please. By being paid in money you cannot be cheated, as with it you can buy what you think proper.

The Queen wishes to offer you the same as was accepted by the Crees. I do not mean exactly the same terms, but equivalent terms, that will cost the Queen the same amount of money. Some of the other Indians wanted farming implements, but these you do not require, as your lands are more adapted to raising cattle, and cattle, perhaps, would be better for you. The Commissioners will give you your choice, whether cattle or farming implements. I have already said we will give you money, I will now tell you how much. If you sign the treaty every man, woman and child will get twelve dollars each; the money will be paid to the head of each family for himself, women and children; every year, forever, you, your women and your children will get five dollars each. This year Chiefs and Councillors will be paid a larger sum than this; Chiefs will get a suit of clothes, a silver medal, and flag, and every third year will get another suit. A reserve of land will be set apart for yourselves and your cattle, upon which none others will be permitted to encroach; for every five persons one square mile will be allotted on this reserve, on which they can cut the trees and brush for firewood and other purposes. The Queen's officers will permit no white man or Half-breed to build or cut the timber on your reserves. If required, roads will be cut through them. Cattle will be given to you, and potatoes, the same as are grown at Fort Macleod. The Commissioners would strongly advise the Indians to take cattle, as you understand cattle better than you will farming for some time, at least as long as you continue to move about in lodges.

Ammunition will be issued to you each year, and as soon as you sign the treaty one thousand five hundred dollars' worth will be distributed amongst the tribes, and as soon as you settle, teachers will be sent to you to instruct your children to read books like this one, which is impossible so long as you continue to move from place to place.

I have now spoken. I have made you acquainted with the principal terms contained in a treaty which you are asked to sign.

You may wish to talk it over in your council lodges; you may not know what to do before you speak your thoughts in council. Go, therefore, to your councils, and I hope that you may be able to give me an answer to-morrow. Before you leave I will hear your questions and explain any matter that may not appear clear to you.[9]

The book to which Laird called attention was, of course, the Bible. After he had finished speaking, there were a few questions; then the council was closed for the day.

Following this session with the commissioners, the councils of the various tribes and bands went into session. The commissioners and other white people had no way of knowing what occurred at these meetings. However, Dempsey has been able to draw on recorded but unpublished interview material which he and others obtained with survivors of the negotiations and their descendants. This material has enabled him to look back through the years and through the walls of the parchment tipis, to eavesdrop on what happened in that of Heavy Shield, where the Blackfoot leaders conferred.

The Blackfoot chiefs were disturbed by Laird's gloomy forecast respecting the imminent disappearance of the buffalo. Since these animals were still relatively common on the Western Plains, as Laird had noted while en route to Fort Macleod, it was virtually impossible for these Indians to realize that they had almost disappeared from the grazing lands of the United States, and would soon be gone from the Canadian prairies. Old Sun, the aged chief of the North Blackfoot band, felt himself too old to decide for his people, and stated that he would abide by the decision of Crowfoot, who was used to dealing with the whites.

Eagle Calf (Eagle White Calf?), chief of the Many Children, favored immediate acceptance, fatalistically resigned to the coming of the white man, but he received no support, even his own band refusing to agree with him. At the opposite extreme, Eagle Ribs, of the Skunks band, not only opposed immediate acceptance but threatened to pull his people out of the negotiations unless better terms were forthcoming. As consensus seemed so distant, as if by common consent all bands and tribes turned to Crowfoot for leadership. Dempsey has succinctly outlined his dilemma:

> He knew that the Mounted Police had saved his tribe from destruction from the whiskey traders and he trusted the words of Col. Macleod. He did not really want to give up the land, to see the mixed-bloods swarm in and kill the buffalo, or to have the whites come in with their herds of cattle and drive the buffalo away. Rather, he wanted to keep and, as long as there were buffalo, to let his people have the exclusive right to hunt them. He wanted to welcome the white people, but not let them come in unchecked. He had heard the words of the commissioner about giving the Indians their own cattle and farming implements, but he could not see the Blackfeet scratching the earth while the buffalo still wandered the plains.
>
> On the other hand, he knew the buffalo were disappearing and that more and more people were settling in his land. Some day the buffalo would be gone and his people would starve. That would be the time they would need to rely on the white man for help.[10]

Crowfoot was not yet ready to commit himself or his people. He wanted to confer with others of the Blackfoot nation, particularly with Red Crow of the Bloods. Consequently, the Thursday session with the commissioners was inconclusive. Thus Laird greeted the chiefs:

> I expect to listen to what you have to say today, but, first, I would explain that it is your privilege to hunt all over the prairies, and that should you desire to sell any portion of your land, or any coal or timber from off your reserves, the Government will see that you receive just and fair prices, and that you can rely on all the Queen's promises being fulfilled. Your payments will be punctually made. You all know the Police; you know that no promise of theirs to you has ever been broken; they speak and act straight. You have perfect confidence in them, and by the past conduct of the Police towards you, you can judge of the future. I think I have now said all, and will listen to you and explain anything you wish to know; we wish to keep nothing back.[11]

Only Button Chief, also named Medicine Calf, a war chief of the Bloods, spoke at any length. In 1855 he had signed treaty with the Americans, only to see the white men repudiate its terms, and he was understandably cautious. He began:

> The Great Spirit sent the white man across the great waters to carry out His ends. The Great Spirit, and not the Great Mother, gave us this land. The Great Mother sent Stamixotokon and the Police to put an end to the traffic in fire-water. I can sleep now safely. Before the arrival of

the Police, when I laid my head down at night, every sound frightened me; my sleep was broken; now I can sleep sound and am not afraid. The Great Mother sent you to this country, and we hope will be good to us for many years. I hope and expect to get plenty; we think we will not get so much as the Indians receive from the Americans on the other side; they get large presents of flour, sugar, tea, and blankets. The Americans at first gave large bags of flour, sugar, and many blankets; the next year it was only half the quantity, and the following years it grew less and less, and now they give only a handful of flour. We want to get fifty dollars for the Chiefs and thirty dollars for all the others, men, women and children, and we want the same every year for the future. We want to be paid for all the timber that the Police and whites have used since they first came to our country. If it continues to be used as it is, there will soon be no firewood left for the Indians. I hope, Great Father, that you will give us all this that we ask.[12]

Stamixotoken (Bull's Head) was the name that the Blackfoot-speakers had given to Macleod, derived from the Police badge with its portrayal of a buffalo bull's head.

Laird poured scorn on Button Chief's suggestion that the Police pay for the wood that they had cut:

I fear Button Chief is asking too much. He has told us of the great good the Police have done for him and his tribe and throughout the country by driving away the whiskey traders, and now he wants us to pay the Chiefs fifty dollars and others thirty dollars per head, and to pay him for the timber that has been used. Why, you Indians ought to pay us rather, for sending these traders in fire-water away and giving you security and peace, rather than we pay you for the timber used.[13]

Laird in his report to the government stated that at this point Crowfoot and the other chiefs laughed heartily at Chief Button's outrageous proposal. But perhaps the governor misinterpreted the Indians' merriment. Perhaps it was not the foolishness of the request but the absurdity of the answer that aroused their laughter. If the Indians owned the land, and the very negotiations for a treaty should seem to imply so (the HBC's Deed of Surrender to the contrary notwithstanding), did they not also own its resources: the fish in the streams, the land, the grass which it nourished, the buffalo that fed thereon, the trees? And if the Indians owned the trees, should they not be paid for them? But of course, wasn't it absurd to expect the rapacious whites to pay for what characteristically and thoughtlessly they simply confiscated for their own use?

But Laird was not finished scolding Button Chief. He continued:

We cannot do you good and pay you too for our protection. Button

Chief wants us to prevent the Crees and Half-breeds from coming in and killing the buffalo. They too are the Queen's children, as well as the Blackfoot and Crees. We have done all we can do in preventing the slaying of the young buffalo, and this law will preserve the buffalo for many years. Button Chief wishes to get the same every year as this year; we cannot make a promise. We cannot make a treaty with you every year. We will give you something to eat each year, but not so much as you will receive now. He says the Americans at first gave the Indians many large sacks of flour, and now they only receive a handful. From us you receive money to purchase what you may see fit; and as your children increase yearly, you will get the more money in the future, as you are paid so much per head.

When your reserves will be allotted to you, no wood can be cut or be permitted to be taken away from them without your own consent. The reserve will be given to you without depriving you of the privilege to hunt over the plains until the land is taken up.[14]

Between Button Chief's requests and Laird's reply, Crowfoot and Old Sun reserved their comments for the morrow. Eagle Tail (Sitting on an Eagle Tail), head chief of the North Peigans, added a few words to those of his brother chiefs:

Great Father, from our Great Mother, Stamixotokon and officers of the Police, the advice and help I received from the Police I shall never forget as long as the moon brightens the night, as long as water runs and the grass grows in spring, and I expect to get the same from our Great Mother. I hope she will supply us with flour, tea, tobacco and cattle, seed and farming implements. I have done at present.[15]

Last speaker of the afternoon was Bear's Paw, who hoped that the commissioners would give his tribe, the Stoneys, as much as possible and as speedily as possible. The *Globe* correspondent editorialized, "This Chief appeared by his speech to be of a mercenary bent of mind."[16] In so commenting, he was not being particularly obtuse. He was, rather, merely reflecting the then-prevalent xenophobic attitude of the white people to their savage, brown-skinned brothers.

So the Thursday session ended. Another day — at least another day — would be needed to persuade the Indians to sign. Probably more, for still the great majority of the Blood tribe had not appeared. Would they come at all? That evening, and far into the night, the council meetings continued. Arguments flew back and forth, became heated. Tempers flared. Button Chief had openly opposed signing; a number of war chiefs vehemently agreed with him. Eagle Calf held an absolutely opposite view. He rode through the camp, threatening to accept the treaty, alone if necessary. No chiefs supported him but many others, their eyes dazzled by the gifts waiting to be distributed, did so. The North Peigan warriors, it was rumored, proposed to wipe out the commission; a prospect which made many of the Indians who heard it extremely apprehensive. Tension mounted. And Crowfoot waited, temporized, procrastinated.

But the tension dissipated and vanished that evening with the news that the main body of the Bloods were on their way. Late in the night they arrived, led by Red Crow; in his following were other prominent leaders of the tribe, such as One Spot and The Moon. Some hours later saw the arrival of the old war chief, Bad Head.

It was a night to remember — and for the staid white Victorians, male and female, one to forget. All night long the hills around re-echoed to the insistent beat of the drums, and the sound of the ancient songs, discordant to white ears, rose and fell. Around the flickering camp-fires the shuffling double-step of the traditional dances continued. Around the lodges the Indian dogs of indeterminate ancestry, excited beyond endurance, added their voices to the noice and turmoil. Tired or not, few slept that night. Yet not all was feasting and dancing and joyous reunions of long-parted friends and relatives. Not all encounters were surreptitious and clandestine courtships in the shadows of trees or tipis. In lodges here and there, chiefs and councillors turned to the medicine men for advice, opened with careful ritual the sacred bundles, and sought the guidance of the Great Spirit. Some moved from group to group, questing always for consensus, for accord.

None prayed for wisdom more assiduously than Crowfoot, for none bore more responsibility. Twice he had gone to the old sachem Pemmican for advice; twice that wise old man had refused to speak. Yet once more the Blackfoot chieftain sought his counsel. But this time the aged medicine man slowly, and feebly gave his advice:

> I want to hold you back because I am at the edge of a bank. My life is at its end. I hold you back because your life henceforth will be different from what it has been. Buffalo makes your body strong. What you will eat from this money will have your people buried all over these hills. You will be tied down, you will wander the plains, the whites will take your land and fill it. You won't have your own free will, the whites will lead you by a halter. That is why I say don't sign. But my life is old, so sign if you want to. Go ahead and make the treaty.[17]

Saturday, 21 September 1877. Yet once more the Police nine-pounder summoned the chiefs and head men to the council tent. When they were all assembled, the commissioners indicated that they were ready to hear the Indians' decision. Crowfoot replied:

> While I speak, be kind and patient. I have to speak for my people,

who are numerous, and who rely upon me to follow that course which in the future will tend to their good. The plains are large and wide. We are the children of the plains, it is our home, and the buffalo has been our food always. I hope you look upon the Blackfeet, Bloods and Sarcees as your children now, that you will be indulgent and charitable to them. They all expect me to speak now for them, and I trust the Great Spirit will put into their breasts to be a good people — into the minds of the men, women and children, and their future generations. the advice given me and my people has proved to be very good. If the Police had not come to the country, where would we all be now? Bad men and whiskey were killing us so fast that very few, indeed, of us would have been left today. The Police have protected us as the feathers of the bird protect it from the frosts of winter. I wish them all good, and trust that all our hearts will increase in goodness from this time forward. I am satisfied. I will sign the treaty.[18]

The next speaker was Button Chief, whom Laird had so scathingly cut down in an earlier meeting. On this occasion the Indian was quite submissive. "I must say what all the people say," he stated, "and I agree with what they say. I cannot make new laws; I will sign."[19]

Red Crow, of the Bloods, spoke at somewhat greater length:

Three years ago, when the Police first came to the country, I met and shook hands with Stamixotokon at Pelly River. Since that time he has made me many promises. He kept them all — not one of them was ever broken. Everything that the Police have done has been good. I entirely trust Stamixotokon, and will leave everything to him. I will sign with Crowfoot."[20]

Another dozen or so chiefs or sub-chiefs spoke their pieces, each in support of Crowfoot. These included Bull's Head, principal chief of the Sarcees, Eagle Head, of the Peigans, and Rainy Chief, of the North Bloods. As each address had to be translated from Blackfoot, Sarcee, or Assiniboine, there was no time for further business that day. Therefore all assembled on the next for the signing, which was preceded by the introduction of Red Crow, great chief of the South Bloods, who had arrived since adjournment the previous day. Some of the Blood chieftains, who to this point had said very little owing to Red Crow's absence, now addressed the assembly; like their leader they accepted the treaty. Then the signing took place, symbolically rather than literally for the Indians. Macleod and Laird affixed their signatures to the document; the natives made their marks, their crosses. Rather, they touched the pen as it was made for them. Meanwhile the nine-pounders boomed out a thirteen-gun salute.

In the end, fifty-one chiefs and councillors' native and translated names apeared on the treaty, the first on the list and the last affixed being

Crowfoot's. The signatures were then witnessed by Assistant Commissioner (Major) A. G. Irvine, six other officers and one non-commissioned officer of the Police, by missionaries McDougall and Scollen, a few other men including Jean L'Heureux, and by a few ladies. These were the wives of Col. Macleod and two police inspectors, young Richard Hardisty's mother, and Anne McDougall, wife of the Reverend John. Their participation, of course, was a courtesy to the fair sex, as it was then so gallantly described, for not even white women in the 1870's were persons, politically speaking, and even less so were Indian women. But the time would come — true, not until the 1950's — when the latter would affix their marks or signatures to treaty adhesions and as principals, not mere witnesses. Not much later a few bands at least would choose female chiefs.

For the Indians, with the signing of the treaty, business was over for the week, but not for David Laird, as he himself reported:

> I was waited upon by a deputation of Half-breeds, who presented me with a petition, expressing the hope that the buffalo law might not be stringently enforced during the approaching winter, and praying that they might receive some assistance to commence farming. With respect to the buffalo ordinance, I told them that the notice having been short, the law would not be very strictly enforced for the first winter, and in regard to their prayer for assistance to farm, I said I would make it known at Ottawa.[21]

Sunday, no work was done. Probably, almost certainly, Scollen and McDougall held services for their respective adherents, but the big event of the day was a sham battle. Parker indicates this took place on the Sunday before the negotiations, but he wrote about it probably some time between 1942 and 1944, over sixty years after the affair. The *Globe* correspondent's account, however, was dated 4 October 1877, only a few days after the event, and his date for the battle was surely the correct one. However, if the date was hazy in Parker's memory, the details were not. As he recalled the affair:

> Having sent word that they would hold a sham battle between the Crees and themselves, everyone with the exception of the camp guard went over to see it. It was a hair-raising affair. They had a big circle about two hundred yards in diameter; the Indian on-lookers, including all the women and chidren, were on the north side, and the lieut. governor and Mounted Police on the south side. A hundred mounted Blood Indians, divided fifty on each side, went at it. Several times an Indian, being shot at, would fall of his horse and the attacking Indian instantly dismounted and rushed to his fallen enemy. He fired a shot close to his head, shipped out his knife and scalped his foe, then tucking the imaginary scalp under his belt, let out his war cry. Several Indians got un-

horsed and there were many fights on the ground with knives. As the Indians were firing ball cartridges it was a miracle nobody was hit. The sham fight lasted about half an hour, the Blackfeet being declared the winners, as they had the most scalps to their credit. This affair, and the galloping parade of the two hundred Blood Indians was all the most thrilling and we would not have missed it for the best farm in Manitoba.[22]

Obviously, Parker was also a little shaky on the number of participants. Aside from this point and the date, his account and that of the *Globe* are on all fours. This is the latter's:

On Sunday afternoon the Indians fought a sham battle on horseback. They wore only the breechcloths. They fired off their rifles in all directions, and sent the bullets whistling past the spectators in such close proximity as to create most unpleasant feelings. I was heartily glad when they defiled past on the way back to their lodges, and the last of their unearthly yells had died away in the distance.[23]

On Monday at 10 a.m. the commissioners met the chiefs of the Blackfoot nation and the Sarcees. They added to the treaty the names of a few minor chiefs who had left the Saturday assembly before completion of the oratory. Then all chiefs were asked to stand as their names were read aloud, and the Indians asked to indicate their recognition of these men as their leaders. After this formality, the lieutenant-governor invested the head chiefs with their flags, uniforms, and medals, and shook their hands. As he did so, the Mounted Police band played "God Save the Queen." Immediately thereafter, the Police began paying out the treaty money. In the afternoon, Laird and Macleod proceeded two miles up the river to the Stoney camp, where the same ceremonial was repeated.

Surely David Laird could now leave for Battleford and a reunion with his family from whom he had been separated so long! It seemed not. Tuesday saw him taking the Cree's adhesions to Treaty No. 6, to which Chief Bob-tail and two councillors, Sometimes Glad and Passingsound, affixed their marks. Laird alone signed for the government, as Macleod's commission presumably did not cover this treaty. However, he affixed his signature as a witness, as did his Assistant Commissioner, A. G. Irvine. The other witnesses were the two missionaries, Scollen and McDougall.

Wednesday witnessed more ceremonial, when the commissioners returned to the council tent to receive an address of thanks, translated by Jean L'Heureux, from the Treaty No. 7 Indians. Laird and Macleod made suitable replies, the latter in the following words:

The Chiefs all here know what I said to them three years ago, when the Police first came to the country: that nothing would be taken away from them without their own consent. You all see to-day that what I told you then was true. I also told you that the Mounted Police were your friends, and would not wrong you or see you wronged in any way. This also you see is true. The Police will continue to be your friends, and be always glad to see you. On your part you must keep the Queen's laws, and give every information to them in order that they may see the laws obeyed and offenders punished. You may still look to me as your friend, and at any time when I can do anything for your welfare, I shall only be too happy to do so. You say that I have always kept my promises. As surely as my past promises have been kept, so surely shall those made by the Commissioners be carried out in the future. If they were broken I would be ashamed to meet you or look you in the face, but every promise will be solemnly fulfilled as certainly as the sun now shines down upon us from the heavens. I shall always remember the kind manner in which you have today spoken of me.[24]

In the evening the Crees tendered similar thanks, with Father Scollen interpreting. Between the two ceremonies the commissioners drove five miles east to inspect a coal seam.

Although Laird left for Battleford Thursday afternoon, payment of treaty money and distribution of presents continued until Friday noon, not without a few minor contretemps. These occurred when some Indians returned to claim money for wives and/or children previously forgotten, or for off-spring conceived but not yet born. In the end, nearly $60,000 were paid out. The traders were notified that they had to leave the Crossing by 10 p.m. the following Tuesday. They had all departed well before the deadline; early enough that the police also were able to leave by noon that day. They reached Macleod in two and one-half days. The weather was intensely cold; the prairies covered with snow as they set out. It was 5 October 1877.

And so David Laird and James Macleod signed a treaty. And Crowfoot, the Blackfoot chief who had been a Blood. Or did he? When he was asked to affix his mark to the treaty, that is, touch the pen in the hand of another, he merely gestured towards it. "As much as he understood the white man's ways, he still was suspicious of any supernatural act which might place him in another man's power, so his hand purposely failed to touch the pen. 'Ah,' said Crowfoot to a companion after signing, 'I did not touch it'."[25]

Did Crowfoot understand the treaty? Perhaps. Did the other Indians? To ask the question is to answer it.

References

1. David Laird, "Special Appendix C" in Canada, *Sessional Papers (No. 10)*, 1878, pp. xxxvii-xxxvii.

2. *Anon.*, Toronto *Globe*, despatch dated 4 October 1877.

3. Hugh A. Dempsey, *Jerry Potts Plainsman*, pp. 16-17.

4. _____, *William Parker Mounted Policeman*, p. 41.
(Other accounts do not identify Lavallee as an interpreter)

5. Frank Oliver, "The Blackfoot Indian Treaty," *Maclean's Magazine*, 15 March 1931, p. 28.

6. Hugh A. Dempsey, Crowfoot Chief of the Blackfoot, p. 95.

7. Laird, *op. cit.*, p. xxxviii.

8. *Globe, op. cit.*

9. *Ibid.* and S. B. Steele, *Forty Years in Canada*, pp. 117-119.

10. Dempsey, *Crowfoot*, p. 98.

11. *Globe, op. cit.*

12. *Ibid.*

13. *Ibid.*

14. *Ibid.*

15. *Ibid.*

16. *Ibid.*

17. Dempsey, *Crowfoot*, p. 102.

18. *Ibid.*, p. 103.

19. *Globe, op. cit.*

20. *Ibid.*

21. Laird, *op. cit.*, p. xli.

22. Dempsey, William Parker, pp. 40-41.

23. *Globe, op. cit.*

24. *Ibid.*

25. C. Scollen to A. G. Irvine, 13 April 1879, no. 14924 in Indian Affairs Archives, Ottawa.

9

Hungry Year

Although the weather was unseasonably cold for early October, David Laird must have been more than usually happy as he travelled across the snow-covered plains on his way back to Battleford. After three years he was to be re-united with his family, from whom he had been separated, except for brief visits, ever since he had been elected to Parliament. Even after he became Minister of the Interior, his home — and his children — remained on the Island. From family tradition it seems that Louisa joined her husband in Ottawa for at least part of one session but she left the children at home. "She told her children on her return that Ottawa was very gay compared to Charlottetown with more more dinner parties and balls than she was used to. I don't know who looked after the children. Likely it was her sister who went to Battleford to help her."[1]

Aside from personal considerations, the lieutenant-governor had reason to feel well satisfied with the previous fortnight's work. He had 'carried the flag,' so to speak, to Fort Macleod, one of the most important settlements in the Territories, and its residents had welcomed him with a warmth and enthusiasm which seemed to go far beyond what strict protocol demanded. He had been much impressed and heartened by the Police, on whom, as governor, he depended for the preservation of law and order. He had had an opportunity to observe them not only on parade and in their quarters but also in the field and to note their steadfastness and tact in dealing with both Indians and others.

The journey to Blackfoot Crossing and his sojourn there had widened his acquaintanceships and initiated friendships with many whom would soon or later play important roles in Laird's life and career. Macleod of course he already knew, since the commissioner was a member of the Territorial council. Assistant Commissioner A. G. Irvine, who had met Laird at Battleford, in 1880 was to succeed Macleod as commanding officer of the Mounted Police and on the council. Inspector Denny would be prominent in the public service of Canada when Laird was Superintendent of Indian Affairs for Manitoba and the North-West Territories at the turn of the century. At the Crossing, if not before, David Laird no doubt met the

McDougalls, David and the Rev. John, and the latter's wife Elisabeth, all
from Morleyville (now Morley). And their in-laws, the Hardistys from
Edmonton — the Chief Factor's wife was a sister of the McDougall men.
And as already mentioned, the governor could not have failed to notice
Sergeant-Major Sam Steele, that Lion of the Frontier.

With his fellow-commissioner James Macleod, David Laird had been
successful in negotiating a treaty with numerous bands of Plains Indians.
Nor were these nice tame aborigines gentled by generations of contact with
the Hudson's Bay Company; they were fiercely independent and had often
proved hostile to and even scornful of the intrusive white man. Laird's and
Macleod's had not been an easy task. Even among the Indians themselves
there had been tensions which had had to be resolved. Mutual distrust had
separated the Blackfoot-speakers and their allies, the Sarcees, from the
Stoneys, even to the extent that these last had prudently located their camp
some two miles away from the others. Even deeper animosities existed towards the Crees, who dared not even camp on the same side of the river as
did the southern bands. Nor could Laird have been unaware that the Blackfoot-speakers had been deeply divided among themselves, so that when
negotations began, it was by no means a foregone conclusion that they
would be successful. Yet through the diplomacy, forbearance, and patience
particularly of Crowfoot on the one hand, of himself and Macleod on the
other, success had been achieved. Further, Ottawa should be pleased that
the terms of this new treaty were substantially the same as or equivalent to
those of previous agreements. No tribe or band could feel that it was receiving unfair treatment in comparison to that accorded to others.

Not only had the two commissioners accomplished the assignment
which they had been given; Laird had also secured the adhesion of an
important group of Crees to Treaty No. 6, one that would remove them
from Treaty No. 7 area and thus lessen the danger of inter-tribal conflict.
In a way, this could not have been as easy as it looked. Bob-tail's band had
had no room to manoeuvre; they had to accept without modification a
treaty the terms of which were already fixed and which they had no part in
negotiating.

Laird was also confident that he had ensured the material security of
the Plains Indians. although the buffalo were decreasing and would inevitably disappear in the future, that future seemed safely distant. As Laird
had seen with his own eyes, the animals were still fairly abundant, and
would last perhaps another decade, long enough for the Indians to learn the
ways of the white man's agriculture and become self-supporting thereby.
No doubt the lieutenant-governor would have been inexpressably shocked
had anyone forecast that within months rather than years the buffalo would
have virtually vanished from the Canadian prairies and parklands.

Their indiscriminate slaughter was the result of the white man's rapacity; for generations, centuries, the Plains Indians had found the buffalo

source of most of life's necessities: food, clothing, shelter. Even bones, sinews, and other organs were put to use. And if at times native methods of hunting were wasteful, as with buffalo jumps and pounds, they never seemed to deplete the supply. But when the procurement and sale of buffalo robes became a commercial enterprise with an apparent unlimited demand to be filled, when rich sportsmen measured their prowess by the number of animals they wantonly killed, the buffalo was doomed.

The Plains buffalo, or some of them, tended to be somewhat migratory, spending the summers on what are now the Western Canadian prairies, drifting south as winter approached, and moving north with the arrival of spring. As their numbers lessened, sometimes Indians on the southern side of the Forty-Ninth Parallel would fire vast stretches of the border grasslands to deny pasturage to the animals and so hold them for their own use and subsistence. It is thus understandable that the Canadian Indians viewed with apprehension and hostility the coming of the fugitive Sioux, who were competing with them for a fast-vanishing food resource.

Some United States Indians could not believe that the disappearance of the buffalo was due to human causes. They ascribed it to the anger of the Great Spirit, who had driven the animals into a hole in the ground to punish the Indians for succumbing to the white man's ways. Only if and when these interlopers were wiped out would the buffalo return. The results of this belief were a number of ferocious and lethal encounters between the Indians and the United States Army.

As he drove through those crisp October days, Laird had no presentiment of the imminence of catastrophe. Still, there were clouds on the horizon. What was to be done about Sitting Bull and his Sioux? Their presence was imposing a toll on the diminishing buffalo herds, to the apprehension of Plains Cree and Saulteaux, the Blackfoot-speakers and their allies, the Stoneys and others. The United States government wanted those fugitives back, safely sequestered on reservations where they would no longer be a threat to the Army and to the flood of settlers whom it was their military duty to protect. Further, some Indian bands were proving quite intransigent when it came to accepting treaties from the Canadian government. Nor were these the bands of the proud, even arrogant Blackfoot nation; they were the usually mild and compliant Crees, men like Big Bear and Chief Beardy. Laird knew that he would have trouble with these stubborn people.

By 13 October 1877 the lieutenant-governor had reached his new, half-furnished home, no doubt delighted to be united again with his family and for the moment heedless of the cares of office. But soon he was involved in the minutiae of work, writing to the Rev. John McDougall regarding the quality of flour being supplied to the Indians[2] or complaining about the slow delivery of furniture and requesting a piano[3] or asking a Dr. Rafferty to see the boy of a Chief Red Pheasant.[4]

A letter to Macleod dated 18 February 1878 indicates the range of the lieutenant-governor's concerns. Marked 'Private' and in his own hand, not his secretary's, it reads:

Dear Col Macleod

Your letter of the 6th Jany came to hand by the last mail. You will have heard ere this that Mr Stipendiary Magistrate Richardson went up to Fort Saskatchewan and disposed of the cases there.

I am sorry that you have had so much trouble with the horse I left behind me. It was scarcely necessary to appoint a Board to report on his fitness to live — but as he was government property, perhaps you took the proper course. All I regret is that we had not ordered him to be shot before we left Bow River, and thus saved much trouble and expense. If there be any bills to liquidate on his account please forward them to me for payment.

The Marsh case, I presume, is all right. Having written to M. I had to make him some reply and thought it best to say that I had called your attention thereto. It is very surprising to me, that the authorities at Ottawa, are so neglectful in sending on copies of the Sessional Statutes. The Indian Act, besides, has been (illegible) and ought to have been sent (illegible) to each Police Station.

I hear from what reports are brought me, that some of your officers are making rather free with the women around there. It is to be hoped that the good name of the Force will not be lost through too open indulgence of that kind. And I sincerely hope that Indian women will not be treated in a way that hereafter may give trouble.

You say nothing about the Blackfeet this winter — whether they are content since the Treaty or not.

Many rumors are in circulation that Sitting Bull has returned to the States. I do not believe them, because I feel he is not such a fool as to seek a fight with the present Forces. But it is now definite that his agents are sending around presents of tobacco and trying to make the Assiniboines (illegible) and unite with him in a general campaign against the Whites (illegible). I have not much confidence in him, and if he could raise a general war — Indian against White, I will not be surprised.

The demand of the U.S. Commission in their reports that he should be removed from our frontier to the interior is cruel in the extreme. The truth is Sitting Bull must make up his mind sonner or later — at least so I think — to return to the States, or starve on this side. Before he will starve he will plunder and fight and there is where the danger lies. The commission made him a very good offer financially — better than Canada can ever do for him. Perhaps giving up his arms and horses was a little more than his pride could bear, but after being out of the fight for a year or two, he will probably not see this demand in the same light. Please write anything you may hear about the intention of the American Government to appoint any additional members thereto, we should have the benefit of their assistance. It is surely possible now at any rate to have a meeting to give members an opportunity before the River break up. We have heard little of our last years work, and perhaps during the Session at Ottawa something new may be said or done, that would give our beings (?) a more useful turn (illegible) delayed until June.

Expect to hear from you (illegible) about Indians affairs for this year.

Yours &c.

D. Laird[5]

Thus Laird passed the winter of 1877-78 in the routine business of his office and in family activities. Fortunately for the most part the weather was comparatively mild, since the buffalo were becoming scarce and the Indians were having to make long treks to find enough meat for themselves and their families. Thus with even more anticipation and eagerness than usual whites and natives alike awaited the coming of spring and return of the buffalo. But, as Mme. Forget, wife of the governor's secretary, relates:

> They never came back, and with the exception of a few stray herds, during the next four or five years, none were seen after the winter of 1878. The Indians whose very existence depended on the buffalo soon found themselves in consequence in the most distressing condition.
>
> We are now in the Spring of 1878. So far pleasure only has been my lot; fear, however, was soon to be a disturbing element in our quiet Western existence. A mild winter was succeeded by an early spring, and every day added a new beauty to the picturesque landscape, so characteristic of Battleford. The plateau extending between the Saskatchewan and the Battlefood River was like a velvety carpet of green and the Eagle Hills were looking so luxuriant after long months of winter whiteness. I was happy in my little home, never for a moment anticipating the days of anxiety that were to follow.
>
> First a rumor from the plains reached us that Indians were coming north. Small bands from numerous points commenced to arrive, all bringing tales of great hardship during the winter. By the mail, which came to Battleford every three weeks, we had the report that the Black-foot Indians had sent a message to the officer in command at Fort Calgary, calling attention to their starving condition. "We have heard," said the message, "that a daughter of our great mother is now on this side of the Great Lake. She has her Mother's heart, let her know that women and little children ask her to give them life, for our great Mother's sake. She is good and will hear us and save us.[6]

The "daughter of our great Mother," of course, was the Marchioness of Lorne, daughter of Queen Victoria and wife of recently-appointed Marquess of Lorne as Governor-General of Canada.

Their prayers were not made in vain, and many cases of distress were relieved by the Mounted Police. But this did not prevent large numbers of Blackfeet finding their way to the Capital. Early in May a deputation from that tribe headed by a Minor Chief, Three Bulls, and the Sarcees with their chief, The Drummer, waited upon His Honor Lieutenant-Governor Laird. They could not realise the disappearance of the buffalo. In fact few did, but attributed their absence from their usual haunts to Americans, Half-breeds and others, killing them and preventing their migration north. The interview was long, but ended satisfactorily in the Indians being presented with some provisions and ammunition for their return to their own part of the country.

So far nothing of an unusual character had occurred to cause alarm. The visit of the Blackfeet Indians had on the contrary been quite welcome. They were the first we saw. Their manners, dresses and language so differed from those of the Crees, attracted our curiosity and helped in breaking the monotony of our peaceful life.

But from now on, during a couple of months, starving Sioux, Sarcees, Blackfeet, Stonies and Crees, kept coming in increasing numbers, until some three or four thousand of them were camped near our houses.[7]

Mme. Forget does not indicate whether the Sioux were followers of Sitting Bull or an earlier group who had fled to Canada in 1862 after a bloody confrontation with Americans in Minnesota Territory. These had been granted reserves in the Treaty No. 2 limits of the North-West Territories, areas in what is now in south-western Manitoba and south-eastern Saskatchewan. As United States 'citizens' they were not accepted as signatories to the treaty nor granted annuities or other benefits. But they could become as hungry as any 'treaty' Indians.

Mme. Forget's story continues:

The most alarming rumors regarding their intentions were circulating. All night long, commencing with the break of day, gangs of Indians kept moving around our houses, chanting weird and monotonous songs, with accompaniment of the inevitable tam tam, and the firing of guns. Assistance, of course, was given to them; but provisions in the few stores of the Town of Battleford became very soon exhausted, and quite a long interval elapsed before any new supply coming all the way from Winnipeg by carts, could be procured. The white population, for that reason, also were not in a much better position. Meat of all kinds was fast becoming scarce. The few head of cattle yet remaining, with the exception of milk cows in the possession of settlers, belonged to the Mounted Police, and none of these could well be spared for general distribution. We had to live, in the main, on milk and bread. Mushrooms were fortunately plentiful that spring and proved quite a change in our meagre diet. The little fresh meat that we procured occasionally from the Police, had to be cooked in the greatest secrecy, with doors locked and blinds drawn, and even the keyhole of the kitchen door stuffed, for fear of exciting the envy of the Indians. When the cows were milked a number of Indians never failed to be around with vessels of all descriptions for a share for their starving children. One morning, breakfast had just been cooked. The door for some cause was accidently left unlocked while I went upstairs. To my great consternation, coming down I found five big Blackfeet squatted on the floor and my breakfast vanished. Everything in sight, in the shape of eatables had also disappeared, even including salt and matches. My husband then went out looking for mushrooms; and desirous of teaching the Indians the use they could make of them, invited a few of them to come and see how to prepare them for the table. The dish was nearly ready and they were about to have a taste of it, when he happened to mention that great caution had to be exercised when picking them on the prairie, as some kinds were poisonous. The words were scarcely out of his mouth when they began to leave one after the other, and none could be prevailed upon to even touch of the new dish.

If the Indians ignored the virtues of the mushrooms, they were well acquainted with the wild turnip and the rhubarb. The prairie abounded fortunately with the former, and great quantities were gathered daily by the women and children. For miles around numerous little lumps of freshly turned soil indicated where these tuberous roots had been found. These with ducks and gold eyes in the Battle River, and such little flour as they could procure in exchange for ponies, they managed to eke out a living. But their grumblings were daily getting louder and louder, and their demands for assistance more pressing. Many interviews they had with the Lieutenant-Governor and the acting Indian Superintendent. Threats were not yet made openly, but everybody felt that the climax was fast approaching, unless assistance was soon given. Yet this could not be had until the arrival of freighters with provisions from the East. These were on the road, but coming slowly. Would they arrive on time?

We were then on June 26th. We had had an anxious night. Indians had kept prowling with but little interruption during the whole night and had come singing death songs under our very windows. In consequence we had but little rest that night. Breakfast as usual had been prepared and speedily despatched within closed doors, and my husband had just left for his office, when a sudden volley of rifle shots quite near the house drew my attention outside. some five of six hundred Indians, painted in the most hideous manner, mounted on their ponies, with rifles in hand, were galloping in all directions and firing at random, apparently taking little care whether any person was hit or not. Fearing to venture outside, I sought refuge in the house, locking doors, and there I was all trembling, not being able to understand what this performance meant, when my husband came rushing back home. This was a war or hungry dance, so he had heard, as a prelude to a last meeting with the Governor. Notice of this had been sent to His Honor, with the assurance that no harm was intended, but no time was given to make it known and the alarm among the white people became very great. Most of them, however, came up the hill from the town to view the strange sight, which lasted about thirty minutes. At the close of the dance the wild riders of the plains drew gradually together and moved in a compact body towards Government House, followed by a great number of women and children. The meeting with the Governor took place in the wide open space near Government House, in a most orderly manner. The Indians themselves formed three lines of a square and the women and children behind. His Honor, for a little time stood alone fronting them, but was soon joined by his few officials and two Mounted Police, and the pow wow commenced. The occasion was most impressive, and none but a firm man could have faced it as did His Honor Governor Laird. The speeches were few, but all of the same tenor. They were starving and unless relieved at once they were to die. As one of the chiefs ended his demands, an Indian standing opposite the Governor at a distance of about 40 yards, knelt down, and lowering his rifle, apparently aiming at the Governor, fired and the bullet was heard whistling close to His Honor. The Governor never made a move, and acted as if nothing had occurred. Whether the shot was fired purposely or by accident was never known. . . The incident, pregnant of consequences as it was, actually, however, helped in bringing the interview to a peaceful closing. On behalf of the Indian Superintendent, the Governor promised the Indians some measure of immediate relief, to be followed with more liberal assistance to take them to their homes as soon as the freighters had arrived. The provisions given after the interview comprised some tea, flour, a small quantity of bacon and a live animal, the latter being contributed by the Police. The steer was shot by the Indians themselves after having been run down as a buffalo, a proportionately divided by the chiefs to individual Indians, each carrying his minute share of beef and bacon on pointed sticks. . . The night was spent in dancing and feasting.

Three or four days later the long expected provisions were finally received, and the authorities were not slow in providing the Indians with sufficient supplies to permit of their returning to their respective parts of the country, and our anxieties were brought at last to an end.

To the credit of the Indians be it said that they all behaved in a remarkably orderly manner during those trying weeks of starvation and suspense, certainly better, as was then often remarked, than a similar body of white people placed in similar position. In fact, we often wondered at their not, for instance, interfering with the cattle of the few settlers around Battleford, which were daily seen peacefully grazing around their tepees, assuredly the temptation must have been great, and had they chosen to do it the few members of the Mounted Police, an officer and twelve men in all, could not have offered much protection, brave and willing as they have always proved to be. As a matter of fact no show of authority was ever attempted during that trying time, and the security of the two or three hundred souls, constituting the white population of Battleford, rested entirely on the personal authority of Governor Laird.[8]

The Treaty No. 6 Indians who accepted supplies of food at Battleford were not recipients of charity; such assistance was their right. A section of their treaty reads:

> That in the event hereafter of the Indians comprised within this treaty being overtaken by any pestilence, or by a general famine, the Queen, on being satisfied and certified thereof by Her Indian Agent or Agents, will grant to the Indians assistance of such character and to such extent as Her Chief Superintendent to relieve the Indians from the calamity that shall have befallen them.[9]

A similar paragraph does not appear in other treaties, and it was accepted by Ottawa only with considerable apprehension.

Under the circumstances outlined by Mme. Forget, it is not surprising that David Laird had soon concluded that as far as being Superintendent for Indian Affairs, the game was not worth the candle — or the $1,000 stipend which the appointment carried for him. On 20 April 1878 he had written privately to the Prime Minister, Alexander Mackenzie, that he was submitting his resignation from the position. "The duties of the office have become very onerous, and quite sufficient to engage a man's undivided attention," he wrote. "There is an amount of drudgery, too, about the office with its present staff which is incompatible with the position of lieut. governor. Besides, I cannot afford it."[10]

The second was probably the more important reason. David Laird's stiff Presbyterian conscience would never let him shirk what he regarded as his Christian duty, no matter at what cost to himself of time and energy and material wealth. For Laird to turn away hungry — starving — Indians without giving them something to eat was unthinkable, impossible. He could invite the odd visitor, or even a great many, to his own table, as he did Gabriel Dumont when that Métis called on him about a ferry licence. But to feed visitors by the hundred, even by the thousand? Only the federal government had the resources to do that, and it was distant, dilatory, uncomprehending, and parsimonious. When government rations and supplies were exhausted, Laird (and others) dug deeply into their own resources to nurture the sad-eyed, big-bellied Indian children, their gaunt, uncomplaining mothers, and their increasingly hungry, frustrated, and angry fathers.

> Laird assured them that supplies would soon be brought to them from the eastward and that in the meantime, though there was not much food among the white people, they would share what they had. He kept his promise, and ordered that flour, fish, and other food be given to the Indians. He telegraphed to Ottawa urging the federal government to send help immediately. The government was slow in realizing the seriousness of the situation, but Laird pressed them to action. By the end of the summer large stocks of provisions arrived which were distributed

among the tribes and helped to ward off a serious famine. Had such a famine occurred, it might have ended in warfare and the destruction of the governments hopes in the West.[11]

No wonder Laird wished to lay down this crushing responsibility. But he could not. Either he withdrew his resignation or it was not accepted for another eighteen months. Mme. Forget was in error when she referred to an acting superintendent for Indian Affairs, as Laird retained that position until the following year. Even then, after Dickieson had been elevated (temporarily) to the superintendency, it was the lieutenant-governor who was the man to see when one was in trouble.

The Indians were not the only people during the 1870's and '80's who turned to the governor and council for help. Greatly out-numbering the whites in numbers were those of mixed and Indian descent. Their forefathers were men of the fur trade, *hommes du nord, Canadien* voyageurs, employed, long before, by the North West Company, Orcadian laborers, Hudson's Bay "people," or English or Scottish clerks, apprentices, or chief traders or chief factors, the "gentlemen" of the Honorable Company. Those who were of French (Canadian) descent — they were usually at least nominally Roman Catholic — were known as Métis, the anglophones, generally Protestant, were designated without any derogatory connotation as half-breeds. The French and English words have exactly the same meaning with respect to descent. To about 1810 the "country marriages" of the fur traders were with Indian women, there being no white female adults in the North-West, with no more than two exceptions, until the arrival of the Selkirk Settlers after 1811. By 1810 the progeny of the white-Indian unions were reaching adulthood. Thereafter, more and more often the brides of the fur traders were Métis or half-breed girls. By the 1870's, their offspring, by then grown to manhood or womanhood, would more properly be called quarter-breeds — some, indeed, such as Louis Riel, were not more than one-eighth Indian in ancestry.

Through their maternal descent they claimed aboriginal rights to the land, and indeed some of their mothers or grandmothers had been members of matrilineal rather than patrilineal tribes. Although the Canadian government had rejected such uncivilized claims, in Manitoba members of the New Nation, as they called themselves, had been granted scrip, redeemable in land or transferable by gift, sale, or otherwise.

Some scions of mixed ancestry were absorbed into their maternal bands; others, mainly anglophone, found places in white society. Many, however, and they mainly Métis, developed a culture neither white nor Indian but borrowing from both. They were less sedentary than the whites, less nomadic than the Indians. Like their maternal forebears, they were buffalo-hunters and trappers, but they also worked for the traders as boatmen, teamsters, drovers, laborers. They fished. Desultorily they dabbled in agriculture, at least to the extent of a bit of gardening. Like the Plains Indians, they too were hard hit by the rapid disappearance of the buffalo, but since they were not so wholly dependent on that resource, their hardship was not so great.

The Métis tended to live in permanent or semi-permanent settlements along the banks of the Red, the Assiniboine, the Saskatchewan, and other bodies of water. There they staked out their little holdings, narrow farms fronting lake or river, their highways, and stretching back two to four miles. Except in Red River (and not always even there) they held no title to their land; legally they were only squatters. Ever since the HBC Deed of Surrender in 1870 they had been appealing to the Canadian government for titles to their little farms and for other assistance, but the Ottawa authorities remained deaf to their entreaties. Now they had their own government, their own governor and council (not the one in far-off Fort Garry acting *ex officio*), the Métis of the North-West renewed their appeals.

They were particularly dissatisfied with the composition of the council, consisting as it did of three white men, all Easterners, none of whom had first-hand knowledge of their problems. Nor could such men really understand them, sympathetic as they might be to the Métis' plight. Accordingly, the latter asked for one of their own people to be appointed to the council. Had they had their choice, they might have picked some one like Gabriel Dumont, illiterate but a leader among the Métis, a sober, responsible, self-supporting Westerner, or Peter Erasmus, like Dumont a one-time ferry owner. It was Erasmus who had saved Treaty No. 6 negotiations from collapse by serving as interpreter after those who had been appointed to the role had proven quite unsatisfactory. George Woodcock comments on the government's choice of a Métis councillor:

> The first response to the urgings of Gabriel Dumont and his fellow Métis was the appointment of a Métis member to the North West Council. But the government was unwise enough to choose a man with a record of obedience rather than a man who represented current Métis feeling. Pascal Breland, the appointed Councillor, had served faithfully on the Council of Assiniboia under the Hudson's Bay Company, had used his influence against Riel both on the Red River and in the Qu'Appelle region when the question of concerted Métis action came up there in 1870, and, with the support of the Canadian authorities, he had been elected to the first Legislative Assembly of Manitoba. He was now an old man, living as a merchant in the Cypress Hills, which gave an excuse to include him in the governing body of the territories. Breland was not ignorant of the problems that disturbed the prairie peoples, and on a few occasions he did present them insistently enough to convince his fellow councillors but in any confrontation he had always been on the side of authority, and most of the Métis had by now come to distrust him.[12]

In short, Breland's appointment was an example of what a later age would declare to be sheer tokenism.

In any event, the enlarged council met at Battleford on 2 August. In many ways, the session must have been frustrating. The Cypress Hills people submitted a petition praying that the ordinance of the previous year for the protection of the buffalo be rescinded. It had become apparent both from this petition and from other evidence that if the ordinance were to be enforced, many Indians and Métis would starve, endangered species though the great ungulate might be. Further, with the natives' desperate need for food, and the thin veneer of police services across the North West, the ordinance was unenforceable. And as every one learned in the law is aware, including no doubt the stipendiary magistrates on the council, an unenforceable law is a bad law. The ordinance was repealed.

Perhaps also the council thought another year would be time enough to save the buffalo from extinction. They were wrong.

Land titles and buffalo regulations were not the only matters concerning the Territories' non-Indian population. In 1877 the people of St. Laurent had petitioned for financial assistance for a school, but Laird had had to reply that the council, without taxation powers, had no funds which could be used for such purpose. However, a request would be made for such an appropriation to be included in the territorial budget and federal grant for the following year. Instead of acceding to this request, Ottawa replied that there seemed to be no obstacle to the formation of school corporations (or districts) by the residents themselves, and the imposition of local taxes to support such schools.

In retrospect, this answer seems particularly obtuse. Schools for the common people have always required outside financial assistance. Only the affluent — of which there were few in the Territories — have ever been able to bear the entire cost of their children's schooling. For fifty years and more the few schools in Rupert's Land had subsidized, and heavily, by the Christian churches, Roman Catholic and Anglican at first, Methodist and Presbyterian also a bit later. But to provide univeral education across the whole North-West was beyond the churches' resources.

For another reason the government's suggestion seems especially ill-considered. The council had no powers of taxation. School districts have never been able to levy taxes or requisitions except on real property, i.e., land or buildings. But if residents of the Territories could not obtain legal title to their holdings, there was no way a school district (corporation) could levy and collect tax revenue. Thus the Cypress Hills people's request to the council in 1878 for assistance to support a teacher had to be rejected as was that of St. Laurent residents the previous year. Apparently, however, Laird continued to pressure the federal government for such help, and it seems to have been forthcoming in 1879.

Probably because they now had their own member on the council, the Métis had many requests. In addition to those respecting buffalo and schools, they also sought seed and especially settlement of their land claims — it was federal disregard of these which was to result in open warfare in 1885. Other council business in 1878 concerned passage of an ordinance respecting marriages and another concerning stallions. It seems that the council was anxious to regularize or limit conjugal unions of both man and beast.

The council session concluded, on 19 August Laird accepted the adhesion to Treaty No. 6 of a band of Cree Indians, the location of the adhesion not indicated. Three of the Indians who signed had truly formidable names: Puskee-Yah-Kay-Wee-Yin, Mah-Kayo, and Pay-Fram-Us-Kum-Ick-In-Um. The more modest cognomen of the fourth was simply 'Isadore.' Their signatures were somewhat easier to read, in each case being simply 'x.' The witnesses were Sub-Inspector John French, NWMP, a brother of the first commissioner of the Police, and Peter Erasmus, who no doubt also served as interpreter.

Erasmus was one of the North-West's best educated and most influential of the country's 'mixed bloods.' He was born at Red River in 1833 of a Danish father and a Métis mother. His father dying when young Erasmus was barely sixteen, he took over responsibility for the family farm, 118 acres, only nine of which were under cultivation. But Peter did not take kindly to playing nursemaid to one horse, four oxen, two cows, four calves, four pigs, and three sheep. Accordingly, in June, 1851, he began a three-year engagement to work with his uncle, Henry Budd, a deacon at Christ Church, Cumberland, and later rector at The Pas. While so employed at Cumberland and elsewhere, young Peter taught school and continued his own studies. These included Greek, his tutor being the Rev. James Hunter. Erasmus also helped Budd with the translation of the Bible and parts of the Book of Common Prayer into Cree. By 1854 he so impressed his uncle, by now the Rev. Henry Budd, and the Rt. Rev. David Anderson, first Bishop of Rupert's Land, that they applied enormous pressure on the young man to study for ordination in the Anglican Church. Although somewhat less than enthusiastic, he seized the opportunity to advance his formal education, spending two terms at St. John's School (later, College) in Winnipeg. Then, realizing that he did not have a calling to the Christian ministry, he abandoned his studies to join the Hudson's Bay Company on the Upper Saskatchewan. Thereafter he worked as "interpreter, voyageur, hunter, builder, freighter, and general assistant. He became a fine horseman and a redoubtable buffalo hunter and traveller."[13] Among his employers, besides the Honorable Company, were the Rev. Robert Rundle, Dr. Hector of the Palliser Expedition, the Rev. H. B. Steinhauer, and the Rev. George

McDougall, from whom he parted when the missionary decided to substantially cut Erasmus' wages. During the Treaty No. 6 negotiations at Carlton in 1876, he was employed by Chiefs Mista-Wa-Sis and Big Child as their interpreter.

Soon after the treaty adhesion of 19 August, the lieutenant-governor was once more on the road. According to the *Saskatchewan Herald,* he spent a week, 15-23 August, on an expedition to Sounding Lake, some 110 miles south-west of Battleford. This little body of water is almost straight east of Red Deer and just west of the present Alberta-Saskatchewan boundary. Here, Laird's party, which included a detachment of Mounted Police under Inspector James Walker, met a number of Treaty No. 6 Indians, to whom Walker paid their annuities or 'treaty money.'

To this day, for many, perhaps most bands, the payment of treaty money is more than just a financial transaction. It is also an important ceremony. The money may be counted out by an Indian Affairs official, but from him it passes to a member of the RCMP, who in turn hands it to the recipient. The policeman must be garbed in his Stetson, scarlet tunic, etc.; no drab brown service jacket and forage cap. The transaction must take place beneath a flag, and the proper one at that. On one occasion a group of Indians in Southern Saskatchewan refused to accept their treaty money because the then-new Canadian maple leaf flag was flying overhead. Hurried arrangements had to be made to bring an appropriate Union Jack from Regina before the ceremonies could continue.

On 29 August 1878 at Battleford, Laird as Indian Superintendent took the adhesion to Treaty No. 6 of the chief and headmen of a band of Stoney Indians. In English their names were Misketo (Mosquito?), Uses Both Arms, Two Child, and Lightning. Witnesses were Inspector Walker, one Hayer Reed, and Peter Ballendine, who presumably served as interpreter. It was he who had proven so inadequate the previous year with the Indians at Fort Carlton; probably his mastery of Assiniboine was superior to his command of Cree.

September saw Laird, Walker, and Forget heading down-river to Fort Carlton. Here the party were guests of the Hudson's Bay Company and Chief Factor Lawrence Clarke, future member of the council. The party also proceeded to near-by Duck Lake, between the North and South Saskatchewan, and to Prince Albert. The primary purpose of the expedition was to pay treaty money, but at Duck Lake there was other business. The governor was anxious to settle Chief Beardy's band on a reserve, but the chief would not discuss boundaries until he was granted some concessions not in Treaty No. 6. These Laird would not, probably could not concede; the result was an impasse. Beardy, his medicine man, and some others would not accept their annuities from Inspector Walker.

At Duck Lake some Métis from St. Laurent waited on His Honor; they were accompanied by their spiritual advisor, Father André. Since Forget acted as interpreter, it appears that the people from St. Laurent spoke French but little or no English. They urged their land claims not be encroached by Indian reserves established on their hay meadows. Norbert Lorance thanked the lieutenant-governor for his consideration, at the same time asking if any reply had been received from Ottawa regarding their representations, probably about schools.

From Carlton and Duck Lake the party went on to Prince Albert, where leading citizens presented Laird with an address of welcome. He replied as follows:

> I thank you for your address welcoming me to this settlement. It is extremely gratifying to me occupying the highest local position in these Territories under Her Majesty the Queen to be assured you entertain towards her feelings of loyalty and devotion. On passing through your flourishing settlement I have been cheered by the many evidences of the industry and thrift of the population and that the Giver of all good has this year blessed them with a bountiful harvest. The generous soil of this locality and your proximity to the great waterway of the Territories must offer great enducements to the emigrant and will likely increase the importance of your settlement. I hope Prince Albert will extend to the valley of the Saskatchewan.[14]

A deputation waited on the lieutenant-governor, clearly apprehensive of trouble with Indians should there be a scarcity of supplies during the coming winter. The residents urged the necessity of establishing a small detachment of the Mounted Police at Prince Albert. Laird promised that he would request Inspector Walker to leave a few men temporarily at the settlement, presumably until the apprehended danger had passed.

The settlers also expressed the desirability of having a representative on the Territorial council in accordance with the North-West Territories Act. Laird stated that he would have a census of the settlement taken, and if the requisite number of adults was found at Prince Albert, or in the St. Laurent/Duck Lake area, steps would be taken to have representation on the council. The relevant section of the N. W. T. Act reads:

> 13. When and so soon as the Lieutenant-Governor is satisfied by such proof as he may require, that any district or portion of the North-West Territories, not exceeding an area of one thousand square miles, contains a population of not less than one thousand inhabitants of adult age, exclusive of aliens or unenfranchised Indians, the Lieutenant-Governor shall, by proclamation, erect such district or portion into an electoral district, by a name and with boundaries to be respectively declared in the proclamation, and such electoral district shall thenceforth be entitled

to elect a member of the Council or of the Legislative Assembly as the case may be.[15]

Laird also visited the McBeth settlement at the lower end of Prince Albert and the grist and saw-mills of one Captain Moore.

While visiting Prince Albert, the governor was the guest of Charles Mair, one time medical student, Canadian nationalist, journalist, adventurer, promoter, merchant, playwright, and poet. Perhaps this was not the first time David Laird had met this remarkable man who was to become his life-long friend. In 1874 when as Minister of the Interior he had passed through Portage La Prairie on his way to Qu'Appelle, Mair had been running a store in that Manitoba centre.

On returning to Battleford, the governor proclaimed 20 September to be day of general thanksgiving and caused a proclamation to be issued to that effect. It had been a hard year for Laird and for many, perhaps most people in the Territories, but one may suppose that they were thankful to have survived.

Three days before that Thanksgiving, an event occurred which was to affect Laird's life from that time forward. This was the re-election of the Conservative party under the leadership of his old political adversary, Sir John A. Macdonald. Sir John also became not only Prime Minister but also Minister of the Interior. Laird would finish his term as lieutenant-governor of the North-West Territories, but there would be no further political preferment for him until Old Tomorrow was in his grave and the Conservatives were banished to the wilderness or at least to the Opposition benches.

References

1. Elizabeth Laird to John W. Chalmers, 22 May 1980.

2. David Laird to John McDougall, 7 December 1877 (Saskatchewan Archives Board).

3. Laird to Alexander Mackenzie, 24 January 1878 (Saskatchewan Archives Board).

4. Laird to Dr. Rafferty, 21 February 1878 (Saskatchewan Archives Board).

5. Laird to James Macleod, 18 February 1878 (Saskatchewan Archives Board).

6. Mme. A. E. Forget, "Disappearance of the Buffalo and Starvation among the Indians," *The Colonist*, 1905 (exact date undetermined).

7. *Ibid.*

8. *Ibid.*

9. Canada, *Copy of Treaty No. 6. . .*, p. 4.

10. Laird to Mackenzie, 20 April 1879 (Saskatchewan Archives Board).

11. Frank MacKinnon, "David Laird of Prince Edward Island," *The Dalhousie Review*, v. 26, no. 4, p. 418.

12. George Woodcock, *Gabriel Dumont* p. 122.

13. Peter Erasmus (as told to Henry Thompson), *Buffalo Days and Nights*, p. xix.

14. Laird family papers.

15. E. H. Oliver, *The Canadian North-West*, v. 2, pp. 1079-1080.

Again
the Third Horseman

In 1877, the Prairie had exported 30,000 buffalo hides to the U.S.A. In 1878 the number dropped to 13,000 and 1879 almost reached the vanishing point, 5,000 hides. It was this wholesale slaughter year after year that brought on the starvation of 1879 . . .[1]

In summary, the winter of 1878-79 was a repetition of that of the previous year. On 15 October, Laird submitted (or resubmitted) his resignation as Indian Superintendent. However, Ottawa apparently took no notice of this action other than to terminate his annual $1,000 stipend for this assignment. Consequently, he had to carry the worry and responsibility of this appointment during the winter as well as attending to his usual gubernatorial duties. Thus in February he was calling for tenders — wheat, barley, potatoes, flour and pemmican — at ten different near-by points as well as four locations in the Swan Hills agency. In March, Mr. W. J. Christie wrote complaining about the problems on the James Seemens and Lentz Bob Indian reserves, specifically about the work of M. G. Dickieson, Laird's clerk for Indian affairs. Apparently Dickieson was getting into bad odor with the Indians, trumping up any excuse to cover his inability to satisfy them. Christie stated that Dickieson was not the man to deal with Indians, and some one was required who could command their respect and know how to treat them.

Such a harsh judgment was not necessarily a just one. Indians then as now tended to hold a very negative opinion of any government official who did not instantly accede to what they regarded as their just and legitimate demands, regardless of the physical impossibility of their so doing. Yet the frustration of the Indian agent or other bureaucrat under such circumstances is usually equalled or exceeded by that of the Indians, who are unable to comprehend the inertia and red tape inherent in governmental bureaucracy. Indeed, it is often incomprehensible to the public servants themselves. Thus Christie's condemnation should not be accepted at face value.

Early in February, the *Saskatchewan Herald* mentioned two Indian appeals to Laird for assistance. On the eighth of the month, chiefs from Eagle Hills sought help from the lieutenant-governor as they were near starvation. The following day, four Indians from the Green Lake reserve asked for such aid. No doubt there were many others, and they were sent not empty away.

On 13 March, Laird wrote to Col. J. S. Dennis, Deputy-Minister of the Interior, respecting both the plight of the Indians and his own unsettled status as Indian Superintendent. He pointed out that the winter was still severe, that Indians at both Battleford and Qu'Appelle were starving, that Sitting Bull's band were competing with the Canadian Indians for the fast-diminishing buffalo. Turning to his own situation, he continued:

> The late government promised $1,000 additional if I undertook the duties of Indian superintendent. I have discharged these duties faithfully. The late government fulfilled their contract on the date of resignation and paid the arrears to Sept. 30 last. (Since that time no money has been received.) Likely this is an omission of the Deputy-Minister of Finance. Ask him about this as I do not want to bother the Minister (by writing directly to him.) This is expensive country to live in as freight from Winnipeg is very high. Price of flour is $11 per bag, about five times what it cost in Ontario. Clothing is higher here as there is no tailor. I have ordered by mail clothing for myself and my children. The new mail regulation is that only 2 lb. parcels will be permitted. I feel I will need much more money for my duties as Lieut. Governor and should receive $9000 to $10,000 per year in order to get supplies, which here cost 6 to 10 cents more per pound. My resignation as Indian Superintendent is before the Minister but until it is accepted I am entitled to the $1,000 allowance.[2]

In effect, Laird was insisting that his resignation as Indian superintendent be accepted, and that he be paid for the period in which he continued to act in that capacity until acceptance. He was also showing that the salary provided by the Indian Act[3] was inadequate for the position and indicating that a raise (or, for Britons, a rise) would be appropriate. A century later, in such a situation as his, a northern, wilderness, or isolation bonus would be forth-coming.

Shortly afterwards, Laird was informed that the stipend as Indian Superintendent was being paid to the end of March, after which date Dickieson would be acting superintendent. As will be noted, however, the Lieutenant-Governor of the North-West Territories could not thus easily escape responsibility to and for the native peoples in his domain.

When P. C. Laurie, editor and publisher of the *Saskatchewan Herald,* learned of Laird's resignation as Indian superintendent, his paper had some very nice things to say about him:

> The public will learn with regret that His Honor the Lieutenant-Governor has resigned the position of Superintendent of Indian Affairs, which he held in conjunction with the Governorship. His loss will be severely felt; and much anxiety will prevail pending the appointment of his successor. Thoroughly acquainted with the details of the whole Indian business of the North-West, most patient and painstaking in mastering the intricities of every case brought under his notice, and with his whole heart engaged in his work, and enjoying the confidence and respect of those who have had to do with him, it will be difficult to find one who can so efficiently fill the office. If at times in the past some of his suggestions and most urgent representations to the Department at Ottawa had been complied with, there is no doubt that many of the difficulties that have arisen might have been obviated, and by the timely expenditure of a little money, a large saving effected in the end. It cannot be too strongly urged upon the Government in Ottawa, that the more the details of the work of this Superintendency are left in the hands of the officers here, the more efficient will be the service, the greater the true economy to the country, and the more beneficial and satisfactory the result to the Indians themselves.
>
> Mr. Dickieson has received instructions to discharge the duties of Superintendent in the meantime.[4]

It is to be noted that the editor took the opportunity to stress that the more governmental decisions are made at the local level, the better; a thesis already promulgated in these pages. The announcement of Dickieson's appointment to be acting superintendent is made without comment despite the fact that for some two years Dickieson had been serving as clerk for Indian Affairs.

Laird's work during the winter of 1878-79 had not been confined wholly to matter affecting Indians. In October he had been concerned with the regularization of marriages and the publication of an ordinance by which the lieutenant-governor could authorize justices of the peace or clergymen to issue appropriate licences. Alternatively, marriages could be performed following publication of banns, the reading aloud in church of notification of an intended marriage for three successive Sundays, or as nearly as circumstances would allow. It is not clear whether the ordinance permitted marriages to be performed by other than ordained clergymen. Apparently they did, for in February Laird received a protest from the Roman Catholic church, objecting to the ordinance. Laird replied that no persecution of the Catholic clergy was implied or intended, but some parts of the Territories were seldom visited by clergymen, and the ordinance was intended to facilitate the legalization of marital unions. Certainly the 'country marriages' traditional to the fur trade had very ambiguous validity, if any at all, in law, just as so-called common law marriages do today. The history of the North-West is replete with stories of 'country wives' and half-breed children being abandoned to the cold comfort of grudging and uncertain charity.

On March 10, the lieutenant-governor appointed a number of prominent westerners to be issuers of marriage licences. Included in the list were his private secretary and clerk of the council, A. E. Forget; Charles Mair, of Prince Albert; Chief Factor Lawrence Clarke, of Fort Carlton; Chief Factor Richard Hardisty, of Fort Edmonton, whom Laird had met at Blackfoot Crossing during Treaty No. 7 negotiations, and the Rev. Henry Bird Steinhauer, the Ojibway with the German name whose descendants are registered Crees. One of them, Ralph Steinhauer, became a lieutenant-governor of Alberta, first Indian to hold such a post.

Another of Laird's concerns, natural for a family man, was the education of the community's children. For fifty years before the Hudson's Bay Company signed the Deed of Surrender, all schooling in Rupert's Land, aside from Indian traditional education (by no means negligible), had been that provided by the Christian missions. Under the B.N.A. Act of 1867, the federal government had assumed responsibility for the education of Indian children, a responsibility which it immediately farmed out to the churches. But as of 1878 the North-West Territories had no policy for the education of non-Indian children. True, in theory, the council had the responsibility, but Ottawa had provided neither funding nor authority to establish districts which could provide the tax revenue necessary to operate the schools.

There remained one approach, and this Laird explored. That was the construction through voluntary contributions of a building for use as a schoolhouse, public meeting hall, and place of worship for all denominations. The lieutenant-governor contributed the first hundred dollars, a much more significant sum then than now. As the *Herald* reported on 21 October, within two weeks the building was almost completed. During the next few years other communities, e.g., Calgary and Edmonton, would establish their first non-denominational schools through similar action.

January found Laird writing to the Minister of the Interior stating the council should have the power to erect municipalities or at least school sections or districts without the requirement of a population of one thousand adults, as was the requirement for an electoral district. Eventually the Territories would have this power, but not during David Laird's tenure as lieutenant-governor.

Other gubernatorial business that winter tended to be routine. On November 11, His Honor proclaimed 4 December to be a Day of Thanksgiving, and had Forget issue a proclamation to that effect. In December he received a letter from James A. Grahame, Governor of the Hudson's Bay Company, respecting liquor permits. The section of the N.W.T. Act dealing with intoxicants runs to three pages, most of which expand on the operant first sentence, which reads in part as follows:

> 74. Intoxicating liquors and other intoxicants are prohibited to be manufactured or made in the said North-West Territories, except by special permission of the Governor in Council, or to be imported or brought into the same from any Province of Canada or elsewhere, to be sold, exchanged, traded, or bartered, except by special permission in writing of the Lieutenant-Governor of the said Territories. . .[5]

Covertly reflecting the common racist view of the era, the section was designed to deny alcohol to the natives, for whom it had proven an unqualified curse, while making it available to white people, who were assumed to be able to drink in moderation. Almost a century was to pass before the Indians were to obtain the legal right to be drunk on or off their reserves.

The problem of land titles, a major cause of the North-West Rebellion in 1885, continued without alleviation. Apparently the federal government was reluctant to act in this matter, partly because it was uncertain what properties would be required for its own purposes. A second reason was that massive land grants would be needed to subsidize the Pacific railroad along its right-of-way, but its route was yet to be finally determined. Meanwhile, residents of Battleford, with no title to their land, erected the most humble buildings thereon, and except for government structures, the community was becoming a collection of shacks. The *Saskatchewan Herald* on 16 December 1878 carried an item respecting a petition for the survey of Battleford, necessary before land titles could be issued. The paper noted that in 1877 an appropriation for such purpose had been made, but nothing had been done.

From time to time the same publication carried news items to indicate that the lieutenant-governor was carrying on farming activities. One can only guess at his motivations. No doubt one reason was to supplement his inadequate salary. Another may have been to demonstrate suitable agricultural practices to the white and native population; after all, his father had been reputed to be one of the best farmers on Prince Edward Island. Finally, as previously noted, once a farmer, always a farmer, at least at heart. In any event, in December the threshing machine which Laird had imported during the fall was reported as working well.

That grain separator was a far cry from the self-propelled combines characteristic of Saskatchewan wheat fields a century later, or even of the stationary monsters of the 1920's. It had neither self-feeder to convey sheaves to the vast, dusty, and vibrating maw of the machine nor blower to blast unwanted straw an appropriate distance from the operation. Nor did steam nor internal combustion engine provide power; that was furnished by a sort of turn-table rotated by four sturdy horses what followed one another on an endless circular path. Finally, the threshing was not done in vast fields of stooked grain but from stacks of sheaves gathered through the fall. The process was not completed within a few autumn days or weeks, but might continue off and on all winter, weather permitting.

It didn't always. The coldest day that winter seems to have been 14 January, with high and low temperatures of -20° F. and -43° F. respectively.

The *Saskatchewan Herald* apparently kept a close eye on David Laird's farming activities. It reported that he sowed some wheat on 12 April, an indication of a remarkably early spring. The issue of 14 July 1879 stated: 'New potatoes of good size and excellent quality were dug in the Governor's garden on the 1st of July. They are the earliest in this neighborhood, if not first in the Territories."[6]

By springtime, the Indians' meagre supplies of food were exhausted, but with the warm weather and the disappearance of snow, the natives were able to abandon their winter camps and wander in search of game or of assistance. On 2 May a deputation of Blackfoot, who found themselves close to Battleford as they searched for buffalo, arrived at the capital to seek help from the governor. They told of absolute destitution in their camps, and of Americans and half-breeds poisoning buffalo carcasses in their eagerness to obtain wolf-hides, with fatal effects on the Indians' dogs. They complained, too, of Crees invading their traditional hunting grounds. Laird stated the obvious: that the use of poison was prohibited, and if the Indians would point out the offenders, their punishment would swiftly and surely follow. As the *Herald* indicates, he had other good advice.

> With respect to other Indians going on their hunting grounds, that was a privilege open to all. It was the privilege of every one to follow the buffalo wherever they went; and if they did not go to where the Blackfeet lived, these must endeavor to help themselves by going to where the herds were to be found.
>
> As to provision for the future, His Honor reminded them that they had a large number of cattle which they had declined to take charge of, but which they had left to be cared for by the police, and strongly advised them to take charge of them for themselves. They were already accustomed to herding their horses, and if the chiefs were to appoint two or three young men to herd their cattle, to see that they did not stray and to take care of the young stock, their cattle would soon so increase in numbers as to afford them an abundant supply of food in time of

scarcity. He did not intend them to live on their cattle all the time, but in the event of buffalo being beyond reach during a month or two of the severer weather in the winter some of these might be killed to supply their families with food. By the young men of the bands taking their turn in herding — say a week or two at a time — the task would not prove at all irksome.[7]

Laird then supplied his visitors with food and ammunition, and after 'recruiting,' i.e., resting their horses for a couple of days, they took their leave. But these were only a few of the Indians who managed to come to Battleford begging for assistance. Through May and June bands of Sarcee, Blackfoot, and others were constantly arriving, all with the same story of destitution and starvation, of subsisting on berries and even gophers with only a rare, thin buffalo providing a little meat. Fortunately the Battle River that spring provided an abundance of fish, but what did buffalo-hunters know about fishing? From all parts of the Great Plains the story was the same. As Col. Macleod observed, "Hungry men are dangerous, whether they be Indian or white."[8] In May the most alarming rumors ran through Battleford: that Indians by the hundred were descending on the capital to wipe it out. On 26 June about one thousand of them united to perform a 'hungry dance' to emphasize their plight on the lieutenant-governor. It was perhaps mainly to impress them that on the Queen's Birthday, 24 May, he held a review and inspection of his troops, that is, the Battleford detachment of the Mounted Police, following which he addressed them with appropriate gubernatorial remarks. They responded with three cheers for the Queen and the same for His Honor.

Starving men are indeed dangerous, the more so when their wives and children are also dying of hunger. That they were indeed starving is recounted in a letter of 15 April 1879 from Father Constantine Scollen to Asst. Com. A. G. Irvine, NWMP:

I have now been acquainted sixteen years with the Blackfeet. I have seen them in all their phases — in their days of prosperity and opulence; when their braves mustered double the number they can muster now: when they were entire masters of the immense prairies from Benton to Edmonton, and the terror of their enemies on every side, North, South, East, and West. I have seen them in those days mourn the loss of numerous relatives fallen in deadly combat against their foes. I have seen them later on, when reduced to the last stage of poverty and disorganization from the effects of intoxicating liquor, but through all these stages I have never seen them so depressed as they are now; I have never seen them before in want of food: last winter for the first time have they really suffered the pangs of hunger, and for the first time in my life have I seen a Blackfoot brave withdraw from his lodge that he might not listen to his crying children when he had not meat to give them! Such,

Dear Sir, has been the state of the Blackfoot Indians last winter. They have suffered fearfully from hunger. Two poor women on Elk River, fell victims to the scourge, a thing never heard of before amongst the Blackfeet. Many sustained life by eating the flesh of poisoned wolves. Some have lived on dogs; and I have known others to live several days on nothing else but old bones which they gathered and broke up, wherewith to make a kind of soup.

This state of affairs has disheartened the Indians wonderfully. They can no longer live together in big camps under the control of their Chiefs. They have been, during the Winter, and are now scattered all over the country. They are in utter dejection, and from a state of dejection, if they continue to suffer, I have no doubt that there will be a transition to a state of desperation.

In fact hunger has driven them to commit many acts of dishonesty which they always abstained from before, around the posts. Many of those whose skeleton horses were able to plod through the deep snow hastened around the settlements in order to live. The consequence is, they have become a burden and a cause of anxiety to the Settlers. They have begged and stolen all they could, and got into the way of helping themselves to white-men's cattle.[9]

In my opinion, give us another Winter like the past, and we are done for. We shall either have to provide for the Indians or fight them; there is no other alternative.[10]

So far, the Indians had proven immensely patient, but each day, each hour the tension increased. For his own safety David Laird had no care. Even an aimed bullet whistling within inches of his head — as one did — could not make him flinch from his duty or scurry for shelter. But, as his daughter has indicated, he felt that he could no longer expose his family to the nameless and unspoken menace that poisoned the atmosphere.

The strain was too much for my father so that summer he sent his wife and family home. Men might in an emergency get away but not women and children. Judge Richardson sent his three daughters with us as far as Ottawa, but Mrs. Scott and Mrs. Forget had to stay with their husbands. It was with a sad heart my father let us go for he could not accompany us. His work was there and he had to see it through.[11]

On our return journey in 1879, we went by boat down the Saskatchewan River as far as Fort Carlton. There we had to wait for a week for another boat. We stayed with Factor 'Lawrence Clarke," also a member of the "Government Council." Governor Grahame of the Hudson Bay Co., and his son were also there and life within the Fort was a new interest.

We took another boat down the Saskatchewan as far as some rapids, then had to portage a short distance to Lake Winnipeg. There we had to embark on another steamer and after a very rough passage arrived at Winnipeg. The railway had by that time reached St. Croix, so we went on from there by rail, but again crossed the Great Lakes by steamer. A wonderful trip to us all.[12]

By 1879 the Great Plains were criss-crossed by the tracks of wheeled vehicles, tracks such as the Carlton Trail, along which Red River carts crept from Winnipeg to Edmonton, or the Whoop-Up Trail, the route of the heavy wagons drawn by bull-teams from Fort Benton to Fort Macleod. But the great highways of the Prairies were still the Red River and the broad Saskatchewan, especially the latter's northern branch. However, the birchbark canoe, fabled in song and story, had virtually vanished from their waters, and even the York boat was fast disappearing. In their place was the fire canoe, the paddle-wheel steamer. Despite constant problems with shallow waters, shifting gravel bars, suddenly-opened new channels and silted-up old ones, despite intransigent engines and leaking boilers, despite these and other handicaps, the stern-wheeler was more efficient, i.e., less expensive than cart or canoe or York boat. "Each cart carried half a ton so that it took 200 to 400 carts to carry as much freight as one stern-wheeler if the waters of the Saskatchewan were in good stage."[13]

In the nineteenth century the river steamers of Western Canada, like those of the Mississippi, were fragile, flat-bottomed vessels built to navigate the country's shallow rivers. Empty, one might draw only a foot of water, and many a boastful captain bragged that he could operate his steamer on a heavy dew. Fully loaded, the draft might be three or three and one-half feet. In appearance, they closely resembled, in a more modest dimension, the craft that Mark Twain immortalized in *Life on the Mississippi* and other books. A significant difference was that they were invariably stern rather than side-wheelers, the better to back off sand or gravel bars, or, with the aid of gin poles, to clamber over them.

The engines were mounted aft, close to the paddle wheels, but the boilers were near the bow. Had they been erected near the engines, the whole vessel would have been stern-heavy, with the bow out of the water. Near the bow and the boilers were usually two, occasionally only one, very tall stacks which belched smoke and glowing embers that occasionally set the prairie afire.

The lower deck, only a few inches above the water line, was a huge, undivided cavern, boiler and engines at either end. The intervening area provided space for freight and baggage, and the dried cordwood required for the insatiable boilers. Periodically the vessel had to stop for fuel, previously contracted for from Métis or Indians, and piled on the river bank. 'Steerage' passengers were also accommodated on the lower deck.

The principal characteristic of the upper deck was the saloon, a long room running almost the entire length of the ship, and serving as dining room, club room, lounge, and bar for the cabin passengers. In the more luxurious vessels, this was sumptuously, even elaborately adorned and furnished. On each side of the saloon and opening thereon were the cabins, tiny bedrooms occupied by the passengers only when they were asleep or sick. The outside deck provided a place to stroll, admire the scenery, or shoot at a bear luckless enough to come within firearm range.

Still higher was the hurricane deck, its principal feature being the bridge and wheelhouse somewhat forward of the stacks. Here the captain, lord of all he surveyed, directed the operation of the ship. But often, perhaps usually, it was the pilot, familiar with the river or a stretch of it, who was in charge of the navigation. It was he who stood behind the big wheel that controlled the rudder which determined in which direction the ship would move. It was his hand on the brass telegraph that signalled 'Full speed ahead,' 'Half speed astern,' 'Finished with engines,' or whatever to the engineer in the bowels of the craft. It was his keen eyes that watched the water ahead, to spot changes in the current since his last voyage. It was his sharp vision that detected the ripple which warned of a hidden rock or submerged log that might rip open the keel, a too-frequent but seldom lethal occurrence. With such possibilities, it is not surprising that the stern-wheelers tied up during the hours of darkness.

On the hurricane deck, so called, there would usually also be a few cabins, quarters for the captain and perhaps some other members of the crew.

First steamer to breast the waters of the upper North Saskatchewan was the Hudson's Bay Company's *Northcote* in 1875. Thereafter, because of its too-great draft and of the uncertain, the erratic water levels on that stretch of the river, it was seldom seen above Fort Carlton. Instead, that portion of the stream was normally served by the Honorable Company's smaller *Lily*. Unlike most paddle-wheelers, it was equipped with but a single stack. This was the vessel on which the Lairds and the Richardsons embarked to begin their long trip east. The Clyde-built *Lily* had been shipped out from England in sections during 1876, and assembled in the North-West the following year. Peel has given a good description of this vessel:

> The *Lily* was a two-decked stern-wheeler, 100 feet in length and 24 in the beam, with a depth of 4 feet. She had a draft of 14 inches, even keel, which was 4 inches more than intended. The boat's machinery included a loco-boiler, and two 13-inch cylinders with a stroke of 36 inches. Her engine power was 31.80 horsepower and her gross tonnage was 207.01. The most notable feature about her was that she had a steel hull, steam

and exhaust pipes of copper, and a brass-fitted engine. Unfortunately, the steel plates of her hull were easily damaged on rocks in the river.[14]

The eastbound passengers expected a speedy connection at Carlton with the *Northcote,* but they had to wait a frustrating week, according to Mary Alice Laird, as already noted. Another authority, however, states that the delay was not one but three weeks and occurred at The Pas and not Carlton.[15]

However, there is no doubt that the Laird children and their friends completed the next stage of their inland voyage aboard the *Northcote.* She was half as long again as the *Lily,* and somewhat broader of beam. Peel gives her vital statistics:

> The new sternwheeler was a prototype of steamboats to be seen on the Mississippi and Missouri rivers, with her forecastle cut down to her main or boiler deck, two tall smokestacks well forward, and the pilot house behind them on the hurricane deck. Her hull was built entirely of Minnesota oak. She was 150 feet from bow to stern, 28.5 feet in breadth, and 4.5 feet deep. Her engines, salvaged from the unnamed boat, were capable of generating 39.72 horsepower. Her gross tonnage was 461.34, while her registered tonnage was 290.63. With a light cargo her draft was 22 inches, but with a load of 150 tons she drew 3.5 feet of water.[16]

But even the *Northcote* was not the ship that would carry Mary Alice to Winnipeg. At the mouth of the Saskatchewan were the Grand Rapids, now submerged in a power dam, most difficult for steamers to descend or climb. Consequently the *Northcote* discharged passengers and cargo above the rapids, to be conveyed overland by Western Canada's first railway (horse-operated) to Lake Winnipeg.

> Before it empties into the northern part of Lake Winnipeg, the Saskatchewan River descends more than seventy feet. About two miles from its mouth is the sharp drop of the Grand Rapids. Here, making a crescent-shaped swing, the river flows between high vertical cliffs of limestone. . .[17]

In 1877 the Hudson's Bay Company's steamer *Colville* carried up Lake Winnipeg to Grand Rapids fifty-five tons of iron rail from the United States, and construction on a narrow gauge railway was immediately begun under the engineer and explorer Walter Moberly. Two twenty-five-foot bridges were built, and a cutting, at times ten feet deep, was made through an old beach line. The three-and-a-half mile track laid through the bush took the place of the longer and more hazardous route.[18]

With four tramcars and a handcar, freighting across the portage went on continuously throughout the summer. The horse-drawn cars hauled loads of six thousand pounds, their movements co-ordinated by what was the most northerly telephone line for years.[19]

Unless beseiged by mosquitoes, black flies, and other such airborne tormentors, the Lairds and Richardsons no doubt thoroughly enjoyed their short railroad jaunt around the Grand Rapids. No doubt it was more pleasant than the next stage of their journey aboard the *Colville,* a somewhat sturdier vessel than the river craft, as was needed for the often-turbulent waters of Lake Winnipeg. Thus the Lairds reached Manitoba's capital, but they were only nicely started on their long journey back to Prince Edward Island. By the time the children reached Charlottetown, their father had made another inland voyage, this one to Fort Edmonton and beyond.

References

1. Mary Alice Mathieson, "Early Days in the North-West Territories" (unpublished typescript in Laird family papers), p. 9.
2. David Laird to J. S. Dennis, 13 March 1879.
3. E. H. Oliver, *The Canadian North-West,* v.2, p. 1076.
4. *Saskatchewan Herald,* 14 July 1879.
5. Oliver, *op. cit.,* p. 1093.
6. *Saskatchewan Herald,* 14 July 1879.
7. *Ibid.,* 5 May 1879.
8. *Ibid.,* 2 June 1879.
9. Constantine Scollen to A. G. Irvine, 15 April 1879.
10. *Ibid.*
11. Mathieson, *op. cit.,* p.7.
12. *Ibid.,* p. 8.
13. Bruce Peel, *Steamboats on the Saskatchewan,* p. 6.
14. *Ibid.,* p. 45.
15. *Ibid.,* p. 58.
16. *Ibid.,* p. 26.
17. Ron Vastokas, "The Grand Rapids Portage," *The Beaver,* August, 1961, p. 22.
18. *Ibid.,* p. 26.
19. *Ibid.*

State Occasions:
West

Hardly had David Laird said good-bye to his family at Fort Carlton than he was again aboard the *Lily,* on its first voyage up-stream from Battleford. This time he was on official, not personal visits. Accompanying him were his secretary Amédée Forget, Mme. Forget, and Col. Richardson, who was en route to Fort Saskatchewan to preside over the trial of an Indian charged with murder and cannibalism. Another ship-mate was Fort Edmonton's Chief Factor Richard Hardisty, who was in charge of the Hudson's Bay Company's western transportation system, which of course included the *Lily.*

The trip up-river to Edmonton was accomplished in six days despite inevitable groundings on sand bars, ". . . but thanks to the skill and admirable energy of Captain (John H.) Smith, these bars caused only a few hours' detention."[1] First official stop was at Fort Pitt, historic fur and later police post. There as elsewhere His Honor and party were cordially received. Next came (Fort) Victoria, now Pakan, the mission which the Rev. George McDougall had established in 1863, to bring Christianity, Methodist variety, to both the Blackfoot south of the river and to the Crees on the north side.

This objective he did not realize as the Indians, especially those of the Great Plains, were too nomadic, not remaining long enough in one place to absorb the teachings of the Prince of Peace. However, the more sedentary half-breeds gradually settled in proximity to the church, parsonage, and school, building their modest log dwellings and establishing Victoria as a base for their far-flung operations. Eventually the Hudson's Bay Company, too, located a trading post in the settlement, which action added the honorific 'Fort' to Victoria's name.

It was commonly agreed that HBC really meant 'Here Before Christ,' in other words, the Company's posts were built at specific locations before the missions. Indeed, the once-omnipotent Company encouraged, even coerced the churches to locate where it was already established, the better that it could provide defense, transportation, hospitality, and other services to the Black Robes and the Praying Men. The Honorable Company welcomed missionaries and teachers, but on its own terms.

Victoria was one of perhaps only two locations in the North-West where the temporal precedence was reversed. The other was Fort Providence, on the Mackenzie River, where the Oblates' mission predated the Company's fort.

Probably Victoria, mission and fort, were little changed from what they were in 1872, when George M. Grant visited them:

> The settlement and Hudson's Bay fort of Victoria is on the river slope of this ridge, and thus travellers, passing along the main trail up the valley, might be in entire ignorance that there was a settlement near.[2]
>
> The church is also used a school-room, the Mission House, and Fort are all at the west end of the settlement. The log-houses of the English and French half-breeds, intermingled with the tents of the Crees, extend in a line from this west end along the bank of the river, each man having a frontage on the river, and his grain planted in a little hollow that runs behind the houses, beneath the main rise of the ridge. Most of their hay they cut in the valley, on the other side of the ridge, where we had camped.[3]

The *Lily's* last stop before Fort Edmonton was at Fort Saskatchewan, the Mounted Police post which Inspector Jarvis had established in 1875. It rather than Edmonton had been chosen because at that time it was commonly understood that the Pacific railway would skirt the northern boundary of the Great Plains and penetrate the Rockies by the Yellowhead, the lowest pass through those great mountains. Jarvis calculated the railway would cross the Saskatchewan at the place where he built the police fort. His judgement was vindicated some years later, but it was not the Canadian Pacific which built its bridge over the river at Fort Saskatchewan.

S. B. Steele has given us a brief description of the fort's log buildings erected in 1875:

> The men's building was 90 feet by 22 feet, whilst the officers' quarters were of a size suitable for two or three. To these were added a guard-room and stables.
>
> We made our own shingles, raised the walls, put on the roof.[4]

By 1883, and probably by 1879, the police post was enclosed in a palisaded rectangle four hundred by one hundred ninety-five feet.[5]

Here Richardson disembarked, for here he had the unpleasant duty to preside over the trial of an Indian in a particularly shocking murder case.

Although Laird was not immediately involved with the administration of justice, naturally as head of government he was concerned about such a serious crime. J. P. Turner has given the salient details of the case:

> Kak-say-kwyo-chin, or Swift Runner, a Cree Indian, had for years lurked off and on in a strip of country about 80 miles north of Fort Edmonton. The Hudson's Bay Company liked him — a fine specimen of his race, over six feet tall and of heavy build. Of good character, he was mild and trustworthy, a considerate husband and exceedingly fond of his children. But Swift Runner suffered abnormally from troubled dreams, one of the most insidious curses of Indian life. He was continually seeing, or thinking he saw, some of the spirits which were wont to haunt every Indian mind. Foremost among these was the Ween-de-go, the Cannibal Spirit, urging him to indulge in cannibalism; among civilized people such a state of mind meant insanity, among Indians it merited death at the stake.
>
> In the autumn of 1878 Swift Runner, his wife and children moved to new trapping grounds on the left bank of Sturgeon Creek some distance north of Fort Saskatchewan. There he profited by his hunting and trapping and was never in need of food. But a little later suspicion fell upon him when he returned to his former location. Upon being questioned by other Indians, he was unable to account satisfactorily for the whereabouts of his wife and children. His wife's people, alarmed at the inexplicable disappearance of members of his family, reported the matter to the Mounted Police. Superintendent Jarvis assigned the investigation to Inspr. Severe Gagnon, who in due course located the trapper's camp and brought back not only Swift Runner but the mangled bones of the victims of his madness.
>
> Exhaustive search on the part of Inspector Gagnon and his helpers had unearthed ample evidence to show that Swift Runner had not only committed wholesale murder but had turned cannibal. He had barely escaped death, the usual penalty for such a crime, at the hands of his tribe. But it caught up with him, and imprisonment at Fort Saskatchewan was merely a prelude to his inevitable execution in the more orderly and humane manner of the white man.
>
> On August 8 a competent jury was empanelled to decide the case, Stipendiary Magistrate Richardson presiding.
>
> A gruesome story was revealed. Swift Runner had taken the police to a little grave near his camp, saying one of his children had died and he had buried it. The grave was opened and the body was found untouched. But human bones were found scattered about the camp, among them a skull which the Indian was not backward in confessing was that of his wife. Upon being pressed, he then readily related the details of the successive murders he had committed. He had killed his wife and eaten her; he forced one of his boys to kill a younger brother and cut him up, and this one he had eaten; he had killed his baby boy by hanging it to a lodge pole, and while at his supper had pulled the baby's legs to hasten its

strangulation. In this manner he had turned for food not only to the body of his helpmate but to his living children. He also confessed that he had done away with his mother-in-law, who, he acknowledged, was a bit tough. It was said by neighboring Indians that a brother had met the same fate. What made his act even more barbarous was the fact that while he was indulging in his ghastly orgy he had plenty of dried meat hanging around the camp.[6]

Naturally under the circumstances only one verdict was possible — 'Guilty' — as was the mandatory death sentence which followed such a verdict. And so on the following 20 December, Swift Runner was hanged by the neck until he was dead. Thus justice was done.

Or was it? Juries often find a prisoner not guilty by reason of insanity, and as Turner has stated, ". . . among civilized people such a state of mind meant insanity."

But as the *Herald* noted, events at Edmonton were in sharp contrast to the gloomy proceedings at Fort Saskatchewan:

On the morning of Tuesday the 5th inst. the steamer, which was gaily decked with bunting, came in view of the Hudson's Bay Company's fort at Edmonton, situated on a steep bank upwards of a hundred feet above the river, numerous flags were seen displayed from the fort and on the residence of Mr. Hardisty, the hospitable and obliging officer in charge of the post.

A salute of thirteen guns from two pieces of ordinance planted on the bank outside the stockade announced the arrival of the Lieutenant-Governor. Mr. Hardisty, whose presence on board the steamer during the passage had in no small degree increased the comfort of the party, offered the hospitality of his house to the visitors, and both he and his amiable wife did everything in their power to make their brief sojourn agreeable.

The next day His Honor, accompanied by Mr. and Mrs. Hardisty and Mr. and Mrs. Forget, proceeded to St. Albert, about nine miles north of the Saskatchewan. The greater part of the land on both sides of the road between Edmonton and St. Albert is already settled, and the magnificent crops of wheat to be seen as the party drove along indicated the industry of the settlers as well as the richness of the soil. Though only aware the day previous of the intended visit of His Honor, everything was prepared for his reception. As the party came in view of this interesting and progressive settlement of the west, the numerous flags which decorated the church, the covent, and the new episcopal palace, and the peal of bells, forcibly reminded one of the thrifty villages on the St. Lawrence. The ladies were greeted by Sister St. Roch, the Lady Superior of the Orphanage, and the Lieutenant-Governor and other gentlemen by Pere Blanchette, in charge of the Mission, and several other Fathers residing at the Bishop's Palace. The day was usefully employed in visiting the Orphanage and attending an improvised examination of the school under the tuition of the Sisters. The orphans, some thirty-five in all, who are with a few exceptions Indians of different tribes, were uniformly and neatly dressed. They presented His Honor a touching address in English, to which he made a suitable and feeling reply. The interview closed with singing by the Orphans.

The examination of the pupils took place in the afternoon. His Honor was gratified to notice that their instruction is conducted with equal care in both English and French. Though they hear more of the latter language spoken, their teachers state that they seem to acquire English more readily. Their knowledge of the geography of Canada proved to be more advanced than that of some of our Dominion newspaper writers. One of the pupils gave the correct boundary of the North-West Territories as distinguished from the District of Keewaydin. The examination concluded with an exhibition of needlework by the little girls, and a short but amusing play. In reply to an address presented him by the pupils, the Lieutenant-Governor expressed his satisfaction at their progress, and pointed out the advantages they enjoyed over most of the children in the country. He also remarked that they ought to show their gratitude to the zealous and benevolent Sisters of Charity by being studious, and thus avail themselves of the opportunity which kind friends had placed within their reach of receiving a superior education.

The party partook of dinner and luncheon at the orphanage, prepared by the sisters with their well-known care and skill. After the latter the Lieutenant-Governor and party took leave of their hosts and returned to Edmonton, carrying with them lasting remembrances of the hearty reception they had received.[7]

In an era when political patronage was even more blatant than it has since become, the federal government's failure to confirm Acting Superintendent Dickieson in the Indian Affairs position in no way can be considered as reflecting unfavorably upon him. It was simply that Edgar Dewdney, a Conservative Member of Parliament from Kamloops, was well and favorably known to Prime Minister Macdonald. Nor did the fact that Dewdney's was a political appointment mean that in any respect was it an unsuitable one. Indeed, Dewdney proved to be a highly competent and energetic Indian superintendent. His ability is evidenced by the record of his activities during the first two and one-half months of his tenure. In company with Commissioner Macleod, NWMP, and a hundred recruits to the Police, he had left Toronto on 19 May 1879, Jean Larmour has recorded his activities from that date until, in company with Supt. Irvine, he reached Edmonton on 6 Aug.

After twenty-two days of travel on railroad and steamboat on the Missouri, the party reached Fort Benton, Montana Territory. Here Dewdney spent a week outfitting. . . and purchasing supplies; then the party moved north to Fort Walsh in the Cypress Hills, a North-West Mounted Police post, arriving June 26.

Dewdney's first task upon arriving in the Territories was to make contact with the Indians. Commissioner Macleod, who had spent considerable time with the Indians and was trusted by them introduced the new Indian Commissioner to the Indians. Dewdney told them that "the Government had heard with great sorrow, the hardships they had suffered, and had sent me to their country to devote my whole time to their interest."

The new Indian Commissioner held innumerable interviews with the chiefs explaining that the government's objective was to try to help the Indians to become independent. He urged them to locate their reserves that they might be surveyed and recorded by the several dominion land surveyors in the Territories for that purpose. These reserves would then be protected from encroachment by the white man. Assistance would be given the Indians in farming their reserves, to help them become self-sufficient. Two of the principal chiefs at Cypress, one an Assiniboin and the other a Cree, agreed to select their reserves.

In earlier times the Cree and Assiniboin Indians had roamed the plains from the North Saskatchewan to the Missouri harvesting the abundant buffalo. Now that the few remaining herds were located near the Missouri, the Indians tended to congregate in the Cypress Hills where supplies would be received from the police post and within easier access to the remnants of these herds. Dewdney interviewed Big Bear, a prominent Cree chief, trying to persuade him to sign the Treaty, but Big Bear refused to do so. However, Little Pine and Lucky Man were persuaded to sign adhesions to Treaty Six. This left Big Bear as the only important chief who had not signed the Treaty.

From July 10-15, Dewdney was in the vicinity of Fort Macleod and Pincher Creek conferring with the chiefs of the Blood, Peigan and other tribes of the Blackfoot confederacy. He sent provisions ahead to Blackfoot Crossing. . . . He was told that they had been selling their horses for a few cups of flour, eating gophers and mice and that they had nearly killed off the antelope. On July 16 he was at Blackfoot Crossing with Chief Crowfoot and other chiefs of the Blackfoot Indians.[8]

The *Herald* continues the story of Laird's western voyage and the shipwreck of the *Lily* — which could hardly be rated as a major marine disaster.

A pleasant evening spent at the residence of Mr. Hardisty brought the visit to a close. The early departure of the steamer on the following morning rendered it more convenient for the party to pass the night on board the boat. During the night Colonel Richardson, Stipendiary Magistrate, and colonel Jarvis, in charge of Fort Saskatchewan, drove up from that post and also came on board. The Lily was fairly underway when the passengers arose the next morning. It was but eight o'clock when Fort Saskatchewan was reached, where Colonel Jarvis and Major Irvine landed — the latter to continue his trip to Winnipeg by land after an inspection of the post. A whistle of the steamer, and again she resumed her course down the Saskatchewan, expecting to reach Battleford in two days from Edmonton if nothing prevented. But the best calculations often miscarry. About ten miles below the fort a boulder was lying under water, the presence of which could hardly be detected by the keenest pilot on account of a ripple on the water occasioned by a slight breeze. Though the captain and the pilot were both in the wheelhouse at their post, the Lily came upon this boulder, which struck her bottom near the centre, about twenty feet from the stern. The captain immediately went below, and finding she was making water rapidly in her rear compartment, at once ran her ashore. But it was ascertained that the leak was inaccessible and too large to be easily stopped, and the bank being steep, notwithstanding energetic efforts were made to stay up her stern on the out or river side with spars, it settled gradually under water. As it was now evident that more men than the crew would be required to raise the steamer, the pilot was sent back to Edmonton for assistance.

His Honor, seeing that some days must elapse before the Lily could be repaired, sent to Fort Saskatchewan for a skiff which would enable his party to reach Victoria or Battleford, if that means of conveyance was found suitable.

The skiff kindly despatched by Colonel Jarvis reached the steamer in the evening. The night was spent on the Lily, but at daybreak next morning, the 8th instant, the Governor, Colonel Richardson, Mr. Dewdney, the Indian Commissioner, Mr. Forget, the Governor's Secretary, and Mrs. Forget, having taken leave of the attentive captain of the steamer, went on board the new craft. The temperature shortly after the new start became intensely hot, rendering rowing a pretty unpleasant task for unaccustomed hands. But the work was kept up remarkably well until Victoria was reached at four o'clock, where the party, after a hearty tea at the Hudson's Bay post, resolved to hire two men and continue their trip by the river as the quickest mode of travelling to get to Battleford, where the Indian Commissioner was anxious to arrive in time for the Indian payments at Sounding Lake. Everything was ready for a fresh start at seven o'clock. The two half-breeds, stimulated by an anxious desire for a rapid trip, pulled hard until dark, when it was found safer to camp for the night. About four o'clock next morning the travellers were suddenly awakened by a shower, threatening to last for some time. A prompt departure was effected but the clouds soon scattered and the weather became beautiful again.

Two days and a half were employed to reach Fort Pitt, the boat shooting down several rapids on the way. After a short stay at that fort, where a new man was hired to replace one returning to Victoria, the voyage was resumed. Between Pitt and Battleford there is only one rapid, but a multitude of sandbars, which rendered the steering rather difficult and increased the distance to be travelled. Two more days and part of the forenoon of the third were occupied by the party in reaching Battleford. The weather was warm during the whole trip, with an occasional eastern breeze. Game was found rather scarce on the river, contrary to expectations. Several black bears, however, were seen feeding on berries on the bank, or coming to drink at the river. Attempts to shoot them by Messrs. Dewdney and Forget were unsuccessful. Once only it was thought one had been wounded on the shore, but a landing for its capture resulted only in discovering where he had made tracks into the thick brush. Captain Smith of the Lily on his way up was more successful. A bear was first seen swimming across the river at some distance; but the Lily being put at greatest speed, Master Bruin was hit as he reached the shore by a bullet from the Captain's rifle and was ultimately captured.

The party landed at Battleford on Thursday, the 14th instant, all looking well, and pleased with their trip to the West and their experience on the river.[9]

Further details of the adventure appear in a letter which Laird wrote on August 30 to his eldest son, (David) Rennie. After mildly complaining that he had not yet heard from his family, although more than a month had elapsed since he had parted from them at Carlton, he continues

Respecting our visit to Edmonton, you will see an account in the Herald of the 25th, which I send you with the two preceding numbers. They were not mailed in my absence. I expected to be back from Edmonton before the last mail left here, but the accident to the Lily prevented me reaching home in time.

We had a pleasant time going up the Saskatchewan. It is not so wide above Pitt. There are but few Islands, and the banks in some places are steep and rocky. We saw several Bears, and the Captain shot one. The steamer was very gay. They had their own flags, and from Battleford, I took an Indian flag, and our big one belonging to the flag staff, and Colonel Richardson took his. When we came to a H. B. co. Post, or a settlement, they were all raised, and the Lily looked very fine. At Edmonton, you will see by the Herald, they fired a salute with big guns. The country above Edmonton is very pretty and the soil rich, but the crops are later than ours.

We received quite an ovation at St. Albert. They rang the Church, Convent and School Bells, and they had white and blue flags displayed from the Church steeple, and a number of poles around the grounds. The orphan boys and girls were very clean and tidy. The school examination was got up in great style. In the new Bishop's palace they had a room fitted up with a platform at one end, which was curtained off, not with a drop curtain like the Police one at our nigger minstrel show, but which was drawn back end-wise. Here when the classes were ready, as a play was to come off, the curtain was drawn. I suppose they would beat you, Gordon and Mary at French, but I think you would have done as well at anything else. The plays consisted chiefly of dialogues in English or French, the actors being dressed in character. One little girl named Robinson did very well. She scolded in French and English and stamped her foot in good style. She also danced across the platform several times to the music of one of the nuns. They have fine currants and gooseberries in their garden there, and altogether it is a pretty place, with the Sturgeon River running by on one side.

Young Richard Hardisty was glad to get home to his mamma. He has a fine looking sister a little older than he is — at least she would be good looking, had she not squint eyes. A baby brother is the only other one of the family.[10]

Young Richard, of course, was the six-year-old who had been present at the signing of Treaty No. 7 two years previously.

Farmer Laird concluded his letter with a report on the family's wheat, oats, and barley crops. Epistles to David Rennie written between 1879 and 1881 are most of the very few of David Laird's personal letters which seem to have survived.

After his western journey, presumably David Laird had something of a breather before the third meeting of the council in September. The *Herald's* issue of 11 August, while the lieutenant-governor was still on the high seas, or rather the low water of the Saskatchewan River, contained a Notice re Prairie and Forest Fires, no doubt a warning to careless settlers to keep their conflagrations under control.

There was also a notice respecting the issuance of liquor permits. Unless an applicant were known to His Honor, he would need a recommendation from a clergyman, magistrate, physician, police officer, or Hudson's Bay Company officer, these evidently comprising the uppermost stratum of territorial society. Although the list does not include some eminently respectable occupations, such as those of merchant or farmer — or editor of the *Herald* — such worthies could be included if they had received magisterial appointments. One so qualified was Charles Mair, of Prince Albert.

The council, which had a heavy agenda, concluded its sessions on 27 September. Its legislations included the following:

1. Respecting Infectious Diseases
2. Dangerous Lunatics
3. Ferries
4. The Prevention of Prairie and Forest Fires
5. Masters and Servants
6. The Licensing of Billiard and other Tables and the Prevention of Gambling

7. Amendment to the Administration of Civil Justice Ordinance of 1878
8. Exempting certain Property from Seizure and Sale under Executions
9. Registration of Deeds and other Instruments relative to Lands
10. Respecting Ordinances of the North-West Territories.

The list suggests that territorial society (non-Indian) was becoming both more sophisticated and more settled. Certainly such men as Presbyterian David Laird and Methodist John McDougall would not regard the advent of pool halls and billiard tables with approbation, but since they could hardly be forbidden, it was important that they be regulated.

The ordinance respecting land ownership indicates that at last the federal government was moving to have surveys completed of at least some real estate holdings, but whether as a result of the *Herald's* fulminations of the previous year is doubtful. By 1878 the latitude and longitude of Winnipeg, Carlton, Battleford, Prince Albert, and Edmonton had been determined by astronomical observations. Thereafter, as Thomson relates, surveying of the North West swung into high gear.

> From 1871 to 1878, with the exception of only two seasons, there were, on the average, only a score of land surveyors employed on Dominion Lands survey work in the western interior of the nation. But in 1879 the numbers rose to 32, heralding a series of impressive annual increases in numbers until 1883 when a peak of 115 was reached, 21 on township outlines, 82 on subdivisions along with one Settlement Belt surveyor and one town-plot surveyor. In addition there were four examiners of contract surveys who were busy in the field.[11]

Editor Laurie did not hesitate to include editorial comment in his news stories, as he did in reporting on the council's deliberations. His observations thereon are interesting evidence that western alienation is no new phenomenon:

> The Council was unable to legislate respecting schools for want of sufficient powers, and to deal with Roads and Bridges for want of funds. It is about time that the people of the Territories, who contribute largely to the general revenue of the dominion, should at least have the allowance of eighty cents per head of the population, which is granted to the Provinces for local purposes. Besides paying the full customs and excise duties exacted in other parts of the Dominion, the people of the Territories have also to pay heavy freight rates for all the goods they import. Would it not, therefore, be common justice to allow them some expend-

iture on roads and bridges, in order to lessen the expense of freighting, in return for the taxes which they pay into the Dominion treasury?[12]

Two letters that Laird wrote in October reveal two very different aspects of his personality. One, to his son Rennie, shows the parental concern of a *paterfamilias*. His previous letter to the boy had shown some slight annoyance that he had not heard from Rennie in more than a month since he had parted from his family at Carlton. This second letter indicates that the boy was not lacking in his filial duty. The letter follows:

> Battleford, N.W.T.
> 16th October 1879

Dear Rennie

I received your letters from Winnipeg, Toronto and Charlottetown. You are a good son to write me so much news. None of you, however, wrote to me of the tumble Harold got. Mr. Straith wrote me that news. I hope my youngest son was not much the worse for his fall, and that he is now showing in school that his head is none the worse. If he does not turn out a good clever boy I will be much disappointed. Of course Weja* is going to be bright too, and learn at home with Mr Mammer (?) so as to be ready for school next spring.

I am very pleased to hear that you passed the examination for Mr Miller's room. He is said to be good Teacher, and I hope you will show yourself a good pupil. Mary and Gordon and Willie will no doubt also be diligent this winter in learning their lessons. If Mary does not take too much "Permit," she ought to be a good French scholar before the spring.

We had snow here on the 9th of this month, but not much. At Prince Albert and Duck Lake, I hear, nearly a foot. Their grain not being all in, is covered with it in the fields.

Planguer (?) had our crop housed before the snow came. He had 170 bushels of Potatoes, and a great many turnips; but we only took up a few of them, and let the cattle eat the remainder in the field. Old Molly went at the turnips so greedily that she got one stuck in her throat and we had to kill her to save the carcase, which, as she was killed before she really died from choking, we sold to Mr Orde for the Indians.

The weather is very fine now and all the snow is gone again here, and we may have some open weather yet.

Geese and ducks are very plenty this fall. I bought Mr Dickieson's gun when we left, but have only been out once to try, and had bad luck.

Oliver came here last night from Prince Albert. He thinks the house terrible quiet without you children. He thinks it too bad that Weja went away and left him in the lurch.

> Your affectn father
> D. Laird[13]

*Family name for Louise

Another letter dated two days later reveals a stiff-necked Presbyterian who valued his honor and his reputation far above material gain:

> Battleford
> 18th October, 1879
>
> Sir
>
> I have told Mr Oliver most distinctly that I make no claim for the three cows which I sent by him to winter at the same rate as the Government cattle at Prince Albert.
>
> I paid Baker & co. $35 each for two of them, and the other was one of my herd all the previous summer, but I will lose them all rather than have the slightest suspicion cast upon my name.
>
> Yours & D. Laird
>
> Mr Palmer, Clerk, &c
> Prince Albert[14]

On 30 October, Laird had two visitors from Prince Albert, Thomas McKay and a man whom he was coming to know quite well and value as a friend. This was Charles Mair. The two were very concerned with the matter of Sioux refugees, who apparently had penetrated as far north as Prince Albert. Laird sent Inspector Walker, NWMP, and Tom Quin, an interpreter, to investigate.

It was perhaps at this time that Laird himself met a deputation of the displaced Sioux. Certainly Mair was present at the meeting, whenever it took place, for he has left us with a first-hand account of it. Referring to Laird, he wrote:

> Perhaps no more trying incident occurred during his regime than the flight of Sitting Bull and his great camp into British territory after the last stand of the Western Sioux against the Americans. Three of their most noted chiefs were sent by Sitting bull to Battleford, to place their grievances, which were great before the Governor, and to implore assistance and protection.
>
> Through the incoming of these wild bands a panic had spread throughout the whole country, extending even to the borders of Manitoba. At Prince Albert the half-breed and white settlers assembled and a volunteer force was enrolled to cope with the anticipated emergency, whilst numbers of the more timid settlers on the outskirts of the Province actually meditated flight. Of course these fears proved to be groundless, but, considering the wild and unsettled condition of the country at the time, and the isolation of its tiny settlements, they were not unnatural.
>
> The interview referred to of the Sioux Chiefs with Mr Laird in the council room at Battleford was a curious and striking scene. Three

bronzed warriors, of noble presence and grave countenance, their breasts — proudly exposed, roped with the transverse scars won at the Sun Dance, their every movement instinct with dignity, knelt, each after each, before they began to speak and breathed a prayer to the Great Spirit. Then each in turn recounted the story of violated treaties, aggression and cruelty which had forced them from their ancient home; and, whilst imploring the shelter and assistance of the Queen, gave earnest assurance of their profound desire for peace. There was unspeakable pathos in the scene. There upon our soil, were the emissaries of the greatest race of Indians on the continent. The Iroquois may be excepted; but, barring their historic contest with the rival French and English, even they, great as they were in many ways, were "canoe Indians" or travelled on foot, whilst the Sioux roamed the Great Plains in all directions on horseback. There was thus a grand freedom in their life which impressed itself upon their very forms and faces, many of which were classic in their beauty. To see in the old days a young Teton or Ogallala warrior in all his appropriate trappings was a sight to be remembered. Fifty years ago the Sioux were very numerous, and together with the Blackfeet and their allied tribes practically ruled the plains. They fared sumptuously, for the bison, and game of all kinds abounded. They lived a free and clean life, for a Sioux Camp, or lodge, in primitive days, was a model of order and cleanliness. Their women were marvels of chastity, presenting a striking contrast to some other races in this particular; and from the Missouri almost to the British line they were lords of all they surveyed. And here, after untold centuries of possession was the end of it all — three broken but dignified old warriors, laying their pitiful tale in the ears of the Canadian Governor, and imploring food and shelter. There is not space to set forth Mr Laird's sympathetic yet unavailing reply; for it had a sting which could not be concealed viz that withal, their true interest was to return to the United States, and accept, in good faith the assurances of the American authorities of protection and fair treatment. But this was delivered with such tact and real kindness that, although, the Chiefs were grieved and disappointed with the reply told; and, in the end, good counsels did prevail and the great mass of their people returned.[15]

It is not surprising that one who could write so sympathetically of Indian people would eventually find himself employed by a Half-Breed Commission.

As for the lieutenant-governor, his next public appearance seems to have been on Thanksgiving Day, 27 November, which opened with divine service in the morning and concluded in the evening with a free musical and literary entertainment. Apparently this was regarded as an Official Occasion, as Laird made the council chamber available for the "large, orderly, and thoroughly appreciative audience." His Honor himself presided. Prof. L. H. Thomas, formerly Saskatchewan Archivist, more recently of the Department of History, University of Alberta, has given a careful evaluation of Laird's remarks on that Day of Thanksgiving so long ago:

> It was a fine speech, full of wise and constructive comment, perceptive in its vision of things to come, with deep feeling for the importance of the pioneer's daily round and common task. Concern for the welfare of the Indians is foremost in the Governor's mind. Coupled with this is his interest in farming progress, both from the economic and social points of view, for to him agriculture is "the most healthful, the most useful, and the most noble employment of man." He concludes with a plea for the recognition of schools and public libraries as essential for the good life. Altogether it is a speech eminently appropriate for the occasion, but possessing also an enduring relevance.[16]

Although Laird's address was a bit ornate and high-flown for twentieth century tastes, with its literary allusions and quotations, it was such a fine speech that it deserves to be quoted in full. And so here it is:

> LADIES AND GENTLEMEN — Our Thanksgiving Day is drawing to a close. In the forenoon we met to render thanks to Him who causeth "the shower to come down in his season" and "the earth to yield her increase." This was proper. But there is also a practical side to the duties of life. We may be serving the great Creator just as faithfully by observing the command "to do your own business and to work with your own hands," as by engaging in a formal service of praise. Of how little avail to us are a fertile soil, refreshing showers, and genial sunshine if we do not use the means to reap the rewards which Providence has placed within our reach.
>
> This evening as we are assembled for an hour's entertainment, it may not be unprofitable to very briefly inquire how the people of the North-West Territories can best promote their own and their country's welfare.
>
> The Territories now may be said to be in a transition state. Until a few years ago, almost the sole occupation of the people was the chase. But the rapid disappearance of the buffalo from the plains has necessitated many who looked to that noble animal for support to turn to some other means of gaining a livelihood. We could have wished, especially for the sake of our Indian brother, that the decrease of the buffalo had not latterly been so rapid. But the crisis sooner or later had to come. Within the memory of old living hunters, that proud denizen of the Plains roamed in thousands eastward to the valley of the Red River. Gradually he receded before his numerous enemies, until this summer scarcely one could be found in Canadian territory. During the autumn some small herds returned to cheer the hunters, and for a few years more they may occasionally cross the International Boundary, but for all practical purposes, as a source of dependence for food, their day is gone by. A few short years more, and they will be numbered with the extinct animals of North America. They will have passed from the history of the period, and will have become the study of the pateontologist

of the future, who will dig us their remains, and place them in his museum side by side with the fossils of the mastodon and the ichthyosaurus of geologic ages. And perhaps Macaulay's New Zealander, on the same tour on which he comes to sketch the ruins of London Bridge, may visit this Western continent to hunt up buffalo skulls, and speculate upon the form and uses of that wonderful quadruped which roamed the prairies away back in the remote centuries of the human era.

But fancy aside, we have to view the disappearance of the buffalo as a solid, sober, serious fact. The Indian of the Plains has for generations solely depended upon this animal for subsistence. The Government is doing much to assist him, and after a sharp trial, during which there will doubtless be not a little suffering, let us hope that the crisis will be overcome. We have all a duty to perform in this matter. I do not say we can afford to any extent out of our own means to assist the aborigines of this country; but we can all speak a kind word. Soft words cost little and are worth much. Further, we should abstain from fomenting dissatisfaction among those sons of the prairie. We may not always think that everything is being done for them by the Department of the Interior, or its agents, that their condition requires; but if so, let us carry our complaints to the proper quarter, and not to the Indian. I can scarcely conceive of a greater enemy to his country, and to the red man himself, than the philanthropist who is continually telling him that he is not receiving justice. Rather let us kindly advise the Indian how he may acquire his own living — and if wrongs or neglect are apparent, there are constitutional means of representing them to the Government and the Parliament at Ottawa, and justice will be done, for the great heart of Canada beats right on this question.

Since plain-hunting is almost a thing of the past, there need be no jealousy between the red man and his pale-faced brother. They can both rejoice soon to see the day, when they may sing with Bryant,

> "The sheep are on the slopes around,
>   The cattle in the meadows feed;
> And laborers turn the crumbling ground
>   Or drop the yellow seed."

Perhaps, however, when we think of the red-man's ancient sway in this "Great Lone Land," there are few amongst us who cannot join with him in sympathetic strain respecting many a sacred spot in its widely-extending area —

> "Hither the artless Indian maid
>   Brought wreaths of beads and flowers;
> And the gray Chief and gifted Seer
>   Worshipped the God of thunders here.

But though the buffalo-chase has well-nigh run its course, in the northern regions of this country the hunter will probably ever hold undisputed possession. The fur trade of the Mackenzie and other rivers of the high latitudes will in all likelihood for many years constitute an important business, forming a source of profit to the trader, a means of living to the trapper, and a market for the productions of the south.

The greatest industry of this country, however, must be agriculture and cattle-raising. Over very extensive districts it has been proved that the principal grains — wheat, oats, and barley — and roots, such as potatoes, turnips, carrots, parsnips, and beets can be raised very successfully. Our wild grasses are also most nutritious. Cattle and horses thrive well on them, and I have no doubt that sheep-raising likewise would be profitable in this country, were their natural enemies — the wolves and husky dogs — sent to the happy hunting grounds of all such carnivorous animals. With, therefore, bread the staff of life, meat which will compare favorably with the roast beef of Old England, potatoes for table use and for starch manufacture, beets, for sugar, wool for warm clothing, coal or lignite for fuel, and a healthy and bracing climate, what is to prevent this country from becoming the home of a great people. The car of progress is on the move. Immigrants are arriving yearly, slowly it may be as yet; but still the cry is "they come." Hark! may we not say of their footsteps —

"I hear the tread of pioneers
   Of nations yet to be;
The first low wash of waves where soon
   Shall roll a human sea."

Let us then be up and doing in the great work that is before us. Let us cultivate the broad acres of the Territories, and multiply our herds, that there may be a sufficiency of food within our borders for all the inhabitants of the country, and also to supply the immigrant as he arrives in our midst. It is not desirable that we should depend any longer upon Montana for a part of our animal food, or upon Manitoba for any of our flour and meal. I am happy to say that within the last two years much has been accomplished in some of our settlements to produce these great necessaries of life. The thousands of bushels of grain raised at Prince Albert, in the Little Saskatchewan country, and in the vicinity of Edmonton, not forgetting Battleford are an earnest of the millions which will yet be produced in these Territories. A late Agricultural Exhibition at Edmonton shows the excellence of the grain and vegetables that can be grown in the Saskatchewan valley. Such shows are commendable, and I hope the day is at hand, when Agricultural Societies, to encourage the procuring of good seed and stock; and to cause a generous rivalry among farmers, will be established in every district.

We need not fear for want of a market. The requirements of the North and of immigrants will consume all the surplus that can be produced for some time. And in a few years we hope to have the railway. The iron horse with his train, setting aside the pony and the Red River cart, will then sweep away to be shipped to Europe our surplus wheat and cattle to feed the millions in the manufacturing towns and cities of the British Isles and the Old Continent. In process of time, this country may also have some manufactures; but for years we ought to give our chief attention to agriculture — with cattle-raising, either as an attendant or independent calling. And a dignified occupation is Agriculture — at once the most healthful, the most useful, and the most noble employment of man. Of it the Poet says:

"The proud throne shall crumble,
   The diadem shall wane,
The tribes of earth shall humble
   The pride of those who reign;
And War shall lay his pomp away —
   The fame that heroes cherish,
The glory earned in deady fray
   Shall fade, decay, and perish.
Honor waits, o'er all the earth,
   Through endless generations,
The art that calls her harvests forth,
   And feeds the expectant nations.

There are other duties, however, which we must not neglect in the race for material prosperity. Our people during the long nights of winter should endeavor to store their minds with useful knowledge. Excellent books and periodicals are now easily procured, and to facilitate their circulation and place them within the reach of all, settlement libraries might be established. Again, those who have children should strive to obtain for them a good education. Kind missionaries of different denominations have done, and are doing, much to place instruction within the reach of not a few in the Territories. Parents should avail themselves of these opportunities to benefit their children, and should assist the teachers by their contributions. Let us hope that ere long the Government will be in a position to aid in this commendable work, and that through the efforts of *all* combined the rising generation may grow up fitted to discharge the duties of good citizens. Let us seek to lay broad and deep in the intelligence and morality of our people, the foundations of free institutins and of a prosperous branch of the Canadian State. Each of us can perform a part in this great undertaking by striving himself or herself to attain a high culture, and by setting a good example to others. Let us sing, and not only sing, but *act* with Longfellow, in his Psalm of Life:

"Lives of great men all remind us
   We can make our lives sublime,
And, departing, leave behind us
   Footprints on the sands of time."[17]

Mention has been made of the fact that the *Saskatchewan Herald* kept a close eye on Laird's agricultural pursuits. An item in the issue of 29 December shows how diligently Editor Laurie noted such activities. It also reveals much more: the inherent honesty of Indians who were going through the third hungry year in a row, and the generous nature of the lieutenant-governor.

Some months ago four head of cattle belonging to the Lieutenant-Governor strayed away from Battleford, and although diligent and extensive search was made no sign of them could be found. Just as hope of recovering them had almost died out they were restored in a most unexpected manner. They had travelled south, and were discovered by some Indians out on the plains about seventy miles from here. Reasoning that they had strayed from the north, two of the Indians were deputed to drive them to Battleford in the hope of finding an owner for them. The conduct of these men, who were non-treaty Indians, in thus undertaking to bring the cattle across the plains in the depth of winter on the mere chance of finding an owner for them, at a time when they were short of provisions and could have killed the animals without any fear of detection, is worthy of the highest praise. In addition to the customary reward of five dollars a head for bringing in the stray cattle the Governor gave the Indians a substantial evidence of his appreciation of their sterling honesty.[18]

A few weeks earlier, the *Herald* had announced that a Mr. Pambrum had raised a 64-lb.-per-bushel wheat from seed obtained from Governor Laird. Since the standard weight of one bushel of wheat is sixty pounds, the quality of this sample was obviously very high.

Probably for both Laird and Richardson the holiday season of Christmas and New Year's was none too festive, with their families in distant Ottawa and Charlottetown. When Member of Parliament for Queen's and even when Minister of the Interior, David Laird had been able to get home regularly or occasionally — in those long-ago days Parliament sat for only a few months in the year, and even a ministerial portfolio was not too onerous. But a century ago, to cross most of the continent was a major, time-consuming venture. Perhaps it was at Christmastide that Laird began to plan for a leave-of-absence in which he could combine business with pleasure, the latter a visit to his wife and children. Certainly he had had no vacation since his appointment as lieutenant governor in 1876.

References

1. *Saskatchewan Herald,* 25 August 1879, "To Edmonton and Back Three Hundred Miles in an Open Boat," also, "Three Hundred Miles in an Open Boat," *Alberta Historical Review,* v. 18, no. 3, p. 24.

2. G. M. Grant, *Ocean to Ocean,* p. 171.

3. *Ibid.,* pp. 171-172.

4. S. B. Steele, *Forty Years in Canada,* p. 89.

5. W. A. Griesbach, *I Remember,* p. 47.

6. J. P. Turner, *The North-West Mounted Police,* v. 1, pp. 500-501.

7. *Saskatchewan Herald* and *Alberta Historical Review, op. cit.,* (latter, pp. 24-25).

8. Jean Larmour, "Edgar Dewdney Indian Commissioner in the Transition Period of Indian Settlement, 1879-1884," *Saskatchewan History,* v. 31, no. 1, pp. 14-16.

9. *Saskatchewan Herald* and *Alberta Historical Review, op. cit.,* (latter, pp. 25-26).

10. David Laird to David Rennie Laird, 30 August 1879, Public Archives of Prince Edward Island.

11. Don W. Thomson, *Men and Meridians,* v. 2, p. 41.

12. *Saskatchewan Herald,* 4 October 1879.

13. David Laird to David Rennie Laird, 16 October 1879, Public Archives of Prince Edward Island.

14. David Laird to Mr. Palmer, 18 October 1879, Saskatchewan Archives Board.

15. Charles Mair, "Mr. Mair's Account of the Meeting with the Sioux Chiefs," handwritten undated account on stationery of Indian Affairs, Regina, N.W.T., Public Archives of Prince Edward Island.

16. L. H. T(homas), "Governor Laird's Thanksgiving Day Address, 1879," *Saskatchewan History,* v. 5, no. 3, p. 107.

17. David Laird, *ibid.,* reprinted from *Saskatchewan Herald,* 1879.

18. *Saskatchewan Herald,* 29 December 1879.

12

Interlude: Letters to the Island, 1880

For 1880, the *Saskatchewan Herald* and certain official documents constitute a chronicle of the activities of the Hon. David Laird, Lieutenant-Governor of the North-West Territories, a man rather austere, dignified, conscientious and able in the performance of his duties, somewhat formal — one cannot imagine even his closest associates calling him "Dave." For many months he was probably a very lonely individual, with his family in distant Charlottetown. And in his position he could hardly afford to have intimates or special cronies, for the very existence of such relationships in the small white community of the Territories could lead to gossip and suspicion of favoritism. Even the occasional conviviality of a shared bottle of wine or more ardent spirits this teetotaling Presbyterian denied himself.

It is in his letters to his son David Rennie during this period that is revealed a more human David Laird, anxious about his children's health and education, yet withal rather parsimonious in his commendation when they did well in their studies. He is interested in and reports on the doings of his neighbors, on farming operations and accidents. He grumbles about irregular and untrustworthy mail service. And occasionally he shows a flash of humor or whimsicality.

Scarcely a letter to Rennie during the first half of 1880 fails to mention the Laird children's progress at school. Thus on 5 February 1880, Laird writes, "The public examinations before the Holidays will have come off long ago. Did any of my dear boys distinguish themselves?"[1] On 18 March this concerned parent devotes a whole page, one-quarter of his letter to Rennie, to matters educational:

> Rev. Mr. Clarke is still keeping school here. He has about 25 pupils. I saw the address of your class to Mr Miller. It was pretty good, but as you say, Mr Seamen helped the boys get it up, I must not give you credit for it. My dear boy, I am always much pleased to receive your letters

but I would like to see you taking more pains to write them nicely and carefully. Your papa is fond of seeing a well-written letter.[2]

This last comment is almost in the category of, 'Do as I say; not as I do.' David Laird's own penmanship fell far short of the Spencerian copperplate ideal of the era.

On 19 May, David Laird returns to the matter of education. "I suppose you have made great progress at school this winter. You ought to be all diligent to learn, for your Papa has gone to great expense to send you home to have opportunities to get Education."[3] In a postscript added three days later, acknowledging the arrival of two more letters from his eldest son, Laird adds the following:

I am glad to hear that you are getting on well in Arithmetic and Geometry. I hope you are a good boy in school, and respectful to your teachers. Teachers have a great many to look after, and may sometimes make mistakes, but pupils also make mistakes, and should always feel kindly and speak well of their Instructors.[4]

Perhaps in the many months since the father had last seen his family, he had forgotten that his two eldest sons were big boys and had rapidly grown bigger. Superscription on at least one letter was to 'Master D. R. Laird,' despite the fact that Rennie was by then fifteen years of age, plus or minus a few weeks or months. In any event, David Laird seems to have been worrying unduly about the academic progress of his progeny. A year later — 15 August 1881 — the *Saskatchewan Herald* cited a Charlottetown *Patriot* report that in his class Rennie stood first in algebra, second in Latin, arithmetic, and geometry, and third in geography. Gordon's record was even more glittering, comprising firsts in grammar, algebra, arithmetic, and geometry, second in Latin, and third in geography.

Did a fond parent in Battleford draw the Charlottetown report to the attention of Editor Laurie?

An interesting omission from the list is French. In several letters, Laird referred to his boys' facility in this subject. As mentioned in chapter 11, on his return from the Edmonton trip, he compared their mastery of the language to that of the St. Albert orphans. On 5 February he states, "I sent Gordon a French letter, which you will give to him. His French was not bad," — barely restrained enthusiasm — "but probably he will do better next time. I hope Mary is well now, and that she, and you too, will write me a few lines in French."[5] And in his 22 May postscript, after acknowledging the recent arrival of two letters from Rennie, his father hurriedly notes, "I have not time to try the great gun puzzle just now, nor to read your French."[6]

Yet the school report from Charlottetown makes no mention of French. Had the boys discontinued its study at the end of the 1880-81 school year? Or was it an 'extra' subject, not required for matriculation, or at least not subject to examination? Or perhaps were the boys, and Mary too, studying it privately, as today's young people may study music, dancing, or figure skating.

Less of a puzzle is the omission of English literature as a subject of school study. Not until the 1870's did it begin to appear on secondary school curricula in North America, and even then rather slowly. At first, its objectives were not mainly the development of literary appreciation but primarily the inculcation of Christian values, Catholic or Protestant depending on the school atmosphere, and secondarily, commitment to the existing system of government and recognition of its inherent superiority over every other system. Of course, that government would be monarchial or republican, depending on whether a particular school was located north or south of the Great Undefended Border. English composition and rhetoric were not neglected, however, being subtended under the omnibus reach of grammar.

In the Laird family, extended as well as nuclear, academic excellence was not considered worthy of special commendation. It was expected, and usually achieved. Of David and Louisa's progeny, Gordon was perhaps the most outstanding scholar, winning a governor-general's medal in 1881. Eventually he was to earn his Ph. D. in Latin and Greek and become a professor of classics in a prestigious American university.

Laird's letters to his sons, of course, dealt with more than the boys' school progress; their health was also a matter of vital concern. On 18 March he wrote to Rennie, "The Island climate does not appear to agree with you now. You must try and avoid getting wet, for I expect that it is wet feet or clothes which give you a cold."[7] Of course, David was quite well aware that Louisa was perfectly able to watch over their children's physical well-being, but he could not help the occasional paternal admonition. "I hope Harold has got quite strong and Magy has become stiff-backed — not stiff-necked again."[8]

Battleford was a capital city — at least, a capital — but lacked somewhat the glitter and glamor of Paris, London, or even Ottawa. Still, it had its occasions, as Papa Laird reported on 5 February 1880:

> There is to be a great Bachelors Ball to-morrow night at the Barracks. They asked for the Council Room but I declined it to them. It is got up in great style. They have the invitations printed. I received one which I enclose for your guidance when you become a bachelor. Just fancy how it will read in most cases — "John Sakeschewen and ladies," "Skeesik and ladies." The hurry is to get it over before Lent when all good people

have to stay at home and fast because of all the sins they committed by kissing girls and eating plum cake the week before.[9]

The idea that one attained rather than abandoned bachelorhood is rather intriguing. Presumably for fifteen-year-old Rennie it would occur when he ceased to be Master and became Mr. D. R. Laird. or perhaps when he fell from grace and committed the sin of kissing girls.

His father's references to "John Sakeschewen and ladies," "Skeesik and ladies" suggest that despite the influence of the Christian missions, polygamy had not wholly ceased among the Indians.

In his only other reference to a Battleford community affair, Laird states, "Next Monday is the Queen's Birthday, but I believe there will be no games here: some are talking of getting up a Pic-nic."[10] Apparently in 1880 there were no plans for the lieutenant-governor to review his troops.

Summer or winter, for all farmers an abiding interest is weather, and most of Laird's letters to his son reflect this concern, e.g.:

5th Feby, 1880. . . The weather was very cold here all December and about half of January. Since then it has not been so bad. For the last few days it has been very mild. Last night the thermometer was only 15° above zero, and today at 2 p.m. it was just at freezing point — vis 32° above zero.[11]

March 18, 1880 . . . It thawed a good deal today, and I think we are going to have spring. There will likely be plenty of water on the Sas-katchewan this year for the steamer, as there is so much snow.[12]

May 19, 1880. . . We have had a good deal of rain this month — more than I ever saw in May before in the North-West. There has been thun-der three of four times — one night a week ago it was very heavy.[13]

As important to the farmer as the weather — more so — are his animals and his crops On 18 March, Farmer Laird wrote, "My two horses have been out all winter, but I will have to get them home now."[14] He also reported the sad and abrupt demise of the horse Lucy, presumably another animal, killed by bot-fly larvae. A happier news item on 9 June concerned Nellie, ". . . so fat and spendid that nearly everybody wants to buy her off me."[15]

But not all living creatures were equally appreciated. "The mosqui-toes are pretty lively and 'smudges' are the order of the day."[16]

The previous August, Laird had reported to Rennie on his crop yield in 1879. The following May he listed his intentions for 1880, somewhat more modest perhaps because he was planning on being away from Battle-ford during the coming harvest season. "I am not putting in much crop this year — only about two acres of wheat, five of Oats, two of barley, and one of Potatoes," he wrote on 19 May. "The wheat is up, the potatoes and barly (*sic*) are not yet planted."[17]

David Laird also reported on others' agricultural efforts. The Rev. Mr. Clarke was planting two acres of oats in the Laird field. Amedée Forget, Laird's secretary and the council clerk, and the sheriff (unnamed) had bought a farm and rented it on a half-crop basis. In fact, the Territorial capital was becoming quite an agricultural centre:

> The Finlaysons are putting in about forty acres of crop out some two miles beyond McFarlane's. ONeill, the Policeman, is putting a little crop out somewhere by the big hay valley. The Police are also putting up a much larger crop this year. So you see Battleford is not altogether asleep.[18]

His children's education and health, the weather, farming operations — these of course did not exhaust the topics about which the affectionate papa wrote to his son. Other subjects were family neighbors and friends. Among the latter was the preacher-cum-teacher, the Rev. Mr. Clarke. "Mr Clarke and I bought Captain French's box sleigh, and put a pole on it. This is lighter than our big double-bob concern," Laird wrote, "and we sometimes have a drive on a fine day. Mr. Clarke goes out much oftener than I do, visiting his parishioners."[19]

In April, the same Mr. Clarke, according to Laird, left Battleford to go to Canada. Apparently the Territories might be part of a Dominion reaching from sea to sea, but these new Nor'Westers had not yet apparently got into the habit of regarding their Territories as part of it. However, whatever they called the East, Clarke didn't reach it. A little beyond Fort Ellice, Clarke's and his companion's horses broke their hobbles, wandered off, and were never seen again. Picking up some loose horses for their wagon, the pair made their way back to Battleford.

> Mr. Clarke was so disgusted with his bad luck that he has given up the trip to Canada for the present. He has been with me ever since; but talks of going out to the reserve to-morrow to help the Indians to hurry in their crop.[20]

With his wife and family on the Island, David Laird was no doubt a lonely man. However, he could at least write to and hear from his beloved Louisa, although no letters seem to have survived. Magistrate Richardson's situation, however, was even bleaker. His daughters were in Ottawa, but his wife had died since she and her girls had come west three years previously. Yet he seemed to have adjusted well to his bereavement, or at least so one might infer from one of Laird's letters:

> Colonel Richardson returned last week to Battleford. He is just the same old sixpence. A young man has come with him by the name of Marigold. What his business is I do not know. He appears to act as a kind of Secretary to the Colonel. I have heard that he came up to join the North West *Temperance* Society![21]

Total abstainer though he was, Laird apparently had no illusions about the prospects for victory in the battle again Demon Rum.

From time to time, Laird mentioned others, some of whom the boys knew. Thus, on 9 June:

> We have not very many Indians here now. It is said, however, that "Mosquito" and a number of others are on the way in. Last week I had a visit from a Sioux Chief called "Iron Dog," and some of his people. I took them over to the Indian office and got Quin to interpret his speech. I replied to him and left him there to get some "grub" and ammunition.
>
> Bourke, Shaw and O'Neill, three Policemen whose time was out last week are going to stay here, they say, and commence farming.[22]
>
> The Sheriff is going to bring up some of his relatives and start a big farm at the Eagle Hills. Dick, Wylde and some of the other Policemen have gone off to Winnipeg. There are very few P. Men here now. Some men came up with the Colonel to repair his house again. It is reported that he is going to have it papered inside and outside. Forget and Scott are going to get foundations put under their houses.[23]

It is hard to imagine the austere, dignified lieutenant-governor, the abstentious Presbyterian elder, the man of complete integrity, as having any human foibles, weaknesses, or minor vices. But his own letters provide evidence to the contrary. On 19 May he wrote to Rennie, "Last mail I received your letter of 3rd March; but the Blanket and the Tobacco did not come to hand."[24] Almost two months later the gifts from the dutiful son had still not appeared.

> I received your two short letters written about the end of April and beginning of May; but I have seen nothing yet of your box and the tobacco. I expect the former has been smashed, and the latter gone to feed the gophers at some of those places where the mail bags were thrown off during the deep snow by the mail carrier.[25]

It would seem that, public opinion to the contrary, postal service in the 1880's was neither faster nor more regular nor more dependable than it was a century later.

David Laird's letter of 9 June was apparently the last one he wrote to his son before departing on 5 July for his long-awaited leave and on his return journey his visit to a number of points in the eastern part of his domain. Of course, between New Year's Day and 5 July he had been engaged in a number of activities, official and probably dull, other than those few mentioned in his letters to Rennie.

References

All references are to 1880 letters, David Laird to David Rennie Laird, in Public Archives of Prince Edward Island.

1.	5 February	14.	18 March
2.	18 March	15.	9 June
3.	19 May	16.	19 May
4.	*Ibid.*	17.	*Ibid.*
5.	5 February	18.	*Ibid.*
6.	19 May	19.	5 February
7.	18 March	20.	19 May
8.	9 June	21.	9 June
9.	5 February	22.	*Ibid.*
10.	19 May	23.	*Ibid.*
11.	5 February	24.	19 May
12.	18 March	25.	9 June
13.	19 May		

13

State Occasions: East

Today, many provincial appointments are made in the name of the lieutenant-governor, although in fact they are the result of action by the executive council or cabinet, and are done only nominally by the sovereign's representative. In parallel cases, however, Laird could act on his own initiative. The Territorial council's function was purely advisory, and the lieutenant-governor did not need to act on its advice. Indeed, except for a few days each year, when the council was in session, seeking such advice was usually impractical, as the majority of members dwelt far from the capital. Thus during 1879 Laird appointed eleven justices of the peace, five issuers of marriage licences, three notaries public, and Printer to the Government of the North-West Territories. Inevitably this last was P. G. Laurie, editor and publisher of the *Saskatchewan Herald,* Battleford's best and only newspaper.

Laurie's paper had been in existence only a couple of years, but already the bracing climate, the crystal-clear atmosphere, the general next-year ambience of the Territories had transferred its owner into as committed a Nor-Wester as ever had the good fortune to come out of Upper Canada. On 23 February 1880 he devoted two and one-half columns of the *Herald* ("Progress" the watchword on its masthead) to smiting the *Toronto Mail* hip, thigh, and cranium. That eastern rag had had the termerity to suggest the dismantling of the Territorial government, or at least, on the completion of Laird's term, the abolition of the office of lieutenant-governor. A single quotation from the long editorial suggests its general tenor:

> Indeed, we believe it can be safely affirmed that the Territories have now a white and half-breed population equal to that of British Columbia. Are the rights and privileges of these people to be ignored? If each of the Provinces requires legislative machinery to enact local laws, should not the Territories, with a respectable and rapidly increasing population, be allowed at least a Lieutenant-Governor and Council?[1]

169

No doubt about it, when it came to the rhetorical question, Laurie was the fastest gun in the West. Nor was he the only resident of the Territories to be exercised by the kite which the *Mail* had flown. In March the *Herald* reported:

> Public meetings have been held at Prince Albert, St. Laurent, and other places, to give expression to the feelings of the people on the subject of the suggested abolition of the Territorial Government. The feeling is all but universal in condemnation of any change, and petitions against such a retrograde step have been almost unanimously signed.[2]

Laird himself, it seems, maintained a discreet silence on the subject.

One of the lieutenant-governor's early official enactments in 1880, as reported in the 9 February issue of the *Herald,* was to make a number of governmental appointments (or re-appointments), as issuers of marriage licences and notaries public. Among those named was Charles Mair, of Prince Albert, and Dr. George Verey, who had taught school at Fort Edmonton, then moved on to McDougall's Morleyville mission in the same role. Apparently, even qualified physicians in those distant days occasionally turned their hands to pedagogy.

All was grist that came to Laurie's word mill. By 1880, the Dominion survey of the Fertile Belt — that vast stretch between the North Saskatchewan and the American Border — was proceeding apace. Thus newcomers and others at last were able to secure title to their homesteads and town lots, or at least a beginning was being made in that direction. However, there still remained problems, as the *Herald* noted in commenting on the 1880 session of the Canadian Parliament:

> The land regulations are to be again brought up. If further changes are to be made we should like to see them take the shape of making the reserves in alternate townships or even large blocks, instead of alternate sections as at present.[3]

Laurie did not give the reasons for his suggestion, probably because they were so obvious to his readers. A century later and to a largely urban population, they may be somewhat obscure. His reference to reserves was not to Indian 'reservations' (United States terminology) but to land set aside or reserved for other purposes.

For the North-West Territories and Manitoba, the federal government had adopted as the basic unit of land measurement a block six miles square. This was and is designated a township. All townships in an east-west strip are given the same number. Township 1 comprises all those immediately north of the Forty-Ninth Parallel; Township 2, those in the next strip north, and so on. The rows of townships running north and south are designated as ranges and, with one exception to be noted shortly, are counted west of designated meridians. Thus all townships immediately west of such a Principal Meridian are denominated as being in Range 1 West of that meridian. The next row is Range 2 West, and so on.

The Prime, or First Principal, or Winnipeg Meridian is located at 97° 27′ 28.41″ west of Greenwich. Why at such an awkward location? Why not at 98° 0′ 0″ West Longitude, especially as the subsequent Principal Meridians, beginning with the Second at 102° West, are at regular four-degree intervals? The reason is that apparently the federal government had directed the Prime Meridian to be surveyed beginning at the International Boundary ten miles west of the intersection of that boundary and the Red River. "It is possible that. . . it was considered that the 10-mile margin would allow ample clearance of settled river properties as well as the wooded area."[4]

In all, there are six Principal Meridians, the fourth, at 100° West, forming the boundary between present-day Saskatchewan and Alberta.

Townships were further divided into thirty-six units, each one mile square, called sections. In each township the sections were numbered according to the indicated scheme.

In turn, sections were divided into quarters designated N.E. (northeast), S.E., S.W., and N.W. A quarter-section, one hundred sixty acres, was the standard size of a territorial homestead, of which more anon.

Legal descriptions under this system were extremely simple, unlike those based on metes and bounds, e.g., "Beginning at a white rock on the bank of the Styx river, thence proceeding in a north-easterly direction. . . and so back to the starting point." A few cryptic symbols could give a complete legal description of a man's farm, e.g., NW 1/4 16-12-4 W 2, which, being translated, means: The North-West quarter of Section 16, Township 12, Range 4 west of the Second Principal Meridian.

31	32	33	34	35	36
30	29	28	27	26	25
19	20	21	22	23	24
18	17	16	15	14	13
7	8	9	10	11	12
6	5	4	3	2	1

The exception mentioned above refers to land in Manitoba described as *east* of the First Principal Meridian, since there is none designated for it to be west of.

Thus this land tenure system, characteristic of the Canadian North-West and a large part of the United States, which established the pattern, differed significantly from that of other countries. Description and title of a holding depending not on terrestial landmarks but on astronomical observations. Rivers might change their courses; floods, forest fires, earthquakes, volcanoes might destroy references on the ground, or bury them, but the sun and the stars were eternal verities by which all surveys could be re-established.

The term 'homestead,' the 'free land' which was ultimately to attract some two million newcomers to the prairies, had a very explicit meaning in the North-West. A homestead has been described as a wager in which a man (rarely a woman) bet ten dollars and three years of his/her life against a farm. For the $10 registration fee the homesteader was assigned, or chose a quarter-section. To obtain title thereto, he was required to live on it for at least six months of the first three years, place a very limited number of acres under cultivation, and erect certain 'improvements,' i.e., buildings, especially a residence. These requirements met, the homesteader was then given a title or patent to the land, and was free to sell it if he wished. It is estimated that not more than half of the homesteaders ever 'proved up' on their land and obtained title to it.

In each township, certain land was reserved (Laurie's reserves) and not available for homesteading. By its Deed of Surrender, in addition to certain areas around its posts, the Hudson's Bay Company retained title to one-twentieth of the land in the Fertile Belt. Thus in one-fifth of the townships the Honorable Company was granted ownership of Sections 8 and 26, in the other four-fifths, to Sections 8 and three quarters of Section 26. Sections 11 and 29 were also reserved, to provide through their future sale funds for the establishment and operation of educational facilities. Commonly they were called 'school sections.'

Nor were these the only reserves. There were also those granted to the Canadian Pacific Railway to make financially possible the construction of its main line. These reserves were made pursuant to an agreement between the government and the company concluded on 21 October 1880 and ratified by Parliament the following February.

> This land grant was to consist of alternate sections carrying uneven numbers and consisting of 640 acres each, these grants extending to a width of 24 miles on each side of the main line from Winnipeg to the Rockies. By far the largest proportion of these reserves came from the territory now contained within the boundaries of Alberta and Saskatchewan.[5]

But the CPR reserves had an even great impact on the availability of land for homesteads. In the East, since most of the land within twenty-four miles of the railroad's main line was already privately owned, the company was granted additional sections in the West. Further, if any of the designated sections were unsuitable for agriculture, the CPR could choose other sections in lieu thereof, more than twenty-four miles from its main line.

Since each township consists of 144 quarter-sections, theoretically it could contain the same number of 160-acre farms, support one hundred sixty families. But some 'land' consisted of lakes and rivers, sloughs, semi-desert, other agriculturally unsuitable terrain. Subtract these areas, subtract school, CPR and HBC reserves (usually the last pieces to be transferred to private ownership), subtract Indian reserves and land held by the government for its own uses. Subtract also pre-emptions, i.e., those quarters next to homesteads which a settler could reserve for purchase when he had 'proved up' his homestead. Thus it can be seen that only a fraction of the townships would have as many as half of its quarter-sections available for homesteaders. Thus the rural population would be sparse indeed, and the per-family cost of local amenities and services — roads, bridges, schools, health and recreation services, etc. — would be very high, thus discouraging settlement.

However, if the various reserves were to concentrated in whole townships or even larger areas, although settlement therein might be delayed, in the remaining areas it could be more concentrated, and local services thus more readily available and affordable. This, to have made a long story still longer, is the reason Editor Laurie advocated the concentration rather than dispersal of the reserves.

Despite the simplicity and elegance of this survey and land tenure system, it did present some problems, some anomalies. These arose because before 1870 the Hudson's Bay Company and Lord Selkirk had granted title to properties which in no way fitted into the later Dominion Lands system, as it was known. Further, many newcomers and native-born had established themselves on little farms without the formality of acquiring land titles. Thus in fact they established *a priori* claims, squatters' rights, to the land, possession being nine points of the law according to popular wisdom. Neither these unpatented pieces of real estate nor the land to which title had been granted were nice square units of one hundred sixty acres or neat fractions thereof, e.g., forty acres, called Legal Sub-Divisions — LSD's for short. Instead, they were narrow strips, two or four miles in length, fronting on rivers or occasionally lakes. Thus it devolved on the transit, rod, and chain men to reconcile the French-Canadian river-lot and the Dominion Lands systems. Ultimately the territory around many of the older settlements, e.g., Edmonton, St. Albert, Prince Albert, Fort Chipewyan, Fort Vermilion was originally surveyed according to the older Canadian tradition.

As is well known, the dilatoriness of the federal government in granting title of their little farms to the Métis squatters was one important cause of the North-West Rebellion in 1885. Of course, by then David Laird was long gone from the Territories. Some of his admirers have suggested that had he remained as lieutenant-governor, the Rebellion might never have occurred.

> Laird constantly communicated with the government in Ottawa, urging the authorities to recognize and alleviate the grievances of the Métis who were becoming more and more restive under the blunt directives from far-away Ottawa. Laird recognized the dangers and exhorted the Government to redress the injustices.
>
> Unfortunately, he was unheeded and in 1885 rebellion and slaughter resulted. Many responsible people regretted that Laird, whom the Indians trusted, was not in Battleford at the time to prevent the outbreak.[6]

It is not surprising that Laird's daughter Mary Alice should hold such an opinion. Her son, David Laird Mathieson, has stated, "She was firmly of the opinion that the North-West Rebellion would not have occurred if her father's advice to Government officers in Ottawa had been followed and his methods carried on."[7] More objective historians, however, would probably agree that if any one man could have prevented the rebellion, that man was not Lieutenant-Governor David Laird but Prime Minister John A. Macdonald.

But in 1880 now "old, unhappy far-off things" were still in the undiscerned future. Laird's daily concerns were more prosaic. As mentioned in a letter to Rennie, he had refused the use of the council chamber for a pre-Lenten ball. This action was not the result of personal antipathy towards the would-be revellers, collectively or severally, but was a matter of principle. For affairs not under control of the governor he thought a town hall more appropriate, as for public meetings, school classes, religious services, or any business of the village.

The *Herald* was surely keeping its eyes on both the public and the private lives of Battleford's residents, including that of the governor. In so doing, Laurie was simply following the tradition that has governed the careers of small-town editors since time immemorial. Of course, wise editors of such organs don't publish everything they know. But the *Herald* issue of 15 March 1880 did include the pleasant intelligence that His Honor had received from William McKay, of Fort Pitt, a Cold Lake trout weighing twenty-two and one-half pounds when cleaned. Incredible though such a fish might seem to twentieth-century Izaac Waltons, this finned denizen of the deep (more or less) by no means constituted a record. That was reputedly held by a trout topping seventy-two pounds.

Not until 29 June, apparently, did Laird make a formal request for leave, when he wrote to the Deputy-Minister of the Interior: "Desire leave-of-absence from the Territories for six weeks from middle of July to visit Ottawa and my family at Charlottetown. Will arrange that little inconvenience as possible will result from absence. Answer by telegraph."[8] Since Laird left Battleford less than a week later, it is hard to understand the delay in submitting the request. Possibly there had been no east-bound mail for some time; certainly the service was irregular. In March the *Herald* had fulminated about it for a good half-column, beginning:

> We are supposed to have a mail once in three weeks. For a long time it has been irregular, and has at last failed us altogether. It has been proved that the mail will not run itself but that proper oversight and proper stock are essential elements to success. Little by little irregularities grew up, but it was always hoped that by "next trip" things would right themselves. Now, however, things have gone so far wrong that nothing short of a reorganization of the line and making a fresh start will extricate it from its present entanglement.[9]

Plus ça change, plus c'est la même chose!

Evidently His Honor received no acknowledgement to his communication, but in any event he left Battleford on 5 July, planning official visits at points down the Saskatchewan, and thence to the Manitoba capital.

He arrived at Carlton aboard the *Lily* the same evening he left Battleford. There he expected to find the deeper draught *Northcote*, but that queen of the inland waters had not yet arrived. However, the delay was not unwelcome, as it gave Laird a chance to meet and confer with Chief Commissioner Grahame and other Hudson's Bay officers, who were holding an annual session of their Company's Canadian council at the fort. "His Honor also visited some of the adjoining settlements and made enquiries respecting roads and other matters of public interest."[10]

"The '*Northcote*' having arrived at Prince Albert on the 20th of July, the Lieutenant-Governor left in her early in the following morning on his downward journey."[11] Whether that stern-wheeler was prevented from proceeding farther up-stream by low water or whether Laird, having travelled overland to join the *Northcote* at Prince Albert as she began her return trip the *Herald* does not indicate. In any event, on 1 August Laird reached Cumberland House, then and now the oldest continuing white settlement in present-day Saskatchewan. It is located on Pine Island in Cumberland Lake, through which the Saskatchewan River flows, not far above The Pas. The original site was about a mile east of the present location which, however, has remained fixed since Laird's visit.

To compete with the aggressive Nor'Westers, Samuel Hearne had established this, the Hudson's Bay Company's first inland post, in 1774. For a hundred years the Honorable Company had been content for the Indians to come to the Bay to trade their furs for the sometimes-dubious blessings of European technology, but competition by the Quebec-based opposition had finally forced the Honorable Company to go to the Indians rather than the reverse. The North West Company soon established its own fort in close proximity to that of the HBC. Captain John Franklin, R. N., on his first expedition to the Arctic, described Cumberland House in 1820:

> The houses of the two Companies, at this post, are situated close to each other, at the upper extremity of a narrow island, which separates Pine Island Lake from the Saskatchewan River . . . They are log-houses, built without much regard to comfort, surrounded by lofty stockades, and flanked with wooden bastions.[12]

Incidentally, the Franklin party determined the latitude and longitude of Cumberland House to be 53° 56' 40" N., 102° 16' 41" w.

In 1821 the two fur companies united under the name of the older one. The post remained active until after 1830, when it declined in importance as Norway House over-shadowed it as a distribution centre. However, the coming of the steam-boats from 1875 revived it somewhat in importance. Pictures of Cumberland House dating from 1875 and 1884 show some six or eight buildings, some of two storeys, set back from the water's edge, but at no great elevation, and back-dropped by spruce trees of the boreal forest. A low palisade of sorts still surrounded at least some of the buildings, but seemed to have more symbolic than defensive significance. Certainly the bastions which Franklin noted in 1820 had disappeared.

On 1 August, the *Northcote* reached Cumberland, where a welcoming arch bearing appropriate sentiments had been erected over the gateway to the Company's post, and another near the Roman Catholic church. Upon landing, the lieutenant-governor received a warm welcome from His Excellency J. Vital, O.M.I., Bishop of St. Albert. In it he alluded to Laird's earlier visit to St. Albert and expressed his thankfulness for good government: ". . . the good words which you have caused to be written to me in different circumstances, lead me to believe that your government, far from placing itself in opposition to the sacred laws which we venerate, will help their accomplishment, as also the work to which we have devoted our lives — the evangelization of the Indians by means of religion and labor."[13]

The address was delivered in French, but it is not clear if the English translation which appeared in the *Herald* and from which the above is quoted was also delivered verbally at that time.

The day being Sunday, no reply from the governor was expected — Bishop Vital was perhaps aware of the Presbyterian aversion to toil on the Sabbath day. Instead, the *Northcote* began the final leg of her voyage, reaching Grand Rapids the next morning. There His Honor had to wait a few days for the arrival of the *Colville,* but he eventually reached Selkirk at the mouth of the Red River on 8 August and from there drove to Winnipeg.

The following day he wired Deputy-Minister Dennis in Ottawa: "Desire leave absence for three or four weeks from territory to visit Ottawa and family at Charlottetown answer."[14] To this telegram Acting Deputy-Minister Russell replied the same day: "Referred your message to Sir Leonard Acting Minister. His view is that formal leave necessitates appointment administrator. He says other Governors absent themselves."[15]

This almost suggests that Tilley, the Acting Minister, is saying: 'Take your leave, but officially I don't want to know anything about it.' Such a gambit is one that every experienced bureaucrat practises occasionally, but in this era of long-distance telephones it is usually done verbally and not in writing.

Departing from the Gateway to the West on 11 August, Laird spent three days in rail travel to Ottawa. As both his Minister and his Deputy were off to England, he conferred with the Acting Deputy, Surveyor-General Lindsay Russell, then pressed on to Prince Edward Island. The *Herald* does not give us the date when he was at last able to rejoin his family. While en route by rail from Summerside to Charlottetown, when he reached his former constituency of Queen's County, he found his old supporters had not forgotten him, as "... he was presented with an Address of welcome from a number of his former constituents, to which he made a suitable reply."[16] He was to make a number of such suitable replies before he reached Battleford again.

Since Laird was in Ottawa on the evening of 14 August, presumably stayed there very briefly, and left the Island on 15 September, his stay there would have been about four weeks. During this time he met the Governor-General, whom he was to entertain the following year at Battleford, but Editor Laurie has given us no further hard information about his activities during his leave. However, knowing something about the kind of man he was, the nature and size of the extended family of which he was a member, the culture and customs of such people in that era, it is not hard to imagine some of the activities of this repatriated Islander.

First, of course, he would be concerned about the health and educational progress of his immediate family. He would question Rennie and Gordon on their school achievement and with great care examine their exercise books. Perhaps he might go so far as to conduct a *viva voce* test of their French, which probably the children spoke better than their dear papa. Likely they had begun their study of that language under the For-gets, back in Battleford. Then the *paterfamilias* would dispense commend-ation and censure with carefully moderated enthusiasm.

On Sunday, inevitably he would herd the whole family to Zion Pres-byterian Church, of which he had been a member and an elder. Probably he retained his membership therein, since his governorship was a limited-term appointment. Possibly, as a mark of esteem to this distinguished Zi-onist, he was asked to read the lesson on at least one Sunday, and on an-other to address the congregation on the great need for missionaries and pastors in the North-West — certainly the Presbyterians were lagging be-hind the Roman Catholics, Anglicans, and Methodists in supplying such personnel to the Territories.

Since David Laird was fast approaching the end of his term as lieu-tenant-governor, and had no prospect of further political preferment under the Conservative government, undoubtedly he was giving thought to his future employment. It is not unreasonable to believe that he would visit the office of the *Patriot,* confer with the editor, Henry Lawson, and perhaps make tentative arrangements for his return to the paper.

But a very large part of his sojourn would be spent visiting his own and his wife's relatives — brothers and sisters, uncles, aunts, cousins, in-laws, Lairds and Owens and many, many others. Each would expect to entertain him and Louisa and their progeny at an enormous meal — a sumptuous repast, to employ the then-current cliché — and to hear from the lips of their distinguished kinsman first-hand tales of the Wild West, of painted and feathered Indians, of the now-vanished buffalo, of the wolves and grizzlies that had roamed the plains, of prairie fires and thunderstorms such as had never been seen (or heard) within the narrow confines of the Island.

Bearded, towering well over six feet in height, gravely carrying the weight of his responsibilities, David Laird was no doubt a formidable figure to those who knew him little or not at all. But to children he could be a charming story-teller. As a young boy, his grandson David Laird Mathie-son remembers him as ". . . one of those who made it appear that he considered a small boy a person of some intelligence, and worth talking to."[17]

Island-bound adults and young people alike must have listened with fascination as the Laird parents and children recounted their adventures in that thrilling, fabulous North-West. How they must have been excited by Uncle David's account of the mock battle at the signing of Treaty No. 7! How interested they would have been as he told them of the calumet used on that occasion! Years later he described it in another context:

The peace pipe, though not always used, was smoked at this treaty with great ceremony. The pipe is made of soft, red American stone which hardens when exposed to the atmosphere. The tobacco is mixed with kinikinik, the inner bark of the wild cornel, which is very abundant in the valley of all streams. 'Haronge' is the name given by the half-breeds to this mixture.[18]

David Laird would also tell his audiences about, perhaps even show them the bow, arrows, and quiver that the Indians had presented to him on that memorable occasion.

And how those numerous relatives would be both shocked and se-cretly delighted with one of Mary's escapades on an occasion when the Indians, hungry and decidedly truculent, were demonstrating at Battleford! As she later wrote:

> At that time I was a young girl and never dreamed of fear. I went in and out among them that day as if it were all a huge joke — even took in an indian fan to show my mother. She was horrified, for it was a human scalp stretched on a stick. It was hastily returned and I was made to stay in the house and watch from the window.[19]

Eventually, however, the Lieutenant-Governor of the North-West Territories had to return to his gubernatorial duties. Stopping at Ottawa, he was still unable to meet with Sir John A., not yet returned from Eng-land. However, he did have an opportunity to discuss various territorial matters with the Deputy-Minister, Col. Dennis, who had got back from overseas only the previous evening. Laird also met the Postmaster-General — one may easily guess the nature of their conversation.

Next stop was Winnipeg, where Laird arrived on 25 September; here he met his secretary, Amédée Forget. Forget and his wife had left Battle-ford on 10 August, he to meet the governor and with him make arrange-ments for the election of members to the Territorial council for the eastern area. Mme. Forget, however, continued on to Montreal, presumably to visit family and friends whom she had not seen since coming to Battleford three years previously.

For Laird and Forget, the territory under consideration was then known as the Little Saskatchewan, after a river of the same name, a minor stream now known as the Dauphin. The region for which the election of either one of two councillors was being planned is now in Western Mani-toba, for in 1880 the "postage stamp province" was indeed that, figuratively at least. Its south and north boundaries were Latitudes 49° and 50° 30′ North respectively; its eastern and western limits Longitudes 96° and 98° 15′ West. The western and northern frontiers, those adjacent to the North-West Territories, in terms of present-day landmarks, were about half-way between Portage La Prairie and Brandon, and cutting the southern tips of Lakes Manitoba and Winnipeg respectively. The province's area of thirteen thousand square miles (some under water), therefore comprised the equivalent of about three hundred sixty townships.

Incidentally, in 1881, Manitoba was to expand to its present western and eastern boundaries — the latter, at least the southern stretch — and to comprise an area of over seventy thousand square miles. In 1912, the boundary was moved to Parallel Sixty, and the province's area reached almost two hundred fifty thousand square miles.

On 1 October, Laird and Forget left for the Territories. On the seventh of the month the governor attended an agricultural show at Rapid City, an event which included the usual public dinner and formal address of welcome. Such literary masterpieces seem to have been produced according to a well-used formula. This formula called for flattering references to His Honor, expressions of continuing loyalty to the Queen and all things British (and even Canadian), and smug and self-satisfied statements about the peace, prosperity, happiness, present well-being, and golden prospects of the local community. The Rapid City oratory was standard, typical of a number of addresses which His Honor would have to endure before again seeing his Battleford domicile.

The gubernatorial reply was equally ritualistic: thanks for the complimentary personal remarks, appreciation for the expressions of loyalty, compliments on the progressive appearance of the whole community, forecasts of a dazzling future for it. Post-prandial addresses, of course, should include commendation for the perfectly splendid meal which had been served, a repast fit for a king, etc. Under no circumstances should the governor say anything which might in any way embarrass the government, i.e., the political party in power at the moment. Nor on any account should the government be committed to any action other than that of giving careful consideration of any representations that good and loyal citizens might care to make. Equally, no public official should make any pronouncement which an elected official might and which would reflect credit on the wisdom, integrity, perspicuity, etc. of said elected official and his party. Only government supporters, not members of the opposition party, had the privilege of making such potentially advantageous pronouncements.

It is thus not surprising that in the 1880's, as a century later, that official speeches tended towards blandness. The only permitted deviation from the whole protocol would be a statement from the local Establishement in their address of welcome when they mentioned, not complaints, but rather prayers of the local populace that their legitimate claims be considered in future government largess.

Indians, however, have commonly and increasingly refused to play this game by the white man's rules. They tend not to request but to demand, and for redress of grievances have the bad taste to appeal to the foot of the Throne itself, or even to United Nations organizations.

On 12 October, Laird proceeded to Minnedosa to grace with his presence the community's second annual Harvest Home. The obligatory addresses, one by Mr. Justice Ryan, high-calorie luncheons, and presentations of local gentry to His Honor were parts of the proceedings.

According to the *Herald,* all was sweetness and light. After leaving Minnedosa,

> . . . The Lieutenant-Governor resumed his journey westward. He was delighted to see the improvements all along the road, especially at Shoal Lake, Birtle, and Fort Ellice. Birtle is quite a rising village and only want of time prevented him from remaining over there a day to inspect the mills and other signs of progress.[20]

Yet for the lieutenant-governor, all was not fun and games. Some of it was work. The Governor-General-in-Council, i.e., the federal cabinet, had authorized the establishment of two electoral districts (for the NWT council) in the Little Saskatchewan area, as already mentioned. Laird was busy, with Forget, in making preliminary arrangements for elections. He was also occupied in learning about the roads in those areas and the need for ferries on the Assiniboine between the Souris and Little Saskatchewan tributaries of that serpentining river.

One significant encounter which Editor Laurie did not report, nor would the Local Board of Trade, if any had existed, occurred at Fort Ellice. There, on 18 October, Laird had an interview with a Stoney (Assiniboine) chief called Ocean Man, who complained that some of his people had been massacred by Gros Ventre and Mandall (Mandan?) Indians while in the United States. This outrage had occurred about the middle of September. Following the interview, Laird immediately sent a report to the Minister of the Interior, along with a covering letter, urging that appropriate action be taken. The text of the report follows. In beautiful penmanship, far different from the governor's crabbed hand-writing, it was perhaps inscribed by Secretary Forget.

> *Ocean Man* — When I see you, Father, I would like to tell you the news. At the time I took Treaty payments this Summer, the Government Agents told me to cut hay, and I did it. The Agent did not give my people food to support them while they were doing this work. Father, listen to me. When my young men were working, I went out to the plains to try & get some food. We went out, but we had not much powder. And two parties of Indians came upon our camp. They killed my first soldier, who was my brother, and altogether eight of our party. I did what you told me when the Treaty was made — I kept my gun in my arm. They

killed two of our horses, and they took away ten others. We had to leave all our carts and tents and come off almost naked. Twelve of our party were wounded, and we had to carry them on our backs. We had to leave everything, even some of our guns. I do not throw away my Reserve; but I do not wish to go on it until the Spring. The place of attack was at the ridge, or Coteau de Missouri, about forty miles South-West of Moose Mountain, and about twelve miles from the United States Boundary. The Indians who made the attack were Gros Ventres and Mandalls. I cannot do anything for myself now, and want some help from the Government. I wish I could only get through the Winter. I desire you to write a letter to the Indian Commission at Shoal Lake to give some assistance this winter, as I have lost everything. I also need a Farm Instructor in the Spring like the other Chiefs. Father, I put all bad things behind my back when the Treaty was made, and I wish you to look after this affair. I will think over it until Spring. I will not go that way until Spring, but if I hear that the Government has done nothing in the case, I may then take a few steps across the Line.

Lieut. Governor Laird — Do you know the names, or could you point out any of the attacking party, if you saw them?

Ocean Man — I do not know the men — I only know the tribe. I could not point out any of the men. My brother went out towards them, and when they asked who we were, we said the Paddling Stony Indians, and they then began to thresh at us with willows, and when my brother went further they shot him down. I think there were about sixty men in their party.

Lieut. Governor Laird — Had any of your people a quarrel with any of those Indians about anything last winter or spring?

Ocean Man — We are aware of nothing. We have been at peace for a long time with those Indians. During the previous Summer we gave a horse as a present to their Chief. I cannot think what caused the attack. We have for a long time been eating and drinking as one nation. I will try and find out the reason that my friends did this to me.

Lieut. Governor Laird — I am glad to hear you say that you are going to try and find out the reason of the attack. I also hope you will endeavour to find out who the leader and chief men of the attacking party were, and if you succeed, report it to me or some other Officer of the Government. If our Government only knew who the men were, they might report it to the United States government and get them punished. But the Government would not wish to harm innocent Indians and can scarcely do anything unless they know the guilty parties. These Indians have committed two great offences — they have killed Indians of a neighboring tribe and have involved the Territory of another country from that under which they live to do their deed of blood. I would advise you not to pursue them across the boundary Line. They are strong, and you might get your people and the Government of this Country into trouble. It is most painful to the Queen to hear of her people — whether her red children or her white children — being killed without provocation and she will see to protect them. I will report what you have stated to the Queen's Councillors at Ottawa. I will also write to Mr. Dewdney, the Indian Commissioner, and say that I consider you people who have lost their ponies, carts and clothing deserve special assistance this Winter. My heart is sore for you. I feel for you, in hearing of your brother and people being shot down, as if they were my own children, and I will at once report the case to the Queen's Government.[21]

Laird's report, with a covering letter, were despatched to the Minister of the Interior on the same day that the interview occurred.

His 1880 visit to Fort Ellice, of course, was not Laird's first; this was one of the points where he had signed Treaty No. 4 with the Indians six years previously. Since then, some changes had occurred in this 1831 fur post located high on the west (right) bank of the Assiniboine, some two hundred road miles west of Fort Garry. In 1874, Fort Ellice seemed to be slipping into a state of desuetude as the buffalo were found farther and farther away on the plains and as a result the post was declining as a centre for the pemmican trade. However, just as the 'fire canoe' had done for Cumberland House farther north, the advent of the stern-wheeler steamer had given Ellice a new lease on life, albeit one destined to be short. "In the early eighties it was the terminus of steamboat navigation on the Assiniboine. . . All imports for a large section of the western country were gathered into its warehouses for reshipment by carts."[22] Thus in 1880, when Laird and Forget visited Fort Ellice, enclosed in a stockade of fifteen-foot pointed spruce pickets, it was again a busy place.

Especially impressive was the Big House, dating from 1863 and providing quarters for the officers and clerks.

It was located at the back of a square opposite the front gates, and was 2 1/2 storeys high, 40 feet by 60 with a large kitchen on the back and a balcony and verandah in front. It was built of eight-inch logs 10 feet long and the entrance opened into a large recreation and council hall. There were five fireplaces and a Carron stove on the ground floor and visitors long remembered the comfort they enjoyed there on cold days and evenings.[23]

However, the death knell of the Fort was already being sounded by the engine-bells of the Canadian Pacific's locomotives. Within five years, that railway would span the continent, rendering the Assiniboine's steamers obsolete and consigning Fort Ellice to the dust-bin of history. by 1901 the Big House, last remaining structure in the post, would be pulled down. Today, of that once-proud fur fort, nothing remains but a memory, that and a cairn to mark where once it stood.

Leaving Fort Ellice, Laird by-passed Qu'Appelle and Riding Mountain because of the lateness of the season. On 29 October be reached St.
Laurent; the following day he arrived at Duck Lake and Carlton. There, as
in the Little Saskatchewan district, he made enquiries and arrangements
for an election of a member of the Territorial council. Then, having rested
over Sunday at Carlton, he continued his safari to Prince Albert. Since his
stop there on the way east was not a State Occasion, this visit was marked
by considerable ceremony.

His host was the Rt. Rev. John McLean, first Anglican Bishop of
Saskatchewan. His Grace was fairly bursting with pride over his mint-new
Emmanuel College, probably the first post-secondary institution of learning in the Territories, and certainly the first Protestant one. Designed for
the preparation of interpreters, teachers, catechists, and clergymen, particularly those of native descent, the college had actually opened its doors in
the fall of 1879. It was first and temporarily quartered in a classroom in St.
Mary's parochial school, about three miles west of Prince Albert. By January, 1880, there were eleven students, all male of course, in residence, only
four wholly of European descent.

McLean decided to erect the college structures in immediate prom-
imity to St. Mary's school, i.e., west of Prince Albert. "The main College
building, a frame structure which the Bishop himself described as the finest
and largest building in the North-West, was ready for use by the summer
of 1880."[24] Largest it may have been, and perhaps finest, depending on the
connotation one places on the word. A plain, rectangular frame structure
of two plus storeys, its one claim to architectural distinction was a pair of
third-level windowed gables. The symmetry of the front facade was destroyed by the off-centre front door and especially by a bay window at one
end, in contrast to a quite ordinary one at the other extremity. Nevertheless,
a building does not constitute an educational institution, and by the time of
the lieutenant-governor's visit, academically Emmanuel was flourishing.

Laird was particularly interested in the college because at that time
he was engaged in correspondence with Ottawa respecting grants for
schools. On 2 November it was the scene of a public meeting, at which the
usual address of welcome was presented to the distinguished visitor. It was
signed by a number of prominent citizens including, inevitably, Charles
Mair. Intriguingly, the second signature is that of one J. Saskatchewan. It
could have been that of a local Cree but was perphaps that of Bishop
McLean himself. In accordance with a quaint ecclesiastical custom, he was
using the name of his diocese instead of his surname.

In one respect, the oratory differed from that of the Standard Address
of Welcome, in that it hinted that support of the lieutenant-governor's policies was not universal. Thus the pertinent paragraph:

That you have been accused by outside critics of partizanship in your conduct of affairs we are aware; and many of us have read with pain and disapproval articles in the eastern press which severely assailed your administration. Yet we who have been close observers of your acts and who know how limited have been the means and patronage at your disposal must readily admit that you have religiously abstained from importing the fiery animus of petty hostility into your proceedings and the spirit which has animated you has been that of a just and impartial administrator.[25]

The *eastern* press? Apparently, western alienation was alive and well in Prince Albert as in Battleford.

Certainly in the field of religion Laird showed himself not only impartial but open and receptive to adherents of all religious faiths and to their beliefs. Here he was receiving more than a formal welcome from the Anglicans, who were expressing almost the same sentiments which he had heard earlier from the Roman Catholics at Cumberland. Rev. John McDougall had visited Laird's family in Charlottetown,[26] and Laird had written to McDougall at Morleyville, closing with kindly enquiries about the Methodist missionary's family and remitting a $25 contribution for his church.[27]

The day following the Prince Albert meeting, the governor left for Battleford, where he arrived to a warm welcome from his fellow-Battlefordians. He had been away from the Territorial capital for exactly four months.

References

1. *Saskatchewan Herald,* 23 February 1880.

2. *Ibid.,* 15 March 1880.

3. *Ibid.*

4. Don W. Thomson, *Men and Meridians,* v. 2, p. 35.

5. *Ibid.,* p. 84.

6. Jack Powell, "David Laird," *The Piper,* 1963, p. 24.

7. D. L. Mathieson to J. W. Chalmers, 3 March 1979.

8. David Laird to Minister of the Interior, 29 June 1880 (Saskatchewan Archives Board).

9. *Saskatchewan Herald,* 15 March 1880.

10. *Ibid.,* "The Lieutenant-Governor's Eastern Tour," 29 November 1880.

11. *Ibid.*

12. John Franklin, *Narrative of a Journey to the Shores of the Polar Sea in the Years 1819, 20, 21, and 22,* p. 55.

13. *Saskatchewan Herald,* "The Lieutenant-Governor's Eastern Tour," 29 November 1880.

14. David Laird to J. S. Dennis, 9 August 1880 (Public Archives of Canada).

15. Lindsay Russell to David Laird, 9 August 1880 (Public Archives of Canada).

16. *Saskatchewan Herald,* "The Lieutenant-Governor's Eastern Tour," 29 November 1880.

17. Mathieson, *op. cit.*

18. R. J. Macpherson, "The Hon. David Laird, Commissioner of Indian Affairs for Manitoba and the Northwest," *The Westminster,* New Series, v. 2, no. 4, p. 188.

19. Mary Alice Mathieson, nee Laird, "Early Days in the North West Territories," unpublished typescript, (Saskatchewan Archives Board SHS 32).

20. *Saskatchewan Herald,* "The Lieutenant-Governor's Eastern Tour," 29 November 1880.

21. David Laird, "Statement of an Interview between Lieutenant-Governor Laird and 'Ocean Man,' a Stony Chief (whose reserve is at Moose Mountain N.W.T.) held at Fort Ellice October 18, 1880 respecting massacre of part of said Chief's Band at the Coteau de Missouri, by Gros Ventres and Mandalls, United States Indian about the middle of September 1880," unpublished manuscript (Public Archives of Canada).

22. G. K. Kinnaird, "An Episode of the North-West Rebellion," *Saskatchewan History,* v. 20, no. 2, p. 71.

23. James McCook, "Frontiersmen at Fort Ellice," *The Beaver,* Autumn 1968, p. 36.

24. Jean E. Murray, "The Early History of Emmanuel College," *Saskatchewan History,* v. 9, no. 3, p. 86.

25. *Saskatchewan Herald,* "The Lieutenant-Governor's Eastern Tour," 29 November 1880.

26. David Laird to David Rennie Laird, 5 February 1880 (Public Archives of Prince Edward Island 2979).

27. David Laird to John McDougall, date illegible (Saskatchewan Archives Board).

14

Farewell to Battleford

Laird's discussions in Ottawa with the Postmaster-General apparently had little effect on the speed of the mail service to the Territories, as it still seems to have taken about two months for a letter to travel from Charlottetown to Battleford. Such at least is the inference that one must draw from the following epistle:

Battleford, N.W. Territories

Dec 9, 1880

My Dear Son

Yours of 30th Sept only came to hand by the last mail. It was old, but I was very glad to hear from you. I am pleased also to see that your writing is improving.

There is very little snow here yet, and we had fine ice for skating for a long time. No one, however, since you left Battleford appear to have skates; or if they have, I never see them skating.

Nellie has not come home yet and I do not expect her up from Ellice this winter. I have four males here, two large and two small ones — the latter about Nellie's size. Sam is around yet; he is a fine big animal now. Strawberry and Rose are around yet also. One of their calves — I forget which — this year, we killed the other day, and it weighed 185 lbs. Beef is very high this winter, as no cattle came in from the United States this year. It is 12 1/2¢ per lb, and you can make up the value of a spring calf at that rate.

Rev Mr Clarke is keeping house in the mission house where Rev Mr McKay used to live. He has got a big bell for the church, hung up on a frame outside. So we can say no longer —

"The sound of the church-going bell
These rocks and valleys never hear."

Barbara Tynan, or Mrs Peonquas'(?) sister is teaching the school. What she *don't* know, I expect, is a good deal, but it keeps the children from going over to the leaning-to-the-river church over the way. Poor Père Hart went out hunting ducks this autumn one day, but did not return. His body was found scarcely cold but he himself had gone where ducks cease from troubling. There is another "father" or "brother" or something of the sort in his place.

A Happy Christmas to all you dear children — and a kiss besides from Papa to Weja

Your loving Papa[1]

David Laird

Evidently Laird was not too impressed with the teacher's mastery of certain aspects of English grammar.

Significantly absent from his letter is any reference to Thanksgiving Day observances in Battleford; there were none. By telegram Ottawa had set 3 November for its general observance, but on that date the lieutenant-governor still had not returned from his eastern tour. Since no one in Battleford had the authority to issue the necessary proclamation, or perhaps there was insufficient time to inform outlying communities, 1880 in the Territories was a year with no official Day of Thanksgiving.

Undoubtedly, Laird's most important official action that fall was to announce government aid for schools. Over a decade since the North-West Territories had come into being, more than five years since passage of the N.W.T. Act, at last the Territories were able to make a start on public education, timid and tentative though this first step might be. It was still not legislatively possible to establish school districts which could levy school taxes, nor was there any Territorial normal schoool for the professional preparation of teachers. For that matter, not even the Provinces of British Columbia and Manitoba had such institutions. Nor was there any leadership from the Territorial Government in the field of education, no provision for authorized courses of study or textbooks, no school inspections, external examinations, licensing of teachers, minimum schoolhouse construction standards, none of the elaborate complex of legislation, regulation, and bureaucratic control that characterizes modern public education in Canada. Not even a start in any of these directions would be made for another five years. Instead, the announcement, dated 4 December, stated that from and after 1 January 1881 His Honor would pay one-half the salary of any territorial teacher, subject to the following conditions:

1st. That a quarterly register of the school be forwarded to this office, showing the names, ages, and studies of the children taught, not being Indian whose education is otherwise aided by the Dominion Government, and that the average daily attendance is not less than fifteen pupils.

2nd. That on some part of the register there be written a certificate signed by the teacher and two of the parents whose children are attending said school, declaring that to the best of their knowledge, they believe the register to contain a true statement of the attendance at the school.

3rd. That accompanying the register there be forwarded to this office a certified copy or statement of the agreement with the teacher, showing by whom he or she was engaged, and the amount agreed to be paid as solely for services as teacher.[2]

The announcement appeared in the *Herald* in French as well as in English, an indication that the latter was not necessarily the language of instruction in the schools. In the same issue of his paper, Editor Laurie expressed his pleasure at the announcement, adding, "It will now be within the power of every settlement to establish within its borders schools for the education of its youth. . ."[3]

In the same editorial, the *Herald* mentioned that in schools on Indian reserves, the maximum salaries paid to teachers was being raised from $300 to $504 per year. Even in an era when beef was high at 12 1/2¢ per pound, such remuneration seemed, and was, meagre. However, during the Great Depression of the 1930's, salaries of some Saskatchewan public school teachers fell even lower. Until 1880, virtually all Indian schools in the Territories, and most others in Canada, were operated by religious organizations, and in some cases their salaries were supplemented by allowances from the sponsoring church bodies. Teachers may also have had other benefits, such as free accommodation and rations.

Schools were usually taught by persons with deep commitment to their churches, and therefore they were minimally interested in financial gain. In Roman Catholic institutions the males were usually priests, deacons, or lay brothers, the deacons on their way to full ordination. The brothers were frequently following the same path. For instance, Father Constantine Scollen, who had been present at the signing of Treaty No. 7, had come west and taught school in Edmonton as Brother Scollen. Only a few, indeed, were laymen. Female Roman Catholic teachers were regularly nuns, although a small number were not.

Protestant school personnel were equally closely associated with their churches. Many were clergymen like the Rev. T. A. Clarke, of Battleford, who had conducted school and taught the Laird children. However, the Praying Men, like the Blackrobes, usually shed the role of school master as fast as they could find some one else to assume it. Some Protestant male teachers, like the Roman Catholic deacons and lay brothers, were on their way to full ordination. When John McDougall first came West at the age of sixteen, he taught school at Norway House. Henry Bird Steinhauer was a teacher before he added 'Rev.' to his name. Female Protestant teachers were frequently sisters, daughters (George McDougall's, for example), wives, or fiancées of current or future preachers — at least, many married such paragons.

Conspicuously absent was any professional preparation in education. Generally, prairie pedagogues did not teach so much as they 'kept school.' Multi-grade classrooms were the rule; thus a teacher would commonly have only one or two pupils in each grade, or, using nineteenth-century terminology, each standard. Thus teaching was largely a matter of individual tutoring or coaching, that, and maintaining order and discipline. Indeed, the territorial schools of the 1880's would have differed little from the one that David Laird had attended at New Glasgow some forty years earlier, except that the Island's teachers were probably better educated.

Not professional but general education was one of the two main criteria by which an instructor was evaluated — after all, the nearest normal school was in Toronto. Not unreasonably, a teacher was expected to know more than his/her pupils. The other principal criterion was an acceptable personal reputation, usually as attested by a clergyman. As implied in Laird's letter reproduced above, the first criterion could be waived, but not usually the second.

Government aid to schools seems to have had two principal consequences. One was an increase in, really a beginning of secular as contrasted with confessional schools; the other an improvement in teachers' salaries and presumably also in their qualifications. Considerable information is available to show the impact of the new grants on education at Edmonton. In the 1840's the Wesleyan, Rev. R. T. Rundle, had operated a school in the Fort, one of his pupils being the daughter of Chief Factor J. E. Herriott, his ten-year-old Peggy. In the 1860's, Brother Scollen taught school within the Fort's palisades — his school he operated for nine years. During the following decade, Dr. George Verey was teaching there. And there were others.

Within months of the governmental aid announcement, the citizens of Edmonton had their school built and operating. They elected as trustees Matthew McCauley, William Rowland, and Malcolm Groat. The first named, a future mayor of Edmonton, was chosen as chairman. The Hudson's Bay Company donated four lots as a school site, still owned by the Edmonton Public School Board. They are located on the south-east corner of 99th (formerly McKay) Avenue and 105th (formerly 5th) Street. The money for the school building, which cost $968, was raised by private subscription. The schoolhouse was erected within one month of the trustees' decision to build.

> It was to be 24 X 30 feet, with a ten-foot ceiling. The inside and outside walls were to be dressed; the outside walls battened; and the walls were to be filled with sawdust, well rammed down. The school was to have a chimney and the doors and windows were both to have two

coats of paint. The room had to have a teacher's desk and twelve forms four feet long and desks four feet long and a blackboard. It was the first lumber building in Edmonton.[4]

It is interesting to note that in this era with its emphasis on building insulation, its importance was recognized a century ago in Edmonton. An early picture of the schoolhouse (and pupils) shows that the siding was vertical rather than horizontal, as is usual today. The battens between the boards, to keep the building watertight, are quite visible covering the cracks where the boards meet. The structure has some modest architectural pretensions, a diamond-shaped lozenge carrying the school's name over the entry porch, and half-diamond mullions over the door and windows. The stove or heater would be near the entrance with the stovepipes running the length of the room, to conserve heat, to meet the brick chimney at the opposite end of the building. As with all early schoolhouses, this one had bilateral lighting, with three windows on each side of the classroom, in addition to at least one in the entry porch. The roof was of simple gable construction, apparently shingled.

The three trustees, together with Chief Factor Richard Hardisty and the Rev. A. B. Baird, first Presbyterian minister in Edmonton, undertook to find a teacher. Since Baird did not take up residence in Edmonton until October, 1881, it would appear that the school did not open until late in the fall of that year. The selection committee eventually chose a schoolmaster named Jack Harris; his salary to be $500 per year, half of which, of course, would come from the government grant. A photograph of the first school and its pupils also reveals a balding, middle-aged gentleman, obviously the teacher. Little is known of him other than that he died soon thereafter. The magnitude of his salary, considerably larger than that paid in Indian schools, indicates the significance of the government aid. However, as it covered only half his salary and not at all the other expenses such as fuel and supplies, private beneficence had to make up the difference. Ten residents, including Hardisty, committed themselves to a total of $500 to provide school services for a year. Interestingly, the list does not include the names of any of the trustees — perhaps their positions as such made them responsible anyway for liabilities and deficits.

A proposal was also made to tax the pupils for the amount necessary if the grant should not be secured and subscriptions fail. The proposal to tax pupils, however, was turned down in favor of the principle of an absolutely free school. Consequently the school was financed by voluntary subscription. . .[5]

Harris' job in the little one-room temple of learning could by no means have been easy. The photograph already mentioned shows no fewer than fifty-one young scholars, and no doubt there were some absentees, as the average attendance in those days seldom reached sixty percent of the enrolment. However, since they were to have their school picture taken, probably most of the children were on hand.

Not more than four-fifths of them were white. Most of the remainder were probably Métis or half-breed; a few perhaps Indian. Until 1870 (and a few years after that), the schools of the Great North-West were racially integrated. But because Indian education became a federal and other education a territorial or provincial responsibility, not for another century did schooling cease to be racially segregated.

Of course, Edmonton's experience in establishing a secular, non-denomination school system was not unique. Another example was that of Calgary, and probably a number of the larger centres followed the same procedure towards the establishment of the first school districts in 1885.

Following his announcement concerning the joyful tidings about school grants, the lieutenant-governor's activities during the winter of 1880-81 seem to have been unexciting. Commissioner James A. Grahame, HBC, wrote from Winnipeg requesting a few signed liquor permits, but with the amounts of spirits, wine, or ale not specified. Laird would no sooner have signed a blank liquor permit than a blank cheque, and for a cautious descended Scots-Canadian named Laird, that would be when hell froze over — not that he would have used that expression. However, the Hon. David did not couch his refusal in such blunt terms. Instead, he explained that he could not comply with Grahame's request because he was required to submit to Parliament an annual return showing not only the number of permits issued, but specifying the kind and quantity of liquor named in each. Instead, he wrote, "I will forward a few permits all made in the Hudson's Bay Company's name filled up for different quantities that can be safely taken by any officer of the Company when in possession by him."[6] He ended his letter by tendering his sincere thanks for the excellent attention he had received on the Company's boats during his return trip from the East.

Replying from Montreal, Grahame thanked His Honor for the permits, promised that they would be used discreetly, and expressed the hope that he would meet Laird during the coming summer at Battleford or elsewhere.[7] He then mentioned that he was having the *Lily* refurbished as there was a rumor that the governor-general would be travelling "your way" and His Excellency might wish to use that boat. This was perhaps the first intimation which Laird had of the possibility of a vice-regal visitation.

On 14 February, the lieutenant-governor issued a proclamation for the election, not of three members to the Territorial council, but of one only. This was to be in the newly-established Electoral District of Lorne, which included Duck Lake, Carlton, and Prince Albert. Evidently Laird had received instructions to postpone or cancel plans for elections in the

Little Saskatchewan area; no doubt arrangements were already underway for its inclusion in the Province of Manitoba. One may wonder what the residents thereof thought of the whole idea. Naturally, as with the Indians, Ottawa would not ask those most vitally concerned for their opinions. It already knew what was best for them; besides, they might give the wrong answer.

The election occurred on 23 March, Lawrence Clarke of Carlton being successful over Captain Moore of Prince Albert. Although officially neutral, Laird must have greeted with much personal satisfaction the success of his friend, one whose hospitality he and his family had more than once enjoyed. In a subsequent battle at the polls, Moore's victory would mean grave disappointment to David Laird.

Almost two years had elapsed since he had given up the superintendency of Indian Affairs, but to many Indians, as to Ocean Man, he was still Father. The 28 March issue of the *Herald* mentioned that two Indians, Mossomin and Mosquito, had called on the governor. "The Chiefs hereabouts don't like the idea of always having to talk to a man they think has no authority," the paper continued, "and frequently take advantage of the patience which the Governor listens, and the kindly way he has of talking with them, to lay their complaints before him, and they always seem to go away satisfied."[8] Since Indian Commissioner Edgar Dewdney had his office in Winnipeg — Manitoba as well as the Territories was his area of responsibility — he was not quite as available as the Territorial lieutenant-governor.

Despite the fact that Laird was nearing the end of his term as lieutenant-governor, his interest in developing western agriculture never seemed to flag. The 25 April issue of Laurie's publication reported that Hungarian grass which Laird had planted the previous spring had proven a success.

No doubt much of Laird's time during that spring of 1881 was spent in preparing the agenda for the council session, which began 25 May and continued until 11 June. Matthew Ryan was not present for the opening meeting, as he was in Ottawa concerning the transfer of his Little Saskatchewan territory to Manitoba. However, he was on hand for at least some of the sittings. All the other members, including newly-elected Lawrence Clarke, were present. The 18 July issue of the *Herald* announced the termination of the appointment as councillor of Little Saskatchewan's Matthew Ryan. Before the year was out, his home territory had been incorporated into Manitoba, no longer the "postage-stamp province."

The 1881 council session was a busy one. Only some of the matters with which it dealt were: Bill to amend Titles Ordinance, Bill to provide a Medical Examining Board and defining Qualifications of Medical Men, Bill respecting Mortgages and Sales of personal property, Bill to incorporate Bishop of the Church of England, Diociase of Saskatchewan, Bill to

amend ordinance respecting Stallions. The council also considered a petition for the opening of a Land Office at Prince Albert, and a memorial
relating to claims of half-breeds to land for scrip.

Half-breed scrip was a certificate entitling the holder to title to crown
land, usually one hundred sixty acres, free and clear, without any obligation
as to residence, cultivation, or erection of buildings.

From 1871 to 1877, by means of the Great Treaties, Nos. 1 to 7, the
Canadian government had moved to extinguish aboriginal rights to the
broad acres of Rupert's Land. This it did despite the fact that Canada had
paid £300,000 to the Hudson's Bay Company for the same real estate, or
most of it. Thus in effect the government admitted the legitimacy of the
Indians' claims, but it refused to concede the validity of the Métis claims to
the effect that they too had aboriginal rights, which they had inherited
through their mothers. Since some at least of these female Indian forebears
were daughters of matrilineal tribes, such claims were not unreasonable.
Yet the federal government refused to allow them. Indeed, outside the
North-West, as in British Columbia and east of Ontario, it has never recognized the validity even of the Indians' claims. International custom rec-
ognizes sovereignty over a territory as being established through any of
four different processes: discovery and occupation (uninhabited lands only),
purchase, conquest, and treaty conceding the disputed territory from one
sovereign power to another. For a good half of Canada, the Indians claim
they have never lost their aboriginal rights through any of these methods.

What of the Métis, the half-breeds? For half a century and more, in
the West they had supplied the muscle for the fur trade. They were buffalo-
hunters and pemmican-makes; they were boatmen and teamsters and drovers. But with the disappearance of the buffalo, the coming of the lake and
river steamers, and ultimately the arrival of the railroads, their livelihood
was swept away. What was to be done with them?

The government had only one answer, the same one it had for the
Indians. Make them into farmers! But instead of sequestering them on
reserves, title to be held in trust for them by the federal government, each
was to have his own farm. So they were given scrip, a certificate exchange-
able for a farm, or rather for a piece of land from which a farm could be
made.

But it didn't work that way. The scrip was transferable, could be sold
— and was — for a song, for a horse and a blanket and a bottle of booze,
for a few dollars more valuable, more urgently needed right now than a
stretch of raw land. So few half-breeds became farmers, and some white
men became rich buying up scrip, claiming and then selling the land —
'scrip millionaires' they were called. Other half-breeds claimed the land as
provided by their scrip but many soon sold it, usually far below its value.
Still others accepted cash instead of scrip. But the little money available

one way or another was soon gone, and the landless Métis were as poor as ever. Of course, some had established little holdings where they did a bit of gardening, perhaps planted a few acres of grain, kept a couple of cows, a few chickens, possibly a pig or two. Those who were able to gain title to their land were the best off in the end — like their brothers, they had no money, but they had their farms — if the government didn't want their land for some other purpose.

Many years later, as will be noted in a subsequent chapter, Laird was to be involved, albeit peripherally, in the whole business of half-breed scrip.

By the beginning of April the rumor of the vice-regal visit had become hard fact. On the eighth of the month Governor-General the Marquis of Lorne had left Winnipeg for the end of steel, west of Portage La Prairie. Here His Excellency was met by a Mounted Police escort under Supt. Herchmer. Next stage of the vice-regal progress was aboard the *Manitoba,* up the Assiniboine to Fort Ellice. Here began the long trek across the prairies. The entourage must have been impressive. Because of ill health, the governor-general's wife, daughter of Queen Victoria, did not accompany her husband. But there was the escort of twenty Mounties under Supt. Herchmer.

> The Governor-General's party consisted of a chaplain, the Rev. Dr. McGregor of Edinburgh; a surgeon, Dr. Sewell; a military secretary, Lieut.-Col. F. De Winton; aides-de-camp, Major and Captain Bagot of the Royal Artillery and Captain Percival of the 2nd Life Guards; an artist, Sidney P. Hall of the London *Graphic;* correspondents of the Toronto *Globe* and the London *Times,* and a French chef and six servants.[9]

The *Herald* noted that Edgar Dewdney accompanied His Excellency on the entire trip (presumably from Winnipeg), and "looked after matters pertaining to his department,"[10] i.e., those involving the Indians visited along the route. At Shoal Lake the vice-regal party were Dewdney's guests.

Travelling across country, the Marquis and company visited Fort Ellice, Qu'Appelle, Duck Lake, and Carlton, ". . . on reaching which historic and romantic spot the party enjoyed a welcome rest under the hospitable roof of Chief Factor Clarke."[11] On 26 August His Excellency received an address "presented by the Officers of the Hudson's Bay Company, the Half-breeds and settlers in the neighborhood, and the Indians,"[12] and made an appropriate vice-regal reply. The following morning, after what was apparently an over-night voyage on the *Lily* — such nocturnal boldness! — he reached Prince Albert. From the citizens there he received a Standard Address of Welcome. Who the signers were the *Herald* does not indicate, but one may be sure that they included Charles Mair. The Warden and Tutorial Staff of Emmanuel College also presented an address to His

Excellency, mostly devoted to bragging about the progress of their estimable institution.

Continuing his tour aboard the *Lily*, Lorne reached Battleford on 30 August. Fine weather and high water had made that inland voyage a delight. Herchmer's Police escort, travelling overland, had arrived the day before. Strictly according to protocol, Lieutenant-Governor the Hon. David Laird greeted Governor-General the Marquis of Lorne. For such an event on its own turf the *Herald* pulled out all stops in describing the welcome which Battleford extended to its distinguished visitor. However, it failed to translate a certain Gaelic expression. No doubt Editor Laurie felt that for his erudite readers no such condescension was necessary. Nor is it for readers of this work.

In view of the approaching visit, the citizens of Battleford erected a handsome arch on the brow of the hill leading up to the Government buildings. On one side it bore a large portrait of Her Majesty, and the words "Welcome to Battleford;" while the other had "Caed Mille Failthe," and a legend in the Indian syllabic character of similar import. On the front of the arch were sheaves of grain, emblematic of the country's wealth, while placed at various points were heads of the Rocky Mountain moose and of elk and various kinds of deer, reminders that but a short time ago the chase was the chief occupation of our people. Crowning the arch were a number of flags, which brightened the scene and set it and the surroundings off to great advantage.

The steamer Lily arrived at eight o'clock on Tuesday morning, when His Excellency was received by His Honor the Lieutenant-Governor and driven to Government House. At the arch, the school children, including many Indian youths, greeted His Excellency and sang "God Save the Queen" as he passed under it.

Shortly after reaching Government House His Excellency was favored with a sight of a "begging dance" by the Stoneys — a dance wherein sparcity (*sic*) of clothing, abundance of grease and paint, and ear-splitting noise are the chief characteristics. In the afternoon the Indian Council was held. From the anxiety displayed by these people for an interview with the Governor General and the Commissioner, and the number of councils and rehearsals they had held on the subject, it was expected that they would make some show of ground for complaint, but their cry was for "more grub" — a repetition of the old story that "Their people were hungry." The only variation was that their demands were more extravagant than usual; and when His Excellency promised that they should have some food and some other provisions, they grunted out their satisfaction and withdrew.

At two o'clock His Excellency received the address of the people of Battleford, after which a number of our citizens were presented to him.[13]

The governor-general made a suitable reply to the Standard Address of Welcome (which the *Herald* carried in full), expressing his regret at not being able to visit Edmonton. Then the Battlefordians took advantage of His Excellency's presence to vent, or ventilate, by way of petition, their increasing frustration with the federal government. The very length of the document, herewith reproduced, is indicative of the depth of these Nor-Westers' feelings:

To His Excellency the Marquis of Lorne,
Governor-General of Canada:

May it please Your Excellency —

We, the citizens of Battleford, wish to lay before you the following statement concerning land in this settlement, and humbly pray that Your Excellency will cause the matter to be brought before your Honorable Ministers at Ottawa, in the hope that more attention may be paid to a petition passing through Your Excellency's hands than representations sent to the Department have hitherto received.

Six years have passed away since the first settlement was made here by white men. The spring following such settlement the Government passed an Order in Council declaring a town-site reserve of four miles square (or 10,240 acres) at the junction of the Battle and Saskatchewan rivers. This was followed by a railway reserve of twenty miles on each side of the surveyed route of the Canadian Pacific railway, which passes through Battleford. The town-site reserve included land taken up by the settlers above mentioned, and who are promised protection in these holdings by the Dominion Lands Act.

Petitions have from time to time been sent to the Department requesting a survey, and a settlement of the matter, but with no result. Some of these petitions have not even been acknowledged.

Government buildings have been placed on said land, and large portions of the claims enclosed for agricultural and other purposes by the officials, under authority, it is supposed, from the Department. To such an extent has this been done on some of the claims that no ground has been left for the settler to farm.

Surveyors have at different times wintered here with full parties under pay, doing nothing when they might have been blocking out townships and surveying the settlement. This was not done because these surveyors were under pay from the Indian branch, while the lands are another branch of the same Department. With due respect to Your Excellency, we suggest that carelessness or red tape should not be allowed to put the people of Canada to such unnecessary expense, nor the settlers of Battleford to such an annoyance.

Many good settlers have passed here to go farther and fare worse because the question of land was unsettled; and today we are without a mill because no one will risk the necessary expense to put a mill in a settlement where nobody knows how soon he may be ordered off by some of the numerous owners of land in the North-West.

Your Excellency has doubtless noticed that the houses in Battleford are hardly such as might be expected in the Capital of the North-West. The cause is the same, namely, that there is no title to land, and people will not put up expensive houses on land that is in dispute.

A person would naturally suppose that having made a town-site reserve at Battleford — having put up public buildings and located the capital here, having built barracks and filled them with police, the Government would survey the land, settle the disputed claims, and make an attempt to build up a town on the town-site. But no; having locked up the most advantageous location for a city in the North-West from sale and settlement, they refuse to sell the land themselves or to let anybody else sell it, and calmly see the settlements on either side of it flourish, but seem to hope that all enterprise here will be choked and Battleford returned to the previous condition as a rendezvous for Indians and buffalo.

Appeals to the Department in person are met with the astonishing answer, that if the railroad comes to Battleford and the land is valuable the Government will take it, but if it is not worth anything the settler can keep it.

While surveys are being made all over the country for the Indians, white men cannot get even a civil answer from the Department. Why is this? Because the white man can be depended on to keep the peace under abuse and tyranny, and the red man cannot.

The land regulations of the railway syndicate and the Dominion Government are well known, and we do not desire exceptional treatment. If we have to pay either of these, or if we get our title by homestead, is all one to us, so that we get it; but a survey and an investigation of title are necessary before we come to that point.

Battleford has more good land in its neighborhood than any settlement in the North-West, with a climate milder in winter and less liable to frosts in summer than either Prince Albert on the east or Edmonton on the west, and it only requires the same favors granted to it that are extended to others to become what its climate, geographical position and fertile soil destined it to be — the premier settlement of the North-West.

In conclusion, we humbly pray that Your Excellency will kindly take an interest in our case and using the influence which your position gives and your abilities grace, end our trouble, and confer a great boon upon a struggling community. We are cut off from many of the commonest pleasures of life, and labor under disadvantages enough without having such hindrance thrown in our way.

It may be that in a few years Your Excellency will be proud to look at Battleford as city, and remember that to your kind offices it owes its prosperity.

And as in duty bound your petitioners will ever pray.[14]

During his stay at Battleford, the Marquis drove through the surrounding area, visiting the principal settlements and points of interest. No doubt he was accompanied by the lieutenant-governor and the press. At some time during his sojourn, the *Graphic's* Hall made an amusing sketch of the Hon. David Laird and the Rev. Dr. Macgregor (Laurie and Turner don't quite agree on the spelling of the latter's name), exaggerating the governor's stature and the other's lack thereof. "Several of the staff took advantage of the excellent shooting to be had in this vicinity to enjoy a few hours' sport, and their success was so great that when they come to tell their exploits, especially among the snipe, we fear they will be met with a smile of incredulity."[15]

On Tuesday and Wednesday evenings, i.e., the 30 and 31 August, Laird entertained the visitors at Government House dinners, to which he invited government officers and leading citizens. The next morning His Excellency set off across country, escorted for several miles by the lieutenant-governor. The Marquis' destination was Morleyville via Calgary, then back to Ottawa by way of Fort Macleod and through the United States. With his departure, Battleford settled down to the more-or-less even tenor of its ways.

If they were disturbed in any manner, it was probably over two questions. Would the lieutenant-governorship be abolished at the end of Laird's term? If not, who would be his successor? The Toronto *Globe* mentioned two possibilities, Senator Skead and Joseph Royal. The latter, a Manitoba Member of Parliament, many years later did in fact become the NWT lieutenant-governor. Laurie made no conjecture of his own, but in the 18 September issue of the *Herald* he criticized Ottawa on two grounds for making no announcement:

> Where movements have to be made covering such distances as exist between the Federal and Territorial capitals, and at a season when unpleasant travelling may be looked for, it is singular, to say the least, that the retiring Governor should be kept in ignorance of the intentions of the Government as to the future. It would seem but ordinary courtesy to give him such timely notice as would permit him to make arrangements either for remaining here or for returning to the east with some degree of comfort; and for the same reason the new Governor should have been appointed before this, that he might avail himself of pleasant weather for travelling to where his duty lies.[16]

The *Herald* issue of 17 October notes that His Honor had travelled down river on the *Lily* to visit Carlton and Prince Albert. Although Laurie does not so indicate, this journey was perhaps somewhat of a farewell tour. If so, the usual gubernatorial addresses and replies did not appear in the *Herald,* but the expedition was to have a lasting benefit to Laird. In the course of his voyage he met a young Presbyterian minister, the Rev. Andrew B. Baird, en route to open the first church of his denomination in Edmonton. This was the same clergyman who in Edmonton participated in the search for talent which resulted in the appointment of Jack Harris as a teacher. The first Laird-Baird Meeting occurred on 6 October; R. C. Russell describes it:

> The river steamer *Lily* stopped at Fort Carlton on its way from Battleford to Prince Albert. Lieut. Governor Laird was a passenger on the boat and Mr. Baird had a very pleasant visit with him. He learned that the Lieutenant-Governor was an ardent Presbyterian from Prince Edward Island and that he was very much interested in learning Hebrew, so that he could read the Bible in what he considered to be the original tongue. Here for a time, and later at home in Battleford, His Excellency obtained some coaching in that language from the young university graduate.[17]

Of course, David Laird was not exactly a beginner in Hebrew, the study of which he had begun as a student at Truro. But that was a long time ago, and one can become a bit rusty. The lessons in Hebrew were resumed at Battleford a few days later. Russell continues the account:

> Mr. Baird reached Battleford about mid-afternoon on Tuesday, October 11th. Here he was hospitably received by the Rev. T. A. Clarke, a missionary to the Indians in the neighborhood. At this time Battleford was the capital of the North West Territories. As the weather remained cold and stormy for several days, Mr. Baird remained here for nearly a week to await milder weather and dry roads. During his stay he obtained a much needed rest and spent a leisurely period reading, visiting new acquaintenances and teaching Hebrew to the Lieutenant-Governor.[18]

The rather accidental meeting of the young preacher and the no-longer-young governor was to ripen into a life-long family friendship when Laird came to Winnipeg as Indian Commissioner and Baird was a member of the faculty of Manitoba College and the minister of a large city church.

Somehow, the fact of David Laird's studying Hebrew, and Greek, too, according to his granddaughter Elizabeth Laird, suggests a rather lonely man with perhaps too little to do, turning back to the intellectual pursuits of his youth to keep himself busy. But this period of loneliness was fast approaching an end.

No doubt by October he was looking to the termination of his governorship and re-union with his family. With no official announcement forthcoming as to the appointment of a successor, Laird seized the initiative. In that month he appears to have submitted his resignation to Prime Minister

Macdonald. In November he shipped four trunks via Qu'Appelle to Winnipeg, care of the Hudson's Bay Company, from which point they would no doubt be forwarded by rail.

"Old Tomorrow" could procrastinate no longer. Activated at last by Laird's resignation, the government provisionally appointed Edgar Dewdney as Laird's successor. Dewdney also retained his Commissionership for Indian Affairs, an economical arrangement for the federal government in that it had to pay only one salary plus a bonus instead of two. It will be remembered that this was the arrangement which Laird had found intolerably heavy. Dewdney's appointment was later confirmed. The 10 December issue of the *Herald* stated that he was expected to leave Winnipeg for Battleford in about six weeks.

Before Laird's departure, on 15 December, his fellow-Battlefordians presented him with an address. At least one of his four trunks must have been full of such documents. A single sentence from this formal farewell expresses the sentiment of the whole. "We regret your departure because we feel not only that we are losing one who has always cheerfully given advice and rendered substantial assistance to each and all of our local and territorial institutions; but because we are losing one who has ever exercised a watchful care over the interests of the country."[19]

His Honor's reply was a model of gubernatorial blandness: thanks for the address and the kind wishes and thoughtful reference to his family, a brief statement of what he had tried to accomplish, especially among the Indians. As with the address, one sentence summarizes the sentiment. "In all my dealings both public and private, I have endeavoured to act in a manner becoming to one occupying the high position which I had the honor to fill in this Country under Her Majesty and the Government of Canada; and it affords me no little gratification that now at the close of my term of office, the inhabitants of Battleford, who know me best, bear testimony that my efforts have not been altogether in vain."[20]

Laird left Battleford on 17 December. Forget, Scott, and many leading citizens "saw him comfortably seated in his cariol and wished him Godspeed through his long and tedious journey over the plains."[21] The editor of the *Herald* seized the opportunity to add his tribute to that contained in the citizens' address:

> On this address it is unnecessary to comment; the respects and esteem of the inhabitants of Battleford for Mr. Laird, are but a faint echo of the feelings of all the people of the Territory, and the sentiments expressed therein will be strongly endorsed in every settlement which has had its growth during his wise administration — his name will always be endorsed by those who have had the privilege of his acquaintance, it will be associated with courtesy, friendship, and with that sympathy which

is not expended in words alone, and his tall frame and hearty laugh, will be connected with many happy recollections of our pioneer days.[22]

Obviously Laurie was not only adept with the Rhetorical Question, he was also a Master of the Interminable Sentence.

Laird's ceremonial send-off was followed by somewhat of an anti-climax. The first and second nights out, the horses slipped their hobbles, deserted their duties, and returned to the familiar environs of Battleford. Laird's driver had to make his way back to the capital to retrieve them, but His Honor remained in camp — it would have been awkward to face his friends again after such a ceremonious farewell. Fortunately, the weather was mild and game plentiful, so that Laird did not find the delay irksome.

But he would not have been able to reach Charlottetown by Christmas.

References

1. David Laird to David Rennie Laird, 9 December 1880 (Public Archives of Prince Edward Island).

2. *Saskatchewan Herald*, "Government Aid to Schools," 20 December 1880 (Advt.).

3. *Ibid.*, "Aid to Schools".

4. G. A. McKee, *The Story of Edmonton School District No. 7 1885-1935*, p. 5.

5. *Ibid.*

6. David Laird to James A. Grahame, 10 February 1881.

7. James A. Grahame to David Laird, 15 March 1881.

8. *Herald*, 28 February 1881.

9. J. P. Turner, *The North-West Mounted Police*, v. 1, p. 591.

10. *Herald*, "The Vice-Regal Journey," 4 September 1881.

11. *Ibid.*

12. *Ibid.*

13. *Ibid.*

14. *Ibid.*

15. *Ibid.*

16. *Ibid.*, "The Lieutenant-Governorship," 18 September 1881.

17. R. C. Russell, "A Minister Takes the Carlton Trail," *The Beaver*, Winter, 1959, p. 10.

18. *Ibid.*, p. 10-11.

19. *Herald*, "Citizens' Address to Governor Laird," 31 December 1881.

20. *Ibid.*, "The Governor's Departure".

21. *Ibid.*

22. *Ibid.*

15

Sojourn
in Charlottetown

For no comparable period in David Laird's adult life is so little hard information available as for his sojourn in Charlottetown from 1882 to 1898. Yet this was a very significant time for the Laird family. The boys and girls grew to adulthood and made a start, for Harold rather abortively, on lifetime careers or as home-makers. Laird himself returned to his vocation as a journalist, and ultimately left it. He re-entered politics, and twice was unsuccessful in his attempts to return to Parliament. In 1895, after thirty-one years of marriage, his Louisa died. Financial security seemed ever beyond his reach; indeed, he remained in harness as long as he lived, which was until he had passed the age of eighty. And this is almost all that is remembered about David Laird's life during the sixteen years between the time he left Battleford and the date when he removed to Winnipeg.

On the surface, these facts seem rather sad, a story, if not exactly of failure, at least of a lack of success which might have been expected in a man of David Laird's intelligence, education, experience, and integrity. Yet such a reckoning must be discarded as superficial and misleading. True, David Laird did not die a wealthy man, as some politicians then and since have done. But to him, material riches were insignificant in comparison with his reputation, his integrity, his Presbyterian principles which he was never known to compromise. So also was his church as an institution important to him. Later in Winnipeg, only the most severe prairie blizzard combined with the entreaties of his daughter could keep him from regular attendance at the kirk. Attending presbytery, conference, and national sessions at Toronto, Montreal, and other points across Canada, David Laird was probably the most influential lay member of his church in the whole country.

David and Louisa were fortunate in their family. Or perhaps it would be more correct to say they were blessed, for fortune implies fortuitousness beyond human control. Of course they were fortunate in the health of their sons and daughters, all of whom reached adulthood with no serious or

Hon. David Laird and Family, c. 1890. Back row: Rennie, Gordon, Mary, Harold. Front row: William, Mrs. Laird, Hon. David Laird, Louise.

lasting illness. The Angel of Death spared their children in an era when typhoid, pneumonia, influenza, tuberculosis took their toll of almost every family. Like all parents, at times the Lairds must have been disappointed with their offsprings' behavior, when son or daughter proved wilful or recalcitrant, chose a path that the parents disapproved of, marched to the beat of a different drummer. But in the end, the younger Lairds grew up to honor their father and their mother and to add lustre to their name. The Honorable David lived to see many of his grandchildren well started on the road which would bring them to goals that a century of life on the North American continent, added to uncounted years beyond the Atlantic, had made steel-strongly traditional for those whose name was Laird. Aspects of this tradition include firm religious faith, respect and tolerance for honestly held but different beliefs, hunger for education, acceptance of social responsibility, an honest day's work for a day's pay, the kind of patriotism which means living as well as dying for one's country, a clear-eyed respect for and pride in the achievements of one's forebears, and a sturdy self-reliance, financial and otherwise, quite different from a greed for wealth. Not all of David Laird's descendants — perhaps none of them — were paragons of every such virtue, and some had their failings. But even unto the third and fourth generation, none has wholly escaped from his or her heritage, and the like heritage derived form the Orrs, the Owens, the Mathiesons, and other Island ancestors.

David Laird's descendants, and those of the other Island Lairds are dispersed through Canada and the United States from the Atlantic to the Pacific. Many have proven themselves leaders in agriculture, business, the professions, and other walks of life; none has ever dishonored the memory of his or her forebears.

But such outcomes were far in the future when David Laird returned to the Island at the beginning of 1882. Immediately, or almost so, he resumed the editorship of the *Patriot*. Whether he had retained part of complete ownership of the paper during the previous eight years, or whether he had to buy back into it is now uncertain. It does appear that while he exercised editorial control, another man directed the financial aspects of the operation, an arrangement which was ultimately to prove little short of disastrous to the editor. But editorial work by no means absorbed all of Laird's energies. No sooner was he back in Charlottetown than he was in the thick of a federal election campaign. Once again he was a candidate in the dual-member constituency of Queen's, whose constituents had given him such a warm welcome on his return to the Island a couple of years before. But he found the public was a fickle master; although his Liberal running-mate, Louis Davies, headed the poll, Laird was defeated.

In 1887 he made another attempt to gain a seat in Parliament. In that year he was a candidate for the newly-created seat of Saskatchewan. But in his five-year absence the North-West had changed. The Canadian Pacific now stretched to the Western Ocean; the capital had been moved from Battleford to Regina. An influx, if not yet a flood, of newcomers was sweeping onto the Prairies, immigrants from Europe and United States and Upper Canada. In the words of another Islander, L. M. Montgomery, they were people who "knew not Joseph."

Despite his success in Island politics and his prominence in the Mackenzie government, David Laird was never really a political person, never a prototype professional politician. He therefore must have been profoundly shocked by the vituperative attack which the *Prince Albert Times* made on him in its edition of 1 February 1887:

> Mr. Laird and some of his friends arrived in Prince Albert to campaign on the Liberal platform. Cast off by his political friends in Queen's County, P. E. I., he has come to try his luck with the people of Saskatchewan. Will he say to himself what part have I taken in building up

Prince Albert or Battleford? What have I done that the people should elect me?

One stain on his record as a public man is the abuse he heaped upon the religion of his Catholic fellow citizens. Elected as an independent he sold himself to the Hon. Alex Mackenzie. Those who support him in Saskatchewan are not the best type. The Liberals in P. E. I. have disowned him, believed he would sell himself again. We want no renegade politican to represent us. The people of Saskatchewan are being asked not only to elect an outsider but one who was false to his friends. He is willing to go to any length, even to stirring up ill blood between the Half Breed and the English speaking people of Saskatchewan. He commenced his campaign by charging Sir John Macdonald with causing the rebellion.[1]

In 1887, Saskatchewan was not a Province but a District of the North-West Territories, its boundaries having been established in 1882.

Laird's successful opponent was the Prince Albert resident, Captain Moore, the mill-owner who in 1881 had suffered defeat in his campaign to win a seat on the Territorial council. Incidentally, in the following century, Prince Albert was to be represented in Parliament at different times by two Canadian Prime Ministers, the Rt. Hon. Mackenzie King, Liberal, and the Rt. Hon. John Diefenbaker, Progressive Conservative. Then, to show their contrariness, the Prince Albert electors chose the candidate of the New Democratic Party.

Frank MacKinnon has given an astute analysis of the reasons for Laird's lack of political success:

The defeats suffered by Laird were serious blows to him after a decade of distinguished public service. Unfortunately for him, he reentered politics at a most inopportune time. His party's fortunes were at a very low ebb in the face of Sir John Macdonald's tremendous popularity and the overwhelming strength of the Conservatives. Laird had been away from his home province for almost eight years, so that to a generation of electors he was almost unknown. Then, too, there were many who still resented the fact that his acceptance of the western governorship, which involved resigning his portfolio as Minister of the Interior, had lost Prince Edward Island a seat in the cabinet. Had he waited a few years after returning to the Island before reentering politics, so that he could have reestablished himself in political circles, his great abilities and experience might again have been used as M.P. for Queen's. The same applies to his defeat in the Territories in 1887, for he had then been away from the West for six years and was personally unknown to the many settlers who had arrived since his administration.[2]

Presumably soon after his return to Charlottetown, David Laird and his family were established in their large house on the east side of Elm (now University) Avenue. Despite the impressive size of their domicile and Laird's prominent position as editor of the *Patriot,* financially life was not easy. Family tradition has it that the most abundant article of food in the Laird household was oatmeal. This tradition calls to mind Dr. Johnson's famous definition of oats: "A grain which in England is generally given to horses, but in Scotland supports the people."[3] The less well-known riposte to the effect that England produces splendid horses and Scotland equally admirable men (and presumably women) would certainly seem as true in P.E.I.'s New as in Scotland's old Glasgow. Perhaps oatmeal was not as prominent in the Laird diet as childhood recollection would have it, but its memory remains undimmed even generations later. The younger and strong-willed daughter, Louise, on reaching adulthood, banished it from her own table forever.

If money was in short supply in the Laird household, its scarcity was not allowed to distort family priorities. One may be absolutely certain that David Laird contributed to the support of Zion Church beyond the call of duty. Second only to religion in importance would be education. Daughter Mary's son, the Hon. David's grandson, writes:

> There was an absolute necessity recognized by any Scot, to ensure that each of the four sons receive a good education. The daughters were to learn to cook and sew and knit and nurse and run a household, as well as to read good literature and memorize good poetry and act like a lady at all times both at home and in society. All of which my mother could and did do with great good humor until within a few days of her long and happy life.[4]

And so, in an atmosphere of plain living and high thinking, the Laird off-spring grew from childhood or youth to maturity. There is evidence that in 1889 David Laird was active in promoting the formation of an Island or Charlottetown scientific society, the unmodified noun 'science' then having a rather wider connotation than that to which it has more recently been restricted. The evidence is the following letter from McGill University's Principal William Dawson:

April 17th 1889

Dear Mr. Laird,

I am very glad to see that you are moving in the promotion of Science and wish all success to your Society.

I shall have much pleasure in asking the Natural History Society of Montreal to place your society on its list of exchanges for the "Record of Science," and in sending you from time to time such papers as I may publish in connection with the Peter Redpath Museum.

You will be entitled to a representation at the meetings of the Royal Society of Canada, and with this object should report to Dr. Bourinot, the Honorary Secretary, House of Commons Ottawa. The Royal Society meets on May 7th in Ottawa.

On application to him he will also place the name of the Society on the list for the Transactions of the Royal Society.

Wishing your effect all success, I remain

Yours Sincerely,

Wm Dawson

Just as the Laird boys and girls were moving from childhood to adulthood, equally inevitably if less perceptibly David Laird was making the transition from maturity to that status which a later generation designates as senior citizenship or some other equally mealy-mouthed euphemism. Equally inevitably, and particularly during the century's last decade, the close ties which bound the Laird family together began to weaken. Even before 1890, William had left the family circle to work on an uncle's farm for awhile, apparently to improve his somewhat uncertain health — but he lived to be almost eighty-eight. Evidently fully recovered, after gaining some shop-keeping experience in Charlottetown, he obtained a position in a Halifax business. Eventually he moved to Rat Portage (now Kenora) and Winnipeg, and to a highly successful career as a chartered accountant.

Since the Island was not to have a degree-granting institution for many years, son Gordon was off to Dalhousie University, Halifax, to continue his study of the classics.

The oldest son was no longer Master Rennie Laird, but 'D. R. Laird, Esq.', as his father addressed the envelopes of the letters that he sent to the young man. On 7 June 1893 he married Aletha Gunn, of Summerside, P.E.I. Despite the fact that both bride and groom were Islanders, the marriage took place in Dorchester, Massachusetts, where the orphaned bride was living with her sister Beatrice. At the time, Rennie was employed in the Boston branch of the Bank of Nova Scotia. Eleven months later, the young couple presented David and Louisa with their first grandchild, a boy named Arthur. Three years afterwards his brother Sidney was born.

By 1890 Harold, at twenty-two, would have begun and perhaps by then he might also have abandoned his study of law, not at a law school but articled under a barrister, as was common in many parts of Canada at that period. Perhaps he found intolerable the pressure to meet the expectations of the Laird family, extended as well as nuclear. Perhaps, as his subsequent career would appear to indicate, he was just naturally an outdoorsman.

On 10 July 1895, Louisa Laird died. No one who has not suffered a similar loss can imagine how devastated David Laird was when his beloved help-mate of over thirty years left him to face the rest of his life without her. Not alone; his two daughters were still at home. However, by this time Mary Alice was probably 'keeping company' with a rising young lawyer whom she had met at a Shakespeare Literary Club meeting. Among those rather staid and proper Scottish-Canadians of that time and place, whirl-wind courtships and short engagements were considered not really in very good taste — and sometimes scandalous as well. Perhaps Mary's marriage to John A. Mathieson was delayed by her mother's death, but on 15 September 1896 she wed her fiancé, a future Premier and Chief Justice of Prince Edward Island. In 1898 their first child, Louise — what happened to Louisa as a family name? — was born.

"The old order changeth. . ." The year 1896 saw the passing of David Laird's brother Alexander and his sister Annie. Two years later his brother James also died.

The 1890's saw other events, their importance to the Lairds at first not completely obvious. In 1891, Sir John A. Macdonald, 'Old Tomorrow," Canada's permanent prime minister (except for an aberrant half-decade in the '70's) ran out of tomorrows and went to the Great Parliament in the Sky, i.e., he died. Slowly it was becoming obvious that the Tories were cursed with a death wish. By permitting the execution of Louis Riel, Mac-donald had alienated Quebec's 'bleus,' apparently forever. With his demise, despite the prophecy, "You'll never die, John A.," his party began its al-most-continuous exile to the political wilderness and its practice of giving short shrift to unsuccessful standard-bearers. Between 1891 and 1896 the party had four leaders; by the latter date it was in complete disarray, and under Wilfrid Laurier the Liberals regained their divine right, that of ruling Canada.

For former Liberal Minister of the Interior the Hon. David Laird, this election at first sight did not seem to have much immediate impact. But by the late '90's the *Patriot* was in serious difficulties. As already mentioned, Laird's attention had been largely or wholly on the editorial aspects of the paper. An associate looked after its financial well-being. For whatever reason, the paper was in serious financial trouble. Thus at an age which a later generation would regard as normal for retirement, David Laird found himself in almost desperate circumstances. He appealed to the silver-haired, silver-tongued Laurier; the claims of such a staunch Liberal could not be denied. On 4 October 1898 he was appointed Indian Commissioner for Manitoba and the North-West. Somewhat unwillingly but Laird-like, recognizing her duty when she saw it and no doubt guided also by deep affection, twenty-four-year-old Louise accompanied her father to establish a new Laird home in Winnipeg.

References

1. *Prince Albert Times,* 1 February 1887.

2. Frank MacKinnon, "David Laird of Prince Edward Island," *The Dalhousie Review,* v. 26, no. 4, p. 420.

3. John Bartlet, *Familiar Quotations,* (11th edition), p. 232.

4. David Laird Mathieson to John W. Chalmers, 3 March 1979.

5. William Dawson to David Laird, 17 April 1889 (Public Archives of Prince Edward Island 2541-66).

16

Treaty No. 8

For the Lairds, papa David, son Harold, and daughter Louise, the move to Winnipeg must have been traumatic. Perhaps not so much for David; in his lifetime he had lived in New Glasgow (or near it), Truro (actually West River), Charlottetown, Fort Livingstone, Battleford, and Charlottetown again. Like men from time immemorial, he went where his work took him and made the best of it. So did Harold, who seems to have been a restless soul, although eventually he was to find a permanent anchorage. But for Louise, the transition must have been most difficult. She had been barely five years old when she left the North-West in 1879. She had grown up and gone to school in Charlottetown, in the midst of friends and relatives. She was completely at home in the Island's capital, where no doubt she knew 'everybody who was anybody.' The whole Island, indeed,

Hon. David Laird explaining terms of Treaty No. 8 at Fort Vermilion, 1899. (R.C.M.P. Museum, Regina)

was narrow, circumscribed, limited, demographically static in size and eth-
nic composition of its population. Now she found herself in a burgeoning
young city, crude, vulgar, materialistic, with an ever-shifting population
speaking a dozen, a score of different European, American, and Asiatic
tongues. Nor were there nice comfortable limits to the physical geography.
Westward the Great Plains stretched almost endlessly hundreds of miles
until they ceased abruptly in the austere, snow-capped mountains. East and
north, almost at the city's outskirts it seemed, began the hostile Canadian
Shield, a land of wood and rock, muskeg and water. One did not need to
leave anglophone Canada to suffer culture shock. And south was a foreign
country, for her truly *terra incognita.*

Almost in the dead centre of the continent, Winnipeg was an environment of extremes, not least of which was the climate. In winter the ground
froze iron-hard and stayed that way for months on end. At -40° F. (or C.)
mercury itself freezes in the thermometer, and often it did. The cold seemed
to penetrate one's very bones. Contrari-wise, summer's hot drying winds
could push temperatures towards and, albeit rarely, beyond 100° F. No
temperature-moderating ocean was near-by to dampen extremes of heat
and cold. Spring brought hordes of mosquitoes, voracious and blood-hun-
gry, and sometimes floods in that misnamed Red River Valley that was as
flat as soup on a plate. Fall could be beautiful — or chilly and rainy.

On Louise's shoulders fell all the responsibility, all the worry and
frustration of trying to make a home in some one else's house, of 'making
do' with (at first) never enough sheets and blankets, china and silver, rugs
and furniture, and of being a gracious hostess to her father's friends and
their wives. Her daughter Elizabeth Laird tells how Louise coped:

> Hon. David Laird came to Winnipeg in October 1898, from Char-
> lottetown, P.E.I., after his appointment as Indian Commissioner with
> his headquarters in the Winnipeg Office of Indian Affairs. This was in
> an office building at the corner of Main St. and Broadway Ave. on the
> opposite side of Main St. from the present Canadian National Station.
> It has since been made into apartments. He took a room in the Empress
> Hotel which was across the street. His daughter Louise and son Harold
> arrived later. My Grandfather sold his house in Charlottetown and re-
> fused to bring many of his belongings. The furniture and household
> articles were sold. My Mother and her brother had to clear out the house
> and come west. My Grandfather had been appalled at the cost of bring-
> ing his family and some of their belongings to Battleford in the 1870s.
> This time they came with their clothes, pictures, a few rugs, and lots of
> books. As Mother said "more books than anything else." They arrived
> after their long journey on Christmas Eve and were both taken by sur-
> prise by the intense cold, although Grandfather had warned them that
> it was colder than Prince Edward Island. After Christmas dinner at the
> hotel, all three started to walk along Main Street. They did not go many
> blocks and before they got back to the hotel, both Mother and Uncle

Harold had frozen noses. She found her coat and winter clothes were not warm enough for a Winnipeg winter and she had to get a warmer coat as soon as she could. I think most of the stock in the stores was pretty low by this time and she had some trouble. She did not, of course know of a dressmaker, nor did her father. David Laird had decided to rent a furnished house. They lived in a succession of these. Sometimes the owner decided to come back sooner than expected and they had to find another place to live. Grandfather wanted to be within walking distance of his office. They lived on Hargrave Ave., and later, as I recall, on Kennedy. My Mother found this a most uncomforable way of living. There were never enough sheets and blankets, and they had to buy some. Often there was barely enough china for the family, let alone having guests for dinner or receiving at a "day," as she was expected, as her Father's daughter to do almost every fortnight. She started to buy china and silver, and finally persuaded her father to buy a house, when they could not find anything suitable to rent one year. This house was at 52 Edmonton St.[1]

And each day, while Louise struggled to make a home for her father, that estimable Indian Commissioner was away to his office, to do whatever an Indian Commissioner did. One example of such activity was an investigation of the conduct of the Rev. J. H. Fairlie, Principal of Rupert's Land Industrial School. This investigation resulted from charges by the chief and councillors of St. Peter's Indian band. These led to hearing on 19 and 26 January and on 16 and 23 February 1899, and were held in the school at Selkirk, near the reserve, and in the Indian Affairs office, Winnipeg. Fairlie had evidently strapped some children (all in the name of good order and discipline) on their bare backs and bottoms so that the marks showed for weeks afterwards. He visited the big girls' dormitories at night, ostensibly to close the windows in summer and adjust the registers in winter, and took the opportunity to kiss some of the young misses good-night — quite paternally, no doubt. He was accused — and surely here his colleagues were equally blameworthy — of using mouldy butter on the pupils' tables and for cooking, while reserving the best for the staff.

At first blush, such harsh, even sadistic treatment and sexual exploitation of pupils in church-operated Indian schools seems unbelievable. However, there are many such instances, well documented, not in the mission records but in oral and written testimony of former students. Nor has any denomination been free of such shameful practices.

With respect to Indian education, mention has already been made of two pertinent facts:

1. Under the B.N.A. Act, the federal government accepted responsibility for all Indian affairs. This responsibility was assumed by both federal and provincial authorities to include Indian education.

2. In each of Indian Treaties No. 1 to 7, the federal government pledged itself to provide education services on the Indian reserves.

Despite these commitments, in 1899 and for many decades thereafter, most Indian schools, including virtually all of those in the North-West, continued to be operated — very badly — by church missions. By the turn of the century, teacher training had been available in normal schools in Winnipeg since 1882, in Regina since 1893. Yet in the Indian schools, professionally qualified instructors were a rarity. Ordained clergymen they might be (occasionally); licensed teachers they usually were not.

True, at Ottawa Indian Affairs did have an education branch — one clerk, to calculate government grants to schools. Not until 1909 would it have a superintendent of education in the person of Duncan Campbell Scott, not an educator but a civil servant and a poet.

In March, Laird was asked to make a recommendation with respect to the Fairlie case. He replied:

> I would be glad were you to relieve me from the task of making a special report. I feel that having to examine witnesses in support of the charges and cross-examine Mr. Fairlie's witnesses in rebuttal of the same, I was, seemingly on account of there being no prosecuting examiner, placed in opposition to the accused. I do not wish to put myself in the position of a judge and would much prefer that you yourself could find time to weigh the evidence and come to your own conclusion.[2]

Quite another category of problems which faced the Indian Commissioner concerned rights-of-way for roads and railways across Indian reserves. Thus in March, 1899, the Selkirk Transportation and Storage Company wished to lay a track across Lots 1 and 2, Parish of St. Peter's (on the reserve). Another seven years were to elapse before the band and the company reached an agreement.

For over a century 'treaty' Indians have been fighting encroachments on their lands, not only for railway and road rights-of-way but for easements for pipelines, drainage and irrigation ditches, and other purposes. In the mid-1880's the Canadian Pacific, without so much as a by-your-leave, surveyed and began construction of its main line through the Blackfoot reserve. On the western edge of expanding Edmonton, a band surrendered certain lands to be used for city roads and streets only, otherwise returned to the band. Under a city replot, the land was not longer used for such purpose. But it was not returned to the Indians either. At Cardston, Alberta, the Blood Indians ceded land to the Canadian Pacific for railway purposes only; CP has leased it to commercial establishments. On their reserve, access to irrigation controls has been assumed by the operating company but never conceded by the band. The first controversy was settled long ago; at this writing the others are still unresolved.

Problems involving land and education were routine for the newly-appointed Indian Commissioner. But in his first year as such, the Hon. David Laird had a much more important task to perform. This was nothing less than the negotiation of a new Indian Treaty, No. 8, which would embrace an area approximately as large as the first seven together.

No Indian treaty had been signed for over twenty years; none apparently had been needed. Native land claims in the Fertile Belt having been extinguished by Treaties No. 1 to 7, white settlement had been proceeding in a more or less orderly manner, except during the three-month North-West Rebellion of 1885. In that same year the Canadian Pacific had reached tidewater; tributary lines soon followed. For example, in 1891 the Calgary and Edmonton (C & E) line was completed — even though construction had halted across the deep, wide valley of the Saskatchewan, south of the old fur Fort.

But north of the Prairies, in the boreal forest, little had changed. The federal and territorial governments treated this area with benign neglect. The former's most visible action was creating the administrative District of Athabasca in 1882, north of the District of Alberta, and enlarging it in 1895, to embrace the northern halves of what are now the Provinces of Alberta and Saskatchewan. Even the Mounted Police did not really penetrate this northern area until 1897. The only permanent white residents were the fur traders, mostly those of the Hudson's Bay Company, the missionaries of the Roman Catholic and Anglican churches, and a few others. Since neither the Honorable Company nor the churches were fly-by-night outfits, here today and gone tomorrow (although some independent traders were), they were careful to respect the customs and traditions, other than religious, of the people, to understand and succor rather than exploit them, to mediate between mutually hostile tribes, and generally to promote peace if not prosperity — the latter was largely beyond their power — among the Northern Cree and Chipewyan, the Beaver and Slaves, the Loucheux and Hare and Inuit. What need was there for more formal governmental machinery?

In many respects these 'canoe' Indians differed widely from the 'horse' Indians of the Great Plains. Perhaps the difference, insofar as the whites were concerned, was their indigenous political structures. The latter — Blackfoot-speakers, Sarcees, Stoneys, Saulteaux, Sioux, Plains Crees — were organized into relatively large bands governed, if not always controlled, by sophisticated councils of chiefs and councillors who, like Crowfoot, could influence and largely commit their followers to treaties.

Commonly, the game of these northern natives was not the gregarious buffalo but the solitary moose, although the former ranged even north of

Parallel Sixty. For two centuries and more these Indians had been trappers and fishermen even more than hunters. In general, their environment's resources caused them to live in small groups, immediate or sometimes moderately extended families. Only infrequently did they gather in large assemblies for religious or trade purposes, to visit, exchange news and gossip, celebrate marital unions. Then it was back to the bush for months of relatively lonely hunting, trapping, and fishing.

Such a life-style did not promote a tribal organization, complete with chiefs and councillors. Indeed, it was often the Hudson's Bay Company's officers who appointed (and dismissed) the chiefs, those to whom it was prepared to render salutes and other honors before trading sessions. These nominated chiefs were those who were the most astute and successful trappers and hunters, and those who had the most influence (but no authority) over their fellow-tribesmen, i.e., those who shared the same mother tongue.

Another significant difference between plain and forest natives was that the latter contained a much larger proportion of individuals of mixed Indian and white descent. For more than a century, in the fur country, white traders had taken native women as (country) wives, their progeny being Métis or half-breeds. It is to be remembered that the latter term, although now considered derogatory, was quite respectable until about 1940. The Great Plains, however, not being productive of fur, produced few individuals of mixed white and Indian descent. Another reason was that their denizens were rather hostile, even belligerent towards white intruders.

Although from time immemorial the northern peoples had lived and died with a minimum of white governmental control, or none at all, times were changing. White homesteaders had begun to seep into the Peace River country, the continent's last agricultural frontier. At twenty-four-mile intervals, surveyors were laying down township base lines. Prospectors were searching for precious and base metals, especially in the Great Slave Lake area; others were already speculating over the possibilities of natural gas and oil development and exploitation of the Athabasca tar sands. More independent traders, out for a fast buck, were invading the boreal forest.

Then, in 1896, gold was discovered in the Yukon. By 1898, thousands of impractical dreamers were on their way to 'the creeks;' hundreds by the all-Canadian route which began in Edmonton, then divided in two there or at Athabasca Landing (now Athabasca). One branch, basically overland, proceeded in a north-westerly direction through northern British Columbia to the instant cities of Whitehorse and Dawson. The other branch was down the Athabasca, Great Slave, and Mackenzie Rivers, then across or through the Richardson mountains and so to the chimerical Eldorado, the glittering Bonanza. J. G. MacGregor estimates that some fifteen hundred Klondikers passed through Edmonton.

Of the many who started along the water route, a few were drowned at Grand Rapids and a few more died from various causes down stream. The vast majority turned back as the difficulties of the way or disagreements in the parties made their positions untenable, and the remainder, a very few indeed, got through.[3]

Of those who set out overland, perhps a dozen in all reached the diggings. A few of the rest died enroute, and the remainder turned back. Few got past Fort St. John.[4]

For the Indians, these romantic wayfarers were little short of a disaster. They killed the game which the natives regarded as peculiarly their own, or frightened the animals into inaccessible valleys of mountain retreats. They shot the Indians' dogs — probably thought they were wolves — stole their few horses, robbed and destroyed their traps, muddied their streams, broke their promises, reneged on their bargains, debauched their women, insulted the men, and treated the whole race with contempt. And the Indians had to endure the invasion of these human locusts not once but twice, both going and returning.

Obviously to keep the wayfarers and the indigenes from each others' throats — and to permit peaceful exploitation of the area's agricultural and other resources — a new treaty was necessary. As early as Janurary, 1898, it was being so recommended by Amedée E. Forget, Indian Commissioner, Laird's former secretary and Territorial council clerk. When his recommendation was accepted, normally it would have been Forget's function to implement it. But that same year he was appointed lieutenant-governor of the North-West Territories — the last, as it was to prove — and Laurier had to find a new Indian Commissioner. With the need for another Indian treaty, who better than the man who had been negotiator for No. 4 and 7, and Minister of the Interior (including Indian Affairs) when No. 5 and 6 were signed? Apparently Laird's appointment was more than a political reward for services rendered to the Liberal party (and, of course, to the country).

But the Indians were not the only ones who had to be placated. Because of their relatively large number — and perhaps because of their capacity for making trouble, as 1885 had indicated — the Métis also had to be considered.

"A treaty cannot be successfully negotiated with the Indians unless the Half-breed claims are also considered." This declaration by Indian Commissioner Forget could not be ignored by Ottawa officials preparing the treaty. It would have been convenient to consider all Métis as white people, who had no rights to special consideration. But such was not the reality.[5]

In the past, many Métis had been permitted to join Treaties 1 to 6. What offer was to be made to the Métis of the Athabasca-Mackenzie District? Of prime importance was that "Their acquiesence in the relinquishment of the aboriginal title should be secured. Finally, it was considered more conducive to their welfare and more in the public interest to take them into treaty than to give them scrip. Métis would be allowed to take treaty, if they so desired, on the judgment of the Commissioners, who would determine which Métis would be dealt with as Indians. Those who were unwilling or not allowed would receive a scrip to either $240 or 240 acres of land.[6]

Accordingly, Ottawa decided to appoint two bodies, the Treaty Commission to deal with the Indians, and the Half-Breed Commission to negotiate with the Métis. The two would, at least initially, operate as a single party, the latter conducting its business immediately following the former's negotiations with the Indians.

Appointment of personnel for the two commissions must have been a major operation in itself as, according to Charles Mair, they totalled "some fifty souls,"[7] not including the boatmen. Of these, Mair has identified twenty-seven by name, the others no doubt being servants, packers, teamsters, laborers, and so on. The Treaty Commission was headed by the Hon. David Laird. His fellow-commissioners were J. A. McKenna, secretary to the Superintendent-General of Indian Affairs, and the Hon. James Ross, Minister of Public Affairs for the Territories. Since Laird's governorship, the Territorial Council had been replaced by a Legislative Assembly. Harrison Young, son-in-law of the Rev. John McDougall, and J. W. Martin served as the Commission's secretaries. Other functionaries were Pierre d'Eschambault, interpreter, Henry McKay, camp manager, and H. A. Conroy, accountant. Reluctantly, because of his age, Father Albert Lacombe had accepted an appointment as advisor. Whether he knew or not, his role was to persuade unwilling or suspicious Indians to accept the proposed treaty. A guest of the Commission was Rt. Rev. E. Grouard, Bishop of Ibora, i.e., of Athabasca and Mackenzie, en route to his see at Fort Chipewyan.

The members of the Half-Breed Commission were Major James Walker, ex-NWMP, and J. A. Coté, of the Land Office, Ottawa. Its French and English secretaries were J. F. Prud'homme and Charles Mair respectively. Serving the whole party on behalf of the Hudson's Bay Company and in charge of transportation was H. B. Round, and a Dr. West acted as medical officer.

The Police escort was commanded by Inspector Edward A. (or A. E.) Snyder. One of its members was Corporal Fitzgerald, who was later to die of exposure while on duty in the Arctic, and in whose memory the name of Smith's Landing was changed to Fort Fitzgerald.

It is difficult to estimate how many of the expedition's half-hundred souls Laird had previously known. Probably Albert Lacombe — *everyone* in the Territories knew that peripatetic priest. Probably also Harrison Young, since Laird's relations with the McDougalls were cordial. Certainly James Walker, who had been in charge of the NWMP post at Battleford when that centre became the capital of the Territories. And equally certainly he knew Charles Mair — one may hazard the guess that it was Laird's recommendation that resulted in Mair's appointment to the Half-Breed Commission.

Since the joint expedition was one that promised to be — and was — physically very demanding, the ages of some members of the group are somewhat surprising. Lacombe had been born in 1827, Laird in 1833, Mair in 1838, d'Eschambault about 1840. Pierre, the most active of the boatmen, was over seventy, "yet agile and firm of step as a man of thirty."[8] ". . . he had accompanied Sir John Franklin on his last journey in Rupert's Land, and Dr. John Rae on his eventful expedition to Repulse Bay, in 1853, in search of Franklin."[9]

Having been preceded by his two colleagues, Laird left Winnipeg on 22 May 1899 and reached Strathcona, the end of the steel, two days later. A short journey brought them across the deep, wide valley of the Saskatchewan to the older but now over-shadowed settlement of Edmonton. But the day would come when it would absorb its upstart rival south of the river.

Because it was the Queen's Birthday, Laird's party found some difficulty in securing hotel accommodation, but eventually were successful. Because of non-arrival of supplies from Winnipeg, and rainy weather, not until the afternoon of 29 May was the expedition able to begin the next leg of its odyssey. But at last it set out, thirteen wagons so heavily loaded that the rate of progress was slowed to a walk. Three days later the party reached Athabasca Landing (now Athabasca).

Laird was now about to embark on the circumnavigation of an area larger than many a European country, two hundred fifty miles from north to south, over two hundred from east to west. Beginning at Athabasca and proceding in a clockwise direction, on the south it is bounded by the Athabasca and Lesser Slave Rivers, Lesser Slave Lake, and its tributary, the South Heart River. Near the latter's source the North Heart rises, on the west side of the area and debouches into the Peace River at the town with that same name. In turn, the Mightypeace — pronounced as one word by residents of the area — forms the principal western and northern limits. The north-east corner of this wilderness is marked by the Rivière des Rochers and the western tip of Lake Athabasca. The eastern and south-eastern boundaries are established by the Athabasca River, back to the starting point. The whole perimeter is navigable, except for the two Heart Rivers, although the Vermilion Chutes, east of Fort Vermilion on the Peace, and a whole series of rapids between Athabasca and Fort McMurray do present formidable obstacles to all except small boats, and even with them, portaging is required.

Even today, to most outsiders, this vast tract is an Unknown Empire. yet several thousand people inhabit it, although the population density is only about one per ten square miles. Some fifteen schools, not counting those on the periphery, and most of them embracing several classrooms, serve the area's few white and many native children.

Already behind schedule, the argonauts were further delayed both because some freight had not yet arrived and because of the non-appearance of some expected trackers. The parties' flotilla consisted of two scows and a York boat, but since the first stage of their voyage was to be against the currents of both the Athabasca and the Slave Rivers, the boats would have to be tracked, i.e., pulled up-stream by the boatmen. Without waiting for the missing helpers, on 3 June the expedition set out with only thirteen trackers in all. Using long, cumbersome sweeps, the trackers first rowed to the north side of the river.

> When the opposite shore was reached, the four trackers of each boat leaped into the water, and, splashing up the bank, got into harness at once, and began, with changes to the oars, the unflagging pull which lasted for two weeks.[10]
>
> But to the harness. This is simply an adjustment of leather breast-straps for each man, tied to a very long tracking line, which, in turn, is tied to the bow of the boat. The trackers, once in it, walk off smartly along the bank, the men on board keeping the boats clear of it, and, on a fair path, with good water, make very good time. Indeed, the pull seems to give impetus to the trackers as well as to the boat, so that a loose man has to lope to keep up with them. But on bad paths and bad water the speed is sadly pulled down, and, if rapids occur, sinks to the zero of a few miles a day. The "spells" vary according to these circumstances, but half an hour is the ordinary pull between "pipes," and there being no shifts in our case, the stoppages for rest and tobacco were frequent.[11]

Without an adequate number of men, progress was desperately slow, but finally help came from an unexpected source.

> So far it had been rain and consequent bad tracking which had delayed us; but still we were too weak-handed to make headway without help, and it was at this juncture that the Police contingent stepped manfully into the breach, and volunteered to track one of the boats to the lake. This was no light matter for men unaccustomed to such beastly toil and in such abominable weather, but, having once put their hands to the rope, they were not the men to back down. With unfaltering "go" they

Members of Treaty No. Eight Commission at Pelican Portage, 1899. L-R: Seated - H.B. Round, transportation manager; Hon. David Laird, commissioner; and Harrison Young, secretary. Standing - Pierre d'Eschambault, interpreter; 2 N.W.M.P. constables; Henry McKay, camp manager; and Lafrance, cook. (R.C.M.P. Museum, Regina)

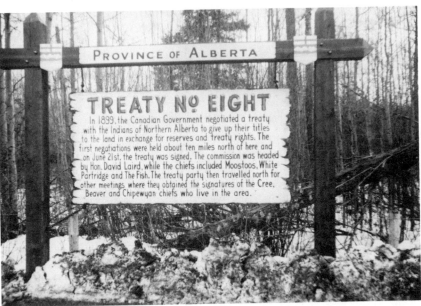

Province of Alberta road sign commemorating Treaty No. 8.

pulled on day after day, landing their boat at its destination at last, having worked in the harness and at the sweeps without relief, from the start almost to the finish.[12]

The old Indian, Peokus, heading the Police line, was a study. His garb was a pair of pants toned down to the color of the grime they daily sank in, a shirt and corduroy vest to match, a faded kerchief tied around his head, an Assumption sash, and a begrimed body inside of all — a short, squarely-built frame, clad with rounded muscles — nothing angular about *him!* — but the nerves within tireless as the stream he pulled against. On the lead, in harness, his long arms swung like pendulums, his whole body leant forward at an acute angle, the gait steady, and the step solid as the tramp of a gorilla. Some coarse black hairs clung here and there to his upper lip; his fine brown eyes were embedded in wrinkles, and his swarthy features, though clumsy, were kindly — a good-humored face, which, at a cheerful word or glance, lit up at once with the grotesque grin of an animated gargoyle.[13]

Nothing indeed, can be imagined more arduous than this tracking up a swift river, against constant head winds in bad weather. Much of it is in the water, wading up "snies," or tortuous channels, plunging into numberless creeks, clambering up slimy banks, creeping under or passing over fallen trees, wading out in the stream to round long spits of sand or boulders, floundering in gumbo slides, tripping, crawling, plunging, and, finally, tottering to the camping-place, sweating like horses, and mud to the eyes — but never grumbling. After a whole day of this slavish work, no sooner was a bath taken, supper stowed, and pipes filled, than laughter began, and jokes and merriment ran round the camp-fires as if such thing as mud and toil had never existed.[14]

If travel up the Athabasca was painfully slow and arduous, the first twenty-five miles of the Lesser Slave, an almost endless succession of rapids, was worse. Still, there were occasional diversions. On a Sunday, after struggling up the Slave for some distance the party encamped on an open grassy point around which the river formed a semi-circle.

It was a lovely and lonely spot, which was soon converted into a scene of eating and laughter, and a drying ground for wet clothes. Towards evening Bishop Grouard and Father Lacombe held a well-attended service, which in this profound wilderness was peculiarly impressive. Listening, one thought of how often the same service, these same chants and canticles, had awakened the sylvan echoes in like solitudes on the St. Lawrence and Mississippi in the old days of exploration and trade . . .[15]

Our camp that night was a memorable one. The day was the fiftieth anniversary of Father Lacombe's ministration as a missionary in the North-West, and all joined in presenting him with a suitable address, handsomely engraved by Mr. Prudhomme on birch bark, and signed by the whole party. A poem, too, composed by Mr. Coté, a gentleman of literary gifts and taste, also written on bark, was read and presented at the same time. Pere Lacombe made a touching impromptu reply, which was greatly appreciated. Many of us were not of the worthy Father's communion, yet there was but one feeling, that of deep respect for the labors of this celebrated missionary, whose life had been a continuous effort to help the unbefriended Indian into the new but inevitable paths of self-support, and to shield him from the rapacity of the cold incoming world now surging around him. After the presentation, over a good cigar, the Father told some inimitable stories of Indian life on the plains in the old days . . .[16]

Eventually the expedition reached Lesser Slave Lake and an end to the drudgery of tracking. Sweeps and oars soon propelled the boats the seventy-five miles to Willow Point, at the head of the lake — total distance from Athabasca Landing, two hundred miles by water.

About three miles from its mouth, the South Heart River flows through a beautiful little body of water known today as Buffalo Bay, then more correctly as Buffalo Lake. On its shore was another small settlement which had developed around the HBC store, whence it was known as Lesser Slave Lake Post. Since 1899, however, many things thereabouts have changed. In the following decade, Willow Point became Grouard, named for the venerable bishop who was hitch-hiking with the Treaty Commission. For a dozen years Grouard was the most populous centre in the Peace River area, partly because it was on the main homesteaders' route, or rather on a principal one, to that Next Year's (i.e., God's) Country. Another reason was that since the Land Office had its location there, settlers were required to come to Grouard to register their homesteads. Soon other institutions appeared and flourished, including hotels, retail stores, saloons, pool halls, barber shops, banks, public and separate schools, and (let it be whispered) brothels.

With the announcement of a railroad to be built to the Peace River country and beyond, Grouard promised to become the Metropolis of the North. Alas, when the Edmonton, Dunvegan and British Columbia (now a branch of the Northern Alberta Railways) was built, instead of being constructed on the high ground on the north side of Slave Lake, it followed the flood-prone south shore. By ten miles it missed Grouard, which almost instantly became a ghost town. Buildings were demolished, abandoned, or moved bodily to Enilda or High Prairie. Both school districts were dissolved. Today, not a single edifice of that once-flourishing centre remains; not even a cellar excavation can be identified with any degree of certainty.

As will be seen, Grouard came to have an enduring significance to the Laird family.

Lesser Slave Lake Post has also disappeared from the map. However, another settlement replaced it on the shore of Buffalo Lake (Bay). This was called Grouard Mission, and is the correct (but unused) name of the settlement known today as Grouard. It became the see of the Vicariate of Grouard, a vicariate, unlike a diocese, being a bishopric which depends on outside support to maintain its existence. In short, it is a mission field. Bishop Grouard himself, and three other bishops are buried in the clergy's cemetery there. In time, a school, a convent, and an orphanage were erected there, as well as accommodation for the bishop and other members of the Oblate order. Most of these structures are long gone, but the parish church still stands, looking much too grand for such a tiny community. Well it might, for it was once a cathedral.

In its latest metamorphosis, the Grouard of today has become an educational centre, largely but not wholly for Indian and Métis children. The wheel has come full circle; the elementary-junior high school is racially integrated. So is the junior college which occupies the facilities which were once those of a vocational-academic high school. And numerous modern houses (staff residences) over-shadow the natives' unserviced log cabins.

Would David Laird have been surprised, could he have foreseen the changes that have occurred at the western tip of Lesser Slave Lake? Probably he never gave them a thought as he made arrangements to talk to the Indians about another treaty. The first decision he had to make was the location for the negotiations. Was it to be Lesser Slave Lake Post or Willow Point? Each hamlet strove for the honor, as might be expected; their rivalry was intense. In a judgment worthy of Solomon, Laird decided that the treaty marquee would be pitched exactly half way between the two centres. The other tents of the two Commissions were located in the same place.

On 20 June, four weeks after Laird had left Winnipeg and twelve days behind the originally-announced schedule, treaty negotiations began. Everyone in the country for miles around, white and Metis as well as Indian, had gathered to witness the historic occasion. It had been over twenty years since there had been such an event. Probably not one of those present, Laird and Walker excepted, had ever been present during the negotiation of an Indian treaty and the activities associated therewith.

Before the start of the formal part of the proceedings, the visitors entertained the local clergy, Anglican and Roman Catholic, at dinner — not lunch in those bucolic days — before the beginning of the serious business of the day. At 2 p.m., after numerous handshakes, the Treaty Commissioners seated themselves along the open front of the marquee. The Indians were seated on the ground before them, and a bit to the rear were the half-breeds. The whites ranged themselves along the perimeter.

The crowd of Indians ranged before the marquee had lost all semblance of wildness of the true type. Wild men they were, in a sense, living as they did in the forest and on their great waters. But it was plain that these people had achieved, without any treaty at all, a stage of civilization distinctly in advance of many of our treaty Indians to the south after twenty-five years of education. Instead of paint and feathers, the scalp-lock, the breech-cloth, and the buffalo-robe, there presented itself a body of respectable-looking men, as well dressed and evidently quite as independent in their feelings as any like number of average pioneers in the East.[17]

Instead of fiery oratory and pipes of peace — the stone calumets of old — the vigorous arguments, the outbursts of passion, and close calls from threatened violence, here was a gathering of commonplace men smoking briar-roots, with treaty tobacco instead of "weed," and those chiefs replied to Mr. Laird's explanations and offers in a few brief and sensible statements, varied by vigorous appeals to common sense and judgement, rather than the passions, of their people.[18]

After the customary distribution of tobacco, Laird presented his proposals, addressed to band members as well as to their chosen representatives, who were Keenooshayoo (The Fish), their chief, and his brother and headman Moostoos (The Bull, or Buffalo, or perhaps The Buffalo Bull). Mair has given an abridged transcript of Laird's talk and the discussion which followed

Red Brothers! we have come here today, sent by the Great Mother to treat with you, and this is the paper she has given to us, to show we have authority to treat with you. The other Commissioners, who are associated with me, and who are sitting here, are Mr. McKenna and Mr. Ross and the Rev. Father Lacombe, who is with us to act as counsellor and adviser. I have to say, on behalf of the Queen and the Government of Canada, that we have come to make you an offer. We have made treaties in former years with all the Indians of the prairies, and from there to Lake Superior. As white people are coming to your country, we have thought it well to tell you what is required of you. The Queen wants all the whites, half-breeds and Indians to be at peace with one another, and to shake hands when they meet. The Queen's laws must be obeyed all over the country, both by the whites and the Indians. It is not alone that we wish to prevent Indians from molesting the whites, it is also to prevent the whites from molesting or doing harm to the Indians. The Queen's soldiers are just as much for the protection of the Indians as for the white man. The Commissioners made an appointment to meet you at a certain time, but on account of bad weather on the river and lake, we are late, which we are sorry for, but are glad to meet so many of you here today.

We understand that stories have been told you, that if you made a treaty with us you would become servants and slaves; but we wish you to understand that such is not the case, but that you will be just as free after signing a treaty as you are now. The treaty is a free offer; take it or not, just as you please. If you refuse it there is no harm done; we will not be bad friends on that account. One thing Indians must understand, that if they do not make a treaty they must obey the laws of the land — that will be just the same whether you made a treaty or not; the laws must be obeyed. The Queen's Government wishes to give the Indians here the same terms as it has given all the Indians all over the country, from the prairies to Lake Superior. Indians in other places, who took treaty years ago, are now better off than they were before. They grow grain and raise cattle like the white people. The children have learned to read and white.

Now, I will give you an outline of the terms we offer you. If you agree to take treaty, every one this year gets a present of $12.00. A family of five, man, wife, and three children, will thus get $60.00; a family of eight, $96.00, and after this year, and for every year afterwards, $5.00 for each person forever. To such chiefs as you may select, and that the Government approves of, we will give $25.00 each year, and the counsellors $15.00 each. The chiefs also get a silver medal and a flag, such as you see now at our tent, right now as soon as the treaty is signed. Next year, as soon as we know how many chiefs there are, and every three years thereafter, each chief will get a suit of clothes, and every counsellor a suit, only not quite so good as that of the chief. Then, as the white men are coming in and settling in the country, and as the Queen wishes the Indians to have lands of their own, we will give one square mile, or 640 acres, to each family of five; but there will be no compulsion to force Indians to go into a reserve. He who does not wish to go into a band can get 160 acres of land for himself, and the same for each member of his family. The reserves are holdings you can select when you please, subject to the approval of the Government, for you might select lands which might interfere with the rights or lands of settlers. The Government must be sure that the land which you select is in the right place. Then, again, as some of you may want to sow grain or potatoes, the Government will give you ploughs or harrows, hoes, etc, to enable you to do so, and every spring will furnish you with provisions to enable you to work and put in your crop. Again, if you do not wish to grow grain, but want to raise cattle, the Government will give you bulls and cows, so that you may raise stock. If you do not wish to grow grain or raise cattle, the Government will furnish you with ammunition for your hunt, and with twine to catch fish. The Government will also provide schools to teach your children to read and white, and do other things like white men and their children. Schools will be established where there is a sufficient number of children. The Government will give the chiefs axes and tools to make houses to live in and be comfortable. The Indians have been told that if they make a treaty they will not be allowed to hunt and fish as they do now. That is not true. Indians who take treaty will be just as free to hunt and fish all over as they now are.

In return for this the Government expects that Indians will not interfere with or molest any miner, traveller or settler. We expect you to be good friends with everyone, and shake hands with all you meet. If any whites molest you in any way, shoot your dogs or horses, or do you any harm, you have only to report the matter to the police, and they will see that justice is done to you. There may be some things we have not mentioned, but these can be mentioned later on. Commissioners Walker and Coté are here for the half-breeds, who later on, if treaty is made with you, will take down the names of half-breeds and their children, and find out if they are entitled to scrip. The reason the Government does this is because the half-breeds have Indian blood in their veins, and have claims on that account. The Government does not make treaty with them, as they live as white people do, so it gives them scrip to settle their claims at once and forever. Half-breeds living like Indians have the chance to take treaty instead, if they wish to do so. They have their choice, but only after the treaty is signed. If there is no treaty made, scrip cannot be given. After the treaty is signed, the Commissioner will take up half-breed claims. The first thing they will do is to give half-breed settlers living on land 160 acres, if there is room to do so; but if several are settled close together, the land will be divided as fairly as possible. All, whether settled or not, will be given scrip for land to the value of $240.00, that is, all born up to the date of signing the treaty. They can sell that scrip, that is, you can do so. They can take, if they like, instead of this scrip for 240 acres, lands where they like. After they have located their land, and got their title, they can live on it, or sell part, or the whole of it, as they please, but cannot sell the scrip. They must locate their land, and get their title before selling.

These are the principal points in the offer we have to make to you. The Queen owns the country, but is willing to acknowledge the Indians' claims, and offers them terms as an offset to all of them. We shall be glad to answer any questions, and make clear any points not understood. We shall meet you again tomorrow, after you have considered our offer, say about two o'clock, or later if you wish. We have other Indians to meet at other places, but we do not wish to hurry you. After this meeting you can go to the Hudson's Bay fort, where our provisions are stored, and rations will be issued to you of flour, bacon, tea and tobacco, so that you can have a good meal and a good time. This is a free gift, given with goodwill, and given to you whether you make a treaty or not. It is a present the Queen is glad to make to you. I am now done, and shall be glad to hear what anyone has to say.

KEENOOSHAYO (The Fish): You say we are brothers. I cannot understand how we are so. I live differently from you. I can only understand that Indians will benefit in a very small degree from your offer. You have told us you come in the Queen's name. We surely have also a right to say a little as far as that goes. I do not understand what you say about every third year.

MR. McKENNA: The third year was only mentioned in connection with clothing.

KEENOOSHAYO: Do you not allow the Indians to make their own conditions, so that they may benefit as much as possible? Why I say this is that we today make arrangements that are to last as long as the sun shines and the water runs. Up to the present I have earned my own living and worked in my own way for the Queen. It is good. The Indian loves his way of living and his free life. When I understand you thoroughly I will know better what I shall do. up to the present I have never seen the time when I could not work for the Queen, and also make my own living. I will consider carefully what you have said.

MOOSTOOS (The Bull): Often before now I have said I would carefully consider what you might say. You have called us brothers. Truly I am the younger, you the elder brother. Being the younger, if the younger ask the elder for something, he will grant his request the same as our mother the Queen. I am glad to hear what you have to say. Our country is getting broken up. I see the white man coming in, and I want to be friends. I see what he does, but it is best that we should be friends. I will not speak any more. There are many people here who may wish to speak.

WAHPEEHAYO (White Partridge): I stand behind this man's back (pointing to Keenooshayo). I want to tell the Commissioners there are two ways, the long and the short. I want to take the way that will last the longest.

NEESNETASIS (The Twin): I follow those two brothers Moostoos and Keenooshayo. When I understand better, I shall be able to say more.

MR. LAIRD: We shall be glad to hear from some of the Sturgeon Lake people.

THE CAPTAIN (an old man): I accept your offer. I am old and miserable now. I have not my family with me here, but I accept your offer.

MR. LAIRD: You will get the money for all your children under age, and not married, just the same as if they were here.

THE CAPTAIN: I am old now. It is indirectly through the Queen that we have lived. She has supplied in a manner the sale shops through which we have lived. Others may think I am foolish for speaking as I do now. Let them think as they like. I accept. When I was young I was an able man and made my living independently. But now I am old and feeble and not able to do much.

MR. ROSS: I will answer a few questions that have been put. Keenooshayo has said that he cannot see how it will benefit you to take treaty. As all the rights you now have will not be interfered with, therefore anything you get in addition must be a clear gain. The white man is bound to come in and open up the country, and we come before him to explain the relations that must exist between you, and thus prevent any trouble. You say you have heard what the Commissioners have said, and how you wish to live. We believe that men who have lived without help heretofore can do it better when the country is opened up. Any fur they catch is worth more. That comes about from competition. You will notice that it takes more boats to bring in goods to buy your furs than it did formerly. We think that as the rivers and lakes of this country will be principal highways, good boatmen, like yourselves, cannot fail to make a good living, and profit from the increase in traffic. We are much pleased that you have some cattle. It will be the duty of the Commissioners to recommend the Government, through the Superintendent-General of Indian Affairs, to give you cattle of a better breed. You say that you consider that you have a right to say something about the terms we offer you. We offer you certain terms, but you are not forced to take them. You ask if Indians are not allowed to make a bargain. You must understand there are always two to a bargain. We are glad you understand the treaty is forever. If the Indians do as they are asked we shall certainly keep all our promises. We are glad to know that you have got on without any one's help, but you must know times are hard, and furs scarcer than they used to be. Indians are fond of a free life, and we do not wish to interfere with it. When reserves are offered you there is no intention to make you live on them if you do not want to, but, in years to come, you may change your minds, and want these lands to live on. The half-breeds of Athabasca are being more liberally dealt with than in any other part of Canada. We hope you will discuss our offer and arrive at a decision as soon as possible. Others are now waiting for our arrival, and you, by deciding quickly, will assist us to get to them.

KEENOOSHAYO: Have you all heard? Do you wish to accept? All who wish to accept, stand up!

WENDIGO: I have heard, and accept with a glad heart all I have heard.

KEENOOSHAYO: Are the terms good forever? As long as the sun shines on us? Because there are orphans we must consider, so that there will be nothing to be thrown up to us by our people afterwards. We want a written treaty, one copy to be given to us, so that we shall know what we sign for. Are you willing to give means to instruct children as long as the sun shines and water runs, so that our children will grow up ever increasing in knowledge?

MR. LAIRD: The Government will choose teachers according to the religion of the band. If the band are pagans the Government will appoint teachers who, if not acceptable, will be replaced by others. About treaties lasting forever, I will just say that some Indians have got to live so like the whites that they would have sold their land and divided the money. But this only happens when the Indians ask for it. Treaties last forever, as signed, unless the Indians wish to make a change. I understand you all agree to the terms of the Treaty. Am I right? If so, I will have the Treaty drawn up, and to-morrow we will sign it. Speak, all those who do not agree!

MOOSTOOS: I agree.

KEENOOSHAYO: My children, all who agree, stand up.

The Reverend Father Lacombe then addressed the Indians in substance, as follows: He reminded them that he was an old friend, and came amongst them seven years ago, and, now being old, he came again to fulfil another duty, and to assist the Commission to make a treaty. "Knowing you as I do, your manners, your customs and language, I have been officially attached to the Commission as adviser. Today is a great day for you, a day of long remembrance, and your children hereafter will learn from your lips the events of to-day. I consented to come because I thought it was a good thing for you to take the Treaty. Were it not in your interest I would not take part in it. I have been long familiar with the Government's methods of making treaties with the Saulteaux of Manitoba, the Crees of Saskatchewan, and the Blackfeet, Bloods and Piegans of the Plains, and advised these tribes to accept the offers of the Government. Therefore, to-day, I urge you to accept the words of the Big Chief who comes here in the name of the Queen. I have known him for many years, and, I can assure you, he is just and sincere in all his statements, besides being vested with authority to deal with you. Your forest and river life will not be changed by the Treaty, and you will have your annuities, as well, year by year, as long as the sun shines and the earth remains. Therefore I finish by saying, Accept!"[19]

After all this discussion, and a few other remarks, the session adjourned until 3 p.m. the following day. There was then some dissension, according to Mair, but this was smoothed over, and the chief and five headmen signed the treaty.

A witness to the negotiations, but not to the signatures, at both Lesser Slave Lake and Peace River Crossing was the legendary James K. (Peace River Jim) Cornwall, steamboat man, farmer, railroad developer, promoter, legislator, soldier. In an affidavit made many years later, he indicated that negotiations were not without problems:

1. I was present when Treaty 8 was made at Lesser Slave Lake and Peace River Crossing.

2. The treaty, as presented by the Commissioners to the Indians for their approval and signatures, was apparently prepared elsewhere, as it did not contain many things that they held to be of vital importance to their future existence as hunters and trappers and fishermen, free from the competition of white man. They refused to sign the treaty as read to them by the Chief Commissioner.

3. Long discussions took place between the Commissioners and the Indian Chiefs and headmen, with many prominent men of the various bands taking part. The discussions went on for days, the Commissioners had unfavorably impressed the Indians, due to lack of knowledge of the bush Indians' mode of life, by quoting Indian conditions on the Prairie.

Chief Moostoos (the Buffalo) disposed of the argument by telling the Chief Commissioner that "a Plains Indian turned loose in the bush would get lost and starve to death."

4. As the Commissioner's instructions from Ottawa required the Treaty to be signed first at Lesser Slave Lake before proceeding North, and

as the white population living in the Indian Territory had been requested by the Government prior to the coming of the Commission, to be prepared to deal with them as such, the whites had done everything in their power to assist the Commissioners, by using every honorable influence that was possible.

5. The Commissioners finally decided, after going into the whole matter, that what the Indians suggested was only fair and right but that they had no authority to write it into the Treaty. They felt sure the Government on behalf of the Crown and the Great White Mother would include their request and they made the following promises to the Indians: —

   a- Nothing would be allowed to interfere with their way of making a living, as they were accustomed to and as their forefather had done.

   b- The old and destitute would always be taken care of, their future existence would be carefully studied and provided for, and every effort would be made to improve their living conditions.

   c- They were guaranteed protection in their way of living as hunters and trappers, from white competition; they would not be prevented from hunting and fishing as they had always done, so as to enable them to earn their living and maintain their existence.

6. Much stress was laid on one point by the Indians, as follows: They would not sign under any circumstances, unless their right to hunt, trap and fish was guaranteed and it must be understood that these rights they would never surrender.

7. was only after the Royal Commission had recognized that the demands of the Indians were legitimate, and had solemnly promised that such demands would be granted by the Crown, also, after the Hudson's Bay Company Officials and Free Traders, and the Missionaries, with their Bishops, who had the full confidence of the Indians, had given their word that they could rely fully on the promises made in the name of QUEEN VICTORIA, that the Indians accepted and signed the Treaty, which was to last as long as the grass grew, the river ran, and the sun shone — to an Indian this means FOREVER.[20]

Most of the witnesses to the signatures of the Commissioners and the Indians were people associated with the Treaty or Half-Breed Commission. However, the names of one witness has appeared in an earlier chapter, both in connection with the establishment of the Edmonton Public School District. He was M. McCauley.

Because the two commissions were now running nearly two weeks behind schedule, and several points had yet to be visited, it was decided that the Treaty Commission would divide into two parties. Accordingly, on 22 June Ross and McKenna, with the two members of the Half-Breed Commission, set out for (Fort) Dunvegan and Fort St. John. A few days later, Laird left for Peace River Crossing, now Peace River. In his circum-navigation of the Unknown Empire, this was the only overland stretch.

References

1. Elizabeth Laird, "Hon. David Laird, Indian Commissioner at Winnipeg 1898-1909," (unpublished typescript), p. 1.

2. David Laird to D. McLean, 13 March 1899 (Information obtained from Public Archives of Canada, in letter from Elizabeth Laird to John W. Chalmers, 11 May 1979).

3. J. G. MacGregor, *Edmonton A History,* pp. 124-125.

4. *Ibid.,* p. 125.

5. Rene Fumoleau, *As Long as this Land Shall Last,* p. 57.

6. *Ibid.,* p. 58.

7. Charles Mair, *Through the Mackenzie Basin,* p. 333.

8. *Ibid.,* p. 335.

9. *Ibid.,* p. 336.

10. *Ibid.,* p. 334.

11. *Ibid.,* p. 335.

12. *Ibid.,* p. 335.

13. *Ibid.,* p. 341.

14. *Ibid.,* pp. 340-341.

15. *Ibid.,* pp. 346-347.

16. *Ibid.,* p. 349.

17. *Ibid.,* p. 356.

18. *Ibid.,* p. 357.

19. *Ibid.,* pp. 356-366.

20. James K. Cornwall, quoted by Fumoleau, *op. cit.,* pp. 74-75.

17

Circumnavigating the Unknown Empire

Ross, McKenna, and members of the Half-Breed Commission never reached Fort St. John, as they learned, twenty-five miles short of their goal, that the Indians there had dispersed in four different directions and would not be returning that season. The group therefore retraced their steps to Dunvegan, where they obtained the adhesions of some Beaver Indians.

Laird, meanwhile, had travelled overland directly to Peace River Crossing, now the Town of Peace River. As he came in sight of that little centre, there unfolded before him what residents of the area consider the most beautiful view in the Land of Twelve-Foot Davis. Here the well-defined valley of the Peace is eight to nine hundred feet in depth, four to five times as deep as that of the Saskatchewan at Edmonton, and perhaps a mile in width. At the top of the valley is the grave of the Yankee gold-miner and trader who gave his name to the whole Peace River Country. Here his friend, Peace River Jim, to fulfil a promise, brought his body, which had originally been interred at Lesser Slave Lake. Looking south, Laird could see a splendid vista which embraced the confluence of the Smoky and the Peace, each adorned with entrancing, tree-covered islands. On a sunny fall day the scene glows with golden autumn colors of poplar and birch, contrasted by the sombre emerald green of spruce trees and accented here and there with the dark red of willows and a few shrubs. However, at the time of Laird's visit, the whole valley would be clothed with summer green.

On 1 July, at the Crossing, the Hon. David obtained agreement of some Crees to the treaty, Father Lacombe acting as one of the two interpreters. He also met a Beaver chief who did not sign; he explained that his people were at Dunvegan.

The next leg of Laird's journey was down the Peace where imperceptibly the high walls of the valley fell back and diminished, until it seems that the river is flowing only a few feet below a vast and level plain. Since steamboats did not run on that stream before 1903, it is probable that his conveyance was a York boat or possibly a scow. From the Crossing all the way around to Fort McMurray, Laird would voyage through a territory whose recorded history antedates that of almost every other part of the North-West. Eight miles up-stream from Peace River Crossing had stood Fort Fork, from which Alexander Mackenzie had departed on his historic sortie to the Pacific in 1793. Down-stream, before reaching the mouth of the Peace, Laird would pass the sites of eight fur posts (seven in existence before 1810) that had been built and abandoned before the foundations had been laid for either Upper or Lower Fort Garry, and at least three-quarters of a century before the intrepid Mounties had erected their Fort Macleod on an island in the Old Man (or Oldman) River.

By 8 July, having descended this long, rapid-free stretch of the Mightypeace — conceived as one word by present-day inhabitants — Laird found himself at Fort Vermilion, a quiet hamlet still in existence. Mair, who followed him by a few days, has recorded a good deal of information about this (nominal) Fort as it was in 1899:

> The place proved to be a rather extensive settlement, with yellow wheat-fields and much cattle, for it is fine hay country.[1] The population interested in farming was estimated at about three hundred souls, thus forming the nucleus of a very promising settlement. . .[2] From Mr. Erastus Lawrence. . . we got definite information regarding the region and its prospects for agriculture. We spent Sunday at his comfortable home, and examined his farm carefully. In front of his house was a field of wheat, 110 acres in extent, as fine a field as we had ever seen anywhere, and of this they had not had a failure, he said, during all their farming experience, the return never falling below fourteen bushels to the acre, in the worst of years, twenty-five being about the average yield. They sowed late in April, but reaped generally about the 15th of August. They had never, he said, been seriously injured by frost since 1884, and in fact no frost had occurred to injure wheat since 1887. There was abundance of hay, and 10,000 head of stock, he believed, could be raised at that very point. Many hogs were raised, with great profit, bacon and pork being, of course, high priced. . . At that time there were about 500 head of cattle, 250 horses, and 200 pigs in the settlement.[4]

After successfully concluding treaty negotiations with some Cree and Beaver Indians, Laird proceeded down the Peace, running or portaging around the Vermilion Chutes, the only obstruction to navigation in over six hundred miles. "The rapids are about four hundred yards in length, and extend across the river, which is here of immense width."[5] "These falls cut somewhat diagonally across the river, the vortex being at the right bank, and close in-shore, concentred by a limestone shelf extending to the bank, flanked on the left, and at an acute angle, by a deeply-indented reef of rock."[6] Laird, accompanied by Bishop Grouard, Father Lacombe, and Brother Jean Marie le Creff, arrived at Fort Chipewyan the evening of 15

July, to be greeted by a general firing of guns along about a mile of the shore.

Just as Cumberland House is Saskatchewan's oldest continuously settled community, so is Fort Chipewyan Alberta's. Its first predecessor was Pond's House, variously named, established on the delta of the Athabasca in 1778. Ten years later it was replaced by the first Fort Chipewyan, on the south shore of Lake Athabasca. This was Alexander Mackenzie's base for his famous journey to the Arctic in 1789. At the beginning of the nineteenth century, the Fort was moved to its present location on the north-west corner of the lake. Known as the Emporium of the North, it served as a fur trade base for the whole Mackenzie Basin and for exploring and surveying expeditions by Franklin, Richardson, Dease and Simpson, Turnor, Rae, Back, Lefroy, and others.

Just a few miles south across the lake is the delta of the Athabasca River, a maze of new and old channels, a level, lacy network wholly devoid of any distinguishing features. But on the north side of what was once called the Lake of the Hills, one abruptly finds himself in the Canadian Shield, its ancient granite in many cases wholly devoid of any earth mantle. Even in the folds of the rock, the soil consists simply of sand which eons of wind and water action and temperature changes have manufactured from the enduring rock.

Originally, Chipewyan was a typical north-western fur fort, built of logs with a palisade and bastions. In the 1870's, however, the bastions, no longer necessary if ever they were, had disappeared, and the palisade had shrunk to a simple fence. The Fort itself, perhaps fifty yards from the edge of the lake, consisted of about half a dozen buildings, mostly of one and one-half or two storeys. There was also a watch tower. Eventually it and the fence as well disappeared, but the main buildings remained for over sixty years. Gradually, west, along the lake-front, a number of little homes were built, and the Anglican church and rectory. Still farther west, a mile or so from the Fort, was the Roman Catholic complex: church (Bishop Grouard's cathedral), presbytery house, Holy Angels school, convent. Around the west end of the lake, in the folds of the granite rocks, could be found little cabins, mainly Métis-owned, built wherever the proprietor fancied and the surface was level enough. Behind the settlement and as a backdrop to it rose the dark spruce-clad stone hills which had given the lake its earlier name. such was Fort Chipewyan in 1899.

The Grey Nuns who ran the school, or rather their pupils, held a reception for the distinguished visitors. David Laird must have recalled the comparable performance he had attended a score of years previously at St. Albert.

Probably the most important provision of the earlier treaties was that concerning the establishment of reserves, on which it was hoped the Indians would learn to become farmers or ranchers. The Government and the Treaty Commission recognized that for most of Treaty No. 8 area, these occupations would not be practicable. Moreover, since the Indians lived not in large bands but in small groups, large reserves would not always be appropriate. The treaty therefore provided an alternative, instead of reserves on previous patterns, small pieces of land, still at the rate of six hundred forty acres per family of five, could be allocated to individual families. Thus to this day there are many small reserves in the North. One at Calling Lake, for example, consists of less than a section. According to Fumoleau, the Indians were not really concerned with land ownership; what mattered to them was that their freedom to hunt, trap, and fish as they always had done be preserved. He quotes Pierre Mercredi, interpreter for the Chipewyans, on this point:

> I interpreted the words of Queen Victoria to Alexandre Laviolette, Chief of the Chipewyans and his band. . . I know, because I read the Treaty to them, that there was no clause in it which said they might have to obey regulations about hunting. They left us no copy of the Treaty we signed, saying that they would have it printed and send a copy to us. When the copy came back, that second clause (that they shall promise to obey whatever regulations the Dominion Government shall set) was in it. It was not there before. I never read it to the Chipewyans or explained it to them. I have no doubt that the new regulation breaks the old treaty. It makes me feel bad altogether because it makes lies of the words I spoke then for Queen Victoria.
>
> Just after the treaty was signed, and the new copy came here, the Indian Agent said that the Chipewyan people could not kill beaver because of a new law. The old Chief came to see me and told me that I had spoken the words for Queen Victoria and they were lies. He said that if she had come and said those words herself, then, and broken them, she would have been an awful liar.[7]

Fumoleau adds that this was but the beginning of a gradual but continuous erosion of Treaty No. 8 promises.[8]

Laird's next port of call was Fond du Lac, one hundred eighty-five miles east of Fort Chipewyan. Despite its name, it is not at the end of Lake Athabasca, which extends another seventy-five miles farther in a narrow arm. In company with Father Gabriel Breynat, Fond du Lac's resident missionary, Laird left Fort Chipewyan on 18 July. As the treaty negotiations did not take place until 25 and 27 of July, he must have spent several days en route.

At first, things did not proceed at all smoothly. As soon as the discussions started, the Chipewyan Chief Moberly (also known as Maurice Piche) almost got into a fight with the interpreter Louis Robillard. Only the intervention of the Police prevented them from coming to blows. The chief jumped into his canoe and paddled off. With tears in his eyes, Laird sought out the priest. "Complete failure!" he said. "We must fold down our tents, pack our baggage and leave."[9] "Evidently there is nothing we can do."[10]

However, Father Breynat offered his services as negotiator, first persuading two councillors, Laurent Dzieddin and Toussaint, to accept the agreement. Eventually he was able to sooth the injured pride of the chief, who had seen the treaty as a threat to his status with his band. In the end, however, he too added his mark to the treaty, the last one at Fond du Lac.

Laird had thus acted as treaty negotiator at Slave Lake, Peace River Crossing, Fort Vermilion, and Fond du Lac. The other two commissioners, singly or together, secured adhesions at Fort Dunvegan, Fort Chipewyan, Smith's Landing, and Wabiscow. In 1900, a few additional bands came into Treaty No. 8, the area of which covers approximately the northern half of Alberta, a corner of Saskatchewan, British Columbia east of the Rockies, and that part of today's North-West Territories south of Great Slave Lake.

Leaving Fond du Lac, Laird returned to Fort Chipewyan in time to board the steamer *Grahame* — its name indicates its HBC ownership. The *Grahame* was a typical river stern-wheeler, built in 1883, length 135 feet, beam twenty-four, cargo capacity ninety tons. It had arrived from Smith's Landing on 9 August, carrying some one hundred twenty disappointed and frustrated Klondikers, one a woman armed with a revolver and a bowie-knife. The craft departed Fort Chipewyan on 11 August with various members of the two Commissions aboard. In his entire circumnavigation of the Unknown Empire, Laird would have found this stretch most comfortable and pleasant. Mair has described the three-day voyage to Fort McMurray:

> When the weather calmed we steamed across to the entrance of one of the various channels connecting the Athabasca River with the lake, and soon found ourselves skirting the most extensive marshes and feeding grounds for game in all Canada; a delta renowned throughout the North for its abundance of waterfowl, far surpassing the St. Clair flats, or any other region in the East.
>
> Next morning, upon rounding a point, three full-grown moose were seen ahead, swimming across the river. An exciting, and even hazardous, scene ensued on board, the whole Klondike crowd firing, almost at random, hundreds of shots without effect. Two of the noble brutes kept on, and reached the shore, disappearing in the woods; but the third, a three-year-old bull moose, foolishly turned, and lost its life in consequence. It was hauled on deck, bled and flayed, and was a welcome addition to the steamer's table.
>
> That night a concert was improvised on deck, in which the music-hall

element came to the front.[11]

On the following day we passed Little Red River, and the next morning reached the fort. . .[12]

Fort McMurray consisted of a tumble-down cabin and trading-store on the top of a high and steep bank, which had yet been flooded at times, the people seeking shelter on an immense hill which overlooked it. Above an island close by is the discharge of the Clearwater River, the old canoe route by which supplies for the district used to come. . .[13]

Fort McMurray was the end of the line as far as the *Grahame* was concerned. From here to Athabasca Landing the river consisted of an almost continuous series of rapids, so it was back to the little boats and the agile, sure-footed trackers.

Both before and after reaching Fort McMurray, Laird would have opportunities to observe the mysterious oil or tar sands which have intrigued and frustrated geologists and engineers for so many years. Peter Pond must have noted them in 1778, although no Pond journals for this period seem to have survived. A description of them appears in Franklin's record of his first journey to the Arctic.[14]

If ascending the Athabasca from the Landing was difficult, return to it was far worse. Mair has listed ten rapids. In order from north to south, i.e., travelling upstream, they were the Mountain, Cascades, Crooked, Long, Middle, Boiler, Brulé (which he also called the Burnt), Grand, Joli Feu, and Pelican. As a rule, these required not mere tracking of the fully or half-loaded boats but portaging of the complete cargo if not the craft itself.

Between the Brulé and Grand Rapids, just opposite Point Brulé, a swift creek, the Little Buffalo, flows into the Athabasca. Here Laird would observe a phenomenon as interesting as the oil sands, and much more spectacular. "The gas escapes from a hole in the ground near the water's edge in a pillar of flame about thirty inches high, and which has been burning from time out of mind. It also bubbles, or, rather, foams up, for several yards in the river, rising at low water even as far out as mid-stream."[15]

Small boats could work their way up through the rapids. Stern-wheelers could travel down-stream through this white water — if they were lucky. Boiler Rapid was so named for a boiler from a steamer of the Honorable Company that had been wrecked there. Once below the rapids, however, steamships operated only between Fort McMurray and Smith's Landing or Fond du Lac. Like the boomerang in the song, to the Landing they never came back.

The Grand Rapids are divided by an island just over a quarter-mile in length, upon which the Hudson's Bay Company had built a man-powered tramway. Freight and even boats could be loaded on its cars and with a minimum of effort pushed the length of the Rapids on the shortest railway in the North-West. The arrangement probably reminded Laird of the much more pretentious railway portage at the mouth of the Saskatchewan.

Above the Pelican Rapids and Portage, the little Pelican River joins the Athabasca on the latter's left marge. Having learned that Ross had been successful in securing adhesion to the treaty by Indians in the interior, the Half-Breed Commission turned up the Pelican en route to Wapiscow (now Wabasca) to distribute scrip to the Métis. Despite the desire of the government for them to acquire and retain possession of their own land, during the entire expedition, of the 1,843 scrip certificates issued, all but forty-three were for instant cash.

Separating from the Half-Breed Commission at Pelican, Laird continued up the Athabasca. He retraced his route from the Landing to Winnipeg, which he reached after an absence of approximately three months. Even then he was not finished with Treaty No. 8; there was still a report to prepare. This the Commissioners managed to have completed and signed by 22 September. Replete with observations on the country and the people, two extracts seem of particular interest:

> There was a marked absence of the old Indian style of oratory. Only amongst the Wood Crees were any formal speeches made, and these were brief. The Beaver Indians are taciturn. The Chipewyans confined themselves to asking questions and making brief arguments. They appeared to be more adept at cross-examination than at speech-making, and the Chief at Fort Chipewyan displayed considerable keenness of intellect and much practical sense in pressing the claims of his band.[16]

> The Indians with whom we treated differ in many respects from the Indians of the organized territories. They indulge in neither paint nor feathers, and never clothe themselves in blankets. Their dress is of the ordinary style and many of them were well clothed. In the summer they live in teepees, but many have log houses in which they live in winter. The Cree language is the chief language of trade, and some of the Beavers and Chipewyans speak it in addition to their own tongues. All the Indians we met were with rare exceptions professing Christians, and showed evidences of the work which missionaries have carried on among them for several years. A few of them have had their children avail themselves of the advantages afforded by boarding schools established at different missions. None of the tribes appear to have any very definite organization. They are held together mainly by the language bond. The chiefs and headmen are simply the most efficient hunters and trappers. They are not law-makers and leaders in the sense that the chiefs and headmen of the plains and of old Canada were. The tribes have no very distinctive characteristics, and as far as we could learn no traditions of any import.[17]

Laird had made an epic circumnavigation of the Unknown Empire, but at no point had he penetrated it. The only Treaty Commissioner to do so was Ross, who negotiated with the Indians at Wapiscow on 14 August.

References

1. Charles Mair, *Through the Mackenzie Basin*, p. 400.
2. *Ibid.*
3. *Ibid.*, pp. 400-401.
4. *Ibid.*, p. 402.
5. *Ibid.*, p. 404.
6. *Ibid.*, p. 405.
7. Rene Fumoleau, *As Long as This Land Shall Last*, p. 79.
8. *Ibid.*
9. *Ibid.*
10. *Ibid.*
11. Mair, *op. cit.*, p. 429.
12. *Ibid.*, p. 430.
13. *Ibid.*
14. John Franklin, *Narrative of a Journey to the Polar Sea, in the Years 1819, 20, 21, and 22*, p. 515.
15. Mair, *op. cit.*, p. 437.
16. Canada, *Treaty No. 8 Made June 21, 1899 and Adhesions, Etc.*, p. 3.
17. *Ibid.*, p. 6.

18

Return
to the Island

Since contact would not be made with all bands in Treaty No. 8 area in 1899, the following year the Superintendent of Indian Affairs, i.e., the Minister in charge of the Branch, the Hon. Clifford Sifton, appointed J. A. Macrae as Treaty Commissioner. His first visit was to Lesser Slave Lake, where he secured the adhesion of the Sturgeon Lake Cree band. Interestingly, one of the signatories was The Captain, who had affixed his mark to the treaty at the same place the year before. Macrae also visited Fort St. John, Fort Vermilion, and Fort Resolution, meeting with the Slaves (Slaveys) of the Upper and Lower Hay River, Beavers of Fort St. John, and Dogribs, Chipewyans, Yellowknives, and Slaves of Great Slave Lake. Since then, no other bands have come under this treaty. In 1899 and 1900 the totals registered under Treaty No. 8 were 2,217 and 1,218 respectively.

David Laird was not responsible for the negotiations in 1900, but as Indian Commissioner for Manitoba and the North-West Territories, thereafter he would be responsible for the welfare of these new signatories. At least, now he knew how many and who they were, if not always where. In Winnipeg he was to find his work relatively stress-free, in contrast to the position of Indian Affairs bureaucrats as the twentieth century drew to a close. For the latter, their work seemed to lurch from crisis to crisis as Indian leaders, usually young, well-educated, and fluent in English, proved adept at exploiting the media to publicize their peoples' grievances. But at the beginning of the century, Indian spokesmen, chiefs and councillors, were usually older men, well educated in their tribes' traditions and cultures (despite Laird's rather harsh judgment of some northern bands), but hopelessly at sea in the white socio- cultural milieu. Fluent in no European language, usually speaking only one or more native tongues, they could read or write neither French nor English. From the white point of view, they were illiterate, although it might be more accurate to describe them as products of a pre-literate culture. Thus none of the original Indian signatories to Treaties No. 4, 6, 7, and 8 was able to sign other than by making his mark. As late as 1950, in the adhesion to Treaty No. 6 signed at Rocky Mountain House, of eighteen Chippewa (Saulteaux) Indians, only one, at that late date, was able to write his own name. The same year, at Witchekan, Saskatchewan, all eight Cree whose names appear on the adhesion made their marks. Thus at the beginning of the twentieth century in no way were the Indians able effectively to bring their concerns to the attention of the government or the public.

They suffered another disability. John Donne to the contrary notwithstanding, each Indian band, in the North, almost each family if not each man was an island, perceiving no common interest one with another, no need to work for common goals, no recognition that in union there is strength. It would be mid-century before truly national organizations of native people were to emerge; another quarter-century before they mastered the white man's communication techniques so they could effectively present their concerns to all the people of Canada and their governments.

Another problem was that there existed between many bands and tribes deep-seated suspicions and hostilities, based on ancient enmities. Traditional foes do not become first friends over-night, and even to this day such antipathies are not unknown. But there was no way they could be expunged, or the different bands work together until they had a common medium of communication. With all their failings as educators — and there were many — this the missionaries provided. In the North-West, of course, it is English.

If today the Indian people are quick to enunciate and defend, by the threat of violence if necessary, what they regard as their rights, at the dawn of the twentieth century the situation was otherwise. Bewildered because of ignorance of Euro-American culture, often giving trust where trust was misplaced, they were a docile people. Indian Affairs officials, therefore, led a relatively tranquil life, not without problems, but problems which were readily solved, or which dissipated with the morning dew. And so as a public officer the Hon. David Laird presented a low profile. If he was awarded no honorary doctorate or knighthood, neither was he subject to libels the like of which the *Prince Albert Times* had heaped on his head in 1887.

When Laird had left Battleford in 1881, the entire Fertile Belt of the North-West had been covered by Indian treaties. But these agreements did not automatically mean that the Indians would immediately be placed on reserves. For one thing, it took some time to secure adhesions from all the Indians in Treaty No. 6 area, the largest of the first seven Great Treaties. Although this one was originally negotiated at or near Forts Pitt and Carlton in 1876, between 9 August 1877 and 11 December 1889, there were no fewer than nine adhesions to it, with Cree and Stoney Indians at Fort Pitt, Edmonton, Blackfoot Crossing, Battleford, Carlton, Fort Walsh, and Montreal Lake.

For the first of these, on 21 August 1877, M. G. Dickieson was the Treaty Commissioner, as Laird was occupied with arrangements for Treaty No. 7. In 1878, as Indian Superintendent, Laird acted as Commissioner for three adhesions; in 1879 that role was filled by newly-appointed Edgar Dewdney. Adhesions for 1882 and 1889 apparently were not signed by a commissioner; only by the Indians and witnesses, including those who explained the treaty to the Indians. In the first case, this was Allan Macdonald, an Indian Agent for Treaty No. 4, and in the second, the Venerable Archdeacon J. A. MacKay.

Incidentally, further adhesions were added to Treaty No. 6 in 1950, 1954, and 1956. Some Indians can be very stubborn.

Even after the treaties and adhesions were signed, it still took considerable time for the Indians to settle down on their reserves. They first had to choose the land they wanted, and in some cases their choices were not acceptable to the government, which had its own plans for the chosen real estate. Perhaps also, once free to roam the whole Prairies, they were reluctant to pin themselves down to the narrow limits of the reserves. Even after they had chosen their tracts, these had to be surveyed, something that could not be done over-night. Thus when Laird left Battleford, the natives were still highly nomandic, as indicated by the frequency with which groups of them visited the Territorial capital, unhampered by fences and other man-made impediments. Some had travelled across the country hundreds of miles from Fort Walsh and Fort Macleod and Blackfoot Crossing for this purpose, to some extent living on the country as they moved over it.

By the time Laird returned to the West (no longer the North-West), the situation had changed very drastically. By and large, with some exceptions the reserves had been delimited, the Indians sequestered thereon — and discouraged from leaving those rural ghettos. Indian agents and farm instructors had been stationed on the reserves, rudimentary (and largely ineffective) health services established, and Roman Catholic, Anglican, and Methodist schools opened, so that for ten months in each year the children lived in such institutions, no longer free to race across the prairies and to learn the skills and traditions of their elders. It wasn't only in Treaty No. 8 area that Indians wore ordinary clothing of the crazywhite man — all one word as far as the aborigines were concerned. For the Blackfoot-speakers, the Sioux, the Plains Cree and others the feathered head-dresses, the buckskin jackets, the women's beautiful white elkskin raiment, the beaded leggings were seldom worn, only on very special occasions. The sacred medicine bundles were hidden away from the eyes of the busy-body missionaries and but rarely opened, with their obligatory songs and ceremonies. The sun dance, with its rites of passage for young men, were discouraged, even outlawed. In the eyes of the Christian clergy, such customs and activities were but reprehensible relics of a pagan past.

The proud peoples of the Great Plains had come wholly under the control of the superordinate or dominant society, and if their native cultures had not been completely obliterated, on the surface it would certainly seem as if they had.

When Laird was Indian Superintendent in the 1870's, although he was distressed by the red tape, so often pointless, connected with his office, most of his work involved first-hand, face-to-face contact with his wards. Indians, like minors, lunatics, aliens, females, and federal judges, were unenfranchised. In the 1900's the Indians were still in the same category, but the job of Commissioner (né Superintendent) had changed. Laird was now a bureaucrat with a bureaucracy: secretary J. A. Lash and Assistant Commissioner A. J. A. McKenna, the same man who had been a commissioner for Treaty No. 8. Instead of dealing with people, to a large extent the Hon. David shuffled papers, relying on the Indian agents to pacify, mollify, and defuse the bands and their chiefs.

Most of Laird's concerns seem to have been, not with Indian affairs, strictly speaking, but with Indian-white relationships. And the majority of these appear to have involved representations — requests — demands — on the part of white entrepreneurs for concessions by the Indians, leading to the exploitation of reserve land for the greater gain, not of the Indians but of the developers. Thus there exists a whole series of communications between the Winnipeg office and the Blackfoot office in Gleichen, District of Alberta (J. A. Markle, Indian Agent) respecting the opening of one or more coal mines on the Blackfoot reserve. Thus in 1900 one J. J. Marshall offered $400 per year for the right to mine four thousand tons, the normal royalty then being apparently ten cents per ton. Since the federal government would generously allow the Indians ten percept of such revenue the band stood to profit to the full extent of forty dollars annually. A proposal that the Blackfoot mine the coal themselves and thus provide extensive employment opportunities nine months a year for numerous adult males seems to have been hung up on the unavailability of working capital. No government money had been appropriated for such a hare-brained venture, but apparently some funds were found for such a purpose and forty Indians were employed. between 10 October 1903 and the following 30 June, about 1,650 tons were mined and $3,541.16 paid in wages.

Relying on political connections in an endeavor to cut red tape, an ambitious or impatient entrepreneur might appeal over the heads of the Indian Agent at Gleichen or the Commissioner in Winnipeg directly to Ottawa for a coal concession or lease. Such a one was Donald H. McDonald in July, 1903. His strategem was self-defeating — counter-productive in modern jargon. It simply resulted in Ottawa writing to Laird and he to Markle for further information and recommendation.

Similarly, in reply to a query from Frank Pedley, Deputy Superintendent-General of Indian Affairs, on 29 July 1903 Laird wrote in part as follows:

> As Mr. Markle, Indian Agent for the Blackfoot Reserve, being now in this city, I have conferred with him upon the matter, and give my views thereon as follows:
>
> I.   The Blackfoot Indians are doubtless opposed to leasing their coal lands, yet if they are offered fair terms, such as can be shown as quite to their advantage, I think their consent to their surrender for lease may possibly be obtained.
>
> II.   The price of 10¢ per ton on all coal mined, offered by D. H. McDonald seems small; but if this amount is the highest received by the Dept. of Interior for leased coal lands, it could be explained to the Indians that they cannot expect more from such than others pay.
>
> III.   Mr. McDonald wants land for a railway spur which would be cut down on Indians getting coal out.
>
> IV.   A great objection to leasing the coal lands and allowing white men, such as miners and others on the reserve, is the demoralizing effect it would have on the Indians by opening greater facilities for drunkeness and licentiousness.
>
> V.   A portion of the coal area should be retained for use by the Indians.
>
> VI.   As Indians are not influenced by the prospect of a remote benefit, the lessee should be prepared to pay a bonus of $2,-000.00 to be distributed among the Indians as soon as surrender is accepted by the Governor in Council and the lease executed by the proper parties.
>
> VII.   There might be clauses in the lease providing if the lessee neglects to operate the mines for any, say 2, consecutive years, or otherwise fails to carry out the terms of the lease, the same should be subject to cancellation by the Department.[1]

Another source of dissatisfaction was inequity of freight rates charged by the Canadian Pacific — a complaint not confined to native people.

From a perusal of official correspondence, it would appear that when Laird wasn't involved with coal matters, he was dealing with rights-of-way for railroads and highways through the reserves. In 1899 some land was withdrawn from the Pelly reserve in the Birtle agency; negotiations continued until 1903. In that year, Laird himself was in Kamsack, busy with the transfer of hay lands between the Assiniboine and Whitesand Rivers, near the Coté reserve. On 13 January he wired to Lash in Winnipeg, "Surrender completed this afternoon. Payments to-morrow. I am well. Phone Louise."² In 1900 the Battleford Agency wanted a road through Moosomin's and Thunderbolt's reserves; the transfer was effected by federal order-in-council.

In 1901, Laird was at Crooked Lake, near Broadview, to complete arrangements for a road allowance to provide access to the Leach Lake reserve. Two years later there was the matter of a bridge over the Qu'Appelle at the east end of Crooked Lakes in the Muscowpetung Agency. In 1904 the Indian Commissioner was concerned about the east end of his territory and settlers in the Wabigoon and Manitou areas, District of Keewatin (part of Ontario since 1912). These worthy citizens wanted a road, or at least a wagon trail through the Wabigoon reserve as travel across and along Little Lake Wabigoon was dangerous, presumably in winter).

Of railway rights-of-way, those desired by the fledgling Canadian Northern (now part of Canadian National) were the most troublesome. In August, 1901, Laird was alerted that he would be receiving a delegation of ten or eleven chiefs and headmen from the Seine River, Coucheking, Red Gut, and Rainy River reserves, east of Winnipeg, to complain about delay in compensation by Canadian Northern for lands used by that system. Apparently, however, this was only part of the reason for their safari; they had not previously had an opportunity to meet the Great Chief who now occupied the Winnipeg tipi, an indication that Laird was rather closely tied to his office. Evidently Laird managed to persuade them that adequate compensation was on the way. But this thrifty Scottish-Canadian was quite up-set at what it was costing Indian Affairs to finance this Indian invasion. He felt that a delegation of two or three would have been just as effective.

In February, 1905, the Indian Commissioner received a letter from one D. H. Laird, of the law firm of Munson, Allan, Laird and Davis, Winnipeg, inquiring about the need of the same railway for its Prince Albert branch through The Pas mission reserve near Erwood (now in Saskatchewan). The correspondence dealt with both the amount of land and the amount of compensation. Rather irrelevantly, the case resulted in a request from Ottawa asking the meaning of the name of The Pas (also known as Le Pas until at least the 1930's). Incidentally, it comes, not from the French, but as an abbreviation of the Indian name of the Pasquia River.

The D. H. Laird of the sesquipedalian-named law firm was to become much more important to the Hon. David's family for personal than for business reasons.

White-Indian relations presented Indian Affairs with constant problems, but they went with the turf, and in the end could be handled through the application of the legal principles embodied in common and statute law, in governmental regulations and precedents — no civil servant ever does anything for the first time. But inter-Indian problems were often more difficult, for they could involve conflict between white and Indian customs, practices, traditions, beliefs and values. Thus from the File Hills agency, Winnipeg was informed that Chief Star Blanket had turned his wife out and taken a young woman in her place. Since Indian Affairs felt that a man holding the important position of chief should be an example to his band, Laird suggested that if Star Blanket did not mend his ways, he be deposed. This case doubly indicates the imposition of white standards on the Indians. A century earlier, a similar contretemps might simply have resulted in a polygamous arrangement, not uncommon among Indian peoples and accepted without qualms by the fur traders. But of course with the coming of the missionaries such a functional institution as polygamy was no longer tolerable. Furthermore, the calm assumption that a chief held his position at the pleasure of the government was a denial of the right of a band to choose its leader according to its immemorial custom.

Another case involved Assiniboine Agency's Nellie Jack, a woman whose mother-in-law had abducted (with the help of the Agent's wife) Nellie's daughter and turned her over to the child's father, who was alleged to be off to the United States with her. Laird's reaction was that he could do nothing for the mother, and she should apply to Mr. Justice Wetmore, Moosomin, for custody. Of course, the judge would decide the custody on the basis of Canadian law, without inquiring as to whether Nellie's band was matrilineal or patrilineal, or in either case, what the tribal custom was in such situations.

In one way, Laird's work as Indian Commissioner could be considered routine; in another, every problem was different. During his tenure in Winnipeg, two more Indian treaties were negotiated, No. 9 in 1905, with the Ojibway and Cree in that part of the District of Keewatin south of Hudson Bay (now Northern Ontario) and in 1905-06 No. 10, with Chipewyan, Cree, and others in the northern half of Saskatchewan, aside from the corner of the province in Treaty No. 8. McKenna acted as Treaty Commissioner for the latter. By 1910, adhesions to Treaty No. 5 had also been secured from Indians at "Nelson House, Split Lake, 'Deer's Lake East,' York Factory, and Fort Churchill."[3] In 1912, Deer's Lake became part of Ontario and the other points were included in Manitoba.

One function which the Hon. David Laird attended must have been, for him, an exercise in nostalgia. A great day for Laird, for the North-West, and for all of Canada was 1 September 1905, when Saskatchewan and Alberta became the Dominion's eighth and ninth provinces. Prime Minister Laurier, now Sir Wilfrid, Governor-General Earl Grey, and other dignitaries travelled west to celebrate the occasion (and perhaps make hay for the Liberal party). First at Edmonton, then at Regina, on 1 and 5 September respectively, the new governments were inaugurated. In charge of the Regina ceremonies was Amedée Forget, last lieutenant-governor of the Territories, first of Saskatchewan. Laird was an invited guest.

> Immediately Governor Forget was sworn in he brought the tall, venerable pioneer from his obscure seat, into a station of special prominence, and all who identified the once majestic figure endorsed the act by the best cheers of the day. In essentials the thing was repeated at the civic luncheon when Mr. Laird spoke. You were in the atmosphere of a sacrament of true Imperialism. Here was a Christian gentleman, to whom in the sunset of life coming events cast their shadows before, glorying with a pathetic modesty in the outcome of his handiwork, acknowledging the qualities of the red man, whom he knows through and through; overflowing with goodwill to newcomers of every kindred and tongue, a model for those who have sat in or may occupy high places of earthly dominion.[4]

Such was Laird's existence as a government official. What about his personal life? No longer a young man — he was sixty-five when he moved to Winnipeg — after his epic inland voyage of 1899, he lived very quietly with his family, i.e., daughter Louise and son Harold. He preferred to spend his evenings at home, reading and occasionally entertaining relatives from the Maritimes or old friends such as Dr. Andrew Baird, Manitoba College, who long ago had coached him in Hebrew. Another such was one whom he had known for many years. "When I called on him. . . I found him sitting with his friend of many Western experiences, Mr. Charles Mair, the Canadian poet of Indian life and author of 'Tecumseh' on his verandah on Edmonton Street."[5]

It would not be on this occasion that the poet Mair showed Laird (and perhaps presented him with) a copy of his principal prose work, which bears the publication date of 1908. Despite its misleading title, *Through the Mackenzie Basin,* it is an account of the travels of the Half-Breed Commission of 1899, and to some extent of the Treaty Commission. Its dedication reads:

TO

THE HON. DAVID LAIRD

LEADER OF

THE TREATY EXPEDITION OF 1899

THIS RECORD

IS CORDIALLY INSCRIBED BY HIS OLD FRIEND

THE AUTHOR

Laird's granddaughter tells of another and memorable Mair visit, which probably occurred in 1904 when Laird was recuperating from pneumonia:

> The Doctor warned Mother that his heart had been affected and he should have a stimulant, like wine or coffee, regularly. Mr. Laird refused to drink coffee; he thought it far too expensive. Mostly he drank hot water or weak tea. Mother did not know what to do. Her father had been a very strong temperance man for years. He had attended Temperance conferences in Toronto as a delegate from Winnipeg. As a concession, his wife had been allowed to use brandy in the sauce on Christmas pudding. Mother knew he was very fond of prunes; in fact, he asked for them for dessert so often that she was very tired of eating them. So she got some sherry and added a little when she stewed the prunes. Her father kept saying how delicious they were. One afternoon his old friend Charles Mair came to call on him and Grandfather invited him to stay for dinner. The dessert that night was prunes and Mother had not asked the maid to make a pudding for her, so the prunes appeared. My Grandfather said, "I know not everyone likes prunes, but Louise has found a new kind of prunes which are delicious. I am sure you will like them." Mr. Mair tasted the prunes, realized what had been added, and winked very suddenly at Mother. She was embarrassed, and thought her Father would see this, or that Mr. Mair would say something. To her relief he said nothing, and she was able to follow the doctor's orders.[6]

But a quiet life is not a hermit's life. Macpherson states:

> It was at the Manitoba College summer meeting of 1901 that I first saw Mr. Laird. Some social question was under discussion, and he rose to speak. It was evidently the arousing of one who had known the battle of debate before; yet the impression was one of power rather than of fire. Most kindly, almost laughingly, he presented his opinion, but with great light, and almost final force. He had unravelled the tangle to get the essentials, and was speaking the last word.[7]

Laird's regular attendance at St. Augustine, no matter how bitter the weather, has already been noted. Nor was his interest confined to the activities merely of its congregation. Naturally, an important topic in his interview with the Rev. R. J. Macpherson was church affairs.

As he had just returned from the General Assembly our thoughts naturally took that direction. "It was my first trip through to the coast," said Mr. Laird. "It is a beautiful trip with those magnificent mountains and gorges. The Assembly itself was well attended; but many of those for whom I had grown to look were no longer there."[8]

While we were thus conversing about Church affairs, Mr. Laird mentioned that he had been a member of two Pan-Presbyterian Councils, Belfast and Toronto, but he went on to say: "One of the most interesting events in Church history with which I have had any connecion, was the beginning of the committee, in 1870, to prepare a basis of union for the Churches. It met in Montreal. . ."[9]

Somewhat over a year after this interview, in December, 1904, Laird requested a fortnight's leave to attend a General Assembly in Toronto. This conference was considered especially important as it would attempt to effect a union of all Presbyterian denominations in Canada.

Just as Laird had been eager to promote the formation of a scientific society in Charlottetown, so in Winnipeg he was soon active in the affairs of the Historical and Scientific Society of Manitoba, serving as president in 1904. In 1905 the Society's *Transactions* contain his paper on "North-West Indian Treaties," probably first presented as an address to the organization. Incidentally, his friend Andrew Baird had been president in 1892.

At infrequent intervals, for example, in 1907, David Laird managed to get away from Winnipeg for a much-needed vacation, for periods of rest and recuperation. Always his heart turned to the Island as a compass needle seeks the North. Despite his long absence from that tiny hamlet, he probably always regarded New Glasgow as his home, and its people as his people. At least the following letter would so suggest:

Indian Commissioner's Office

Winnipeg, Man., Jany 3, 1903

Dear Mr. Moffat —

I was very pleased to receive your Christmas letter and heartily reciprocate your good wishes for the season. I am glad to hear of George Smith and other old friends being well, and especially your father. I often think of New Glasgow, and would like once more to have a walk on the banks of the Clyde. Perhaps I may be able to pay the dear old settlement a visit this year — but I am not sure.

Remember me kindly to your worthy Father, your brother William, Mrs. Archibald, and George Smith. Mrs. Archibald is acting bravely to carry on the Hotel. We are all well here. My son Gordon paid us a visit at Christmas.

Mr. Artemas Moffat   Your sincere friend

New Glasgow
P. E. I.   David Laird[10]

With his work, his books — lots and lots of books — his church and other interests, his visits with friends and no doubt with his son William, then in Winnipeg with the *Free Press,* David Laird was no doubt as contented as he could be after the loss of his wife. But he still had one continuing worry: his son Harold. That young man had come west with his father and sister, and seems to have been employed, at least seasonally, for several years by Indian Affairs. His niece Elizabeth states that he was in the Indian Affairs office "and in the summer went out west. He bought a canoe, learned to paddle. . .[11] When he left in May, 1908, however, he did not return. The reason for his departure that year is contained in a letter his father wrote to Rennie, then in the Bank of Nova Scotia at Amherst, Nova Scotia, on 1 May:

> Harold is away again on a trip to the Peace River. With hard work I got him the position - there were so many applicants. He gets $100.00 per month and will be on this job for about six months.[12]

Then or later, Harold was posted to Grouard, formerly Willow Point, where his father had been nine years before. Here he married a local girl, Métis or Indian, named Rose Desjardins, and here he remained for the rest of his life, a life apparently undistinguished at least by Laird standards. At Grouard he raised his family — one son served in World War II — in straitened circumstances, dying in 1943. The Hon. David and other Lairds continued to help the family financially and with gifts of food, even after Harold's death, but otherwise it was almost as if he had ceased to exist for his brothers and sisters.

David Laird no doubt worried about his son, but one may wonder if he was equally concerned about Louise. On the surface, she led a pleasant if not luxurious life. Her brother taught her conoeing, but she never learned to swim more than a few strokes. However, as Harold was a strong swimmer, she knew that he would always look after her. They both belonged to the Winnipeg Tennis Club, and Louise also found time for Good Works, e.g., she joined the Ladies Auxiliary formed to raise money for a children's hospital. The members did so by holding silver teas and serving meals every summer at the Winnipeg Exhibition, both genteel middle-class activities.

And yet, Louise grew up in an era when the usual destiny of well-educated middle-class young women was to enter teaching or nursing or matrimony. Rather, *and* matrimony. The usual, ultimate goal, confessed or unrecognized, of every well-bred young lady was to become a wife and mother, not that all were so — fortunate? Sometimes it must have seemed to Louise that wedded bliss was not for her. She was twenty when her mother died, and when she found herself, like many another loving and dutiful daughter, with the responsibility of looking after an aging and widowed parent. Romance and marriage would have to be deferred.

She was twenty-five when she came to Winnipeg, where she knew no one her own age. Her filial responsibilities did not become lighter; indeed, they increased, at least when her father was not well, as in 1904. Soon Louise was pushing towards thirty, towards spinsterhood, towards, in the cruel jests of the time, becoming an old maid, an unclaimed jewel, being on the shelf.

William, Louise's brother, was not the only Laird relative in Winnipeg. There was also David Henry, the D. H. Laird, attorney-at-law, who had written to the Indian Commissioner about a railway right-of-way. He was the son of the Rev. Robert Laird, therefore the Hon. David's nephew and Louise's cousin, and had reached Winnipeg in 1898. Laird family bonds being what they were, he came to call on his uncle when the latter arrived from Charlottetown. Soon it was Louise that he was really wishing to see on his visits. Before long, the two first cousins were wanting to marry each other, although at first Louise refused David Henry's suit. The two fathers were very, very cool to the whole idea. The young people were ouside the prohibited degrees, but barely just. However, David and Louise were old enough to know their own minds, and eventually the two *paterfamilias* consented. Remembering the opposition to his own marriage, Louise's father at last agreed, providing the ceremony was held at home. It took place on 29 December 1906; Louise had just turned thirty-one. Her husband was almost exactly a year younger.

Now Louise had to reconcile her duty to her father with that to her husband. The problem was resolved by the young couple's moving in with the Commissioner in the Edmonton Street house. Here they remained for about a year after the Hon. David moved to Ottawa in 1909, and here their elder daughter Mary Louise was born on 7 July 1910, named, obviously, after her mother and her aunt.

In 1909, Laird was seventy-six years old — and still working as a civil servant. There was no compulsory retirement age then for public servants, nor any pension, or vitually none. It was cheaper for the government to keep people in harness as long as they could handle their jobs, then turn them out to pasture — if they could find a pasture — than to pay both salaries and pensions for the same positions. Since Laird was both willing and able to continue working, the government was happy for him to do so. However, for whatever reason, he was moved to Ottawa. He left most of his furniture in the Edmonton Street house for his daughter and son-in-law; they continued to live there for about a year. At that time, he sold the place, Louise and David Henry moving to another part of the city.

Meanwhile, in Ottawa, David Laird took two rooms in a boarding house on Bay Street near Wellington; the structure has since been demolished. His office was in the Parliament Buildings, probably in the Centre Block which was destroyed by fire in 1916. His grandson D. L. Mathieson recalls a visit to Ottawa when he was eight or ten years old, i.e., in 1911 or 1913. Speaking of his grandfather, Mathieson writes, "He personally showed me his office in the Parliament Building. I have no recollection of the building except the Parliamentary Library, which quite over-awed me."[13]

There is little readily available information as to Laird's duties in Ottawa. Perhaps he was a trouble-shooter, rushing like a fireman from crisis to crisis — and as all Branch personnel know, crises are endemic in Indian Affairs. F. J. Newson tells of a small one which Laird travelled to Prince Edward Island to resolve:

> I remember as a small boy meeting David Laird. It happened in this wise. My grandfather, John Newson, owned Warren Farm at Rocky Point, across the harbor from Charlottetown, a fair sized farm for the Island. We were told that he had bought it for sentimental reasons because it was there at a picnic that he first met our grandmother. A band of Mic-Mac Indians had squatted on a corner of the farm some years before. . . My grandfather finally asked the Indian Department either to remove the Indians or to buy the land, and was advised in due course that Mr. Laird, who still had some official position in Indian Affairs, would call to discuss the matter with him. This was either in 1910 or 1912 : . .
>
> I never knew whether the Government bought the land or whether the Indians moved off.[14]

Laird's visit would be more than a business call. The two men had been active in the formation of the Prince Edward Island Natural History Society in 1889, and when Laird was president the following year, the other man served on his executive. Newson was also to have the sad honor of being a pall bearer at Laird's funeral.

It is probable that the date of the Island visit was 1910, as there is reason to believe that in 1912 he was in the West. Elizabeth Laird states: "He did return to Winnipeg to see his granddaughter, because there were snapshots of the two of them in the garden. He was holding her hand, and she was still so small, and he was 6 feet 6, that she could barely reach his hand."[15]

This granddaughter would be Mary Louise, who seems from the above snapshot to have been about two years old. Since she was born on 7 July 1910, the visit would have been most probably in 1912. There is evidence that he went even farther west that year.

Laird family papers contain a photocopy of a newspaper story, date and source not indicated, but the head, "Appreciation of Good Works," appears the acknowledgement "(Calgary Herald)." The story follows:

> The Royal party has come and gone and the day will long be remembered by the people of Calgary and all those who had the opportunity and pleasure of being present and among the many attractions of the day that will remain the longest in the minds of the people and be quoted to the limit of the generation will be: "The great Indian demonstration held at Shagganappi Point when the Duke and Duchess were here."
>
> The Royal party were greatly attracted and interested in it, and expressed themselves greatly pleased at the unique and wonderful display of Indians and Indian life, on horse and foot. Also in the orderly and quiet manner in which the whole body of them conducted themselves during the visit of the Royal party, and expressed their gratitude in unstinted terms to the officials of the Indian department for giving them one of the most enjoyable and delightful days of their tour.
>
> There is no doubt this same feeling was in the mind of everyone present on the occasion. Anyone who knows Indian character will realize the amount of trouble, anxiety and responsibility attending the bringing together (many of them from a long distance) maintaining and controlling such a large body of Indians under the circumstances, and we feel we are greatly in debt to the Hon. David Laird, Indian commissioner, and the agents of the various reserves, who assisted him, and that too much credit cannot be given to the honorable gentleman for his admirable and satisfactory conduct in the demonstration.
>
> It was particularly fitting that this great Indian demonstration should have been directed and managed by the Hon. David Laird, who was formerly lieutenant-governor of the Territories, and when acting in this capacity made the treaty with these Indians and is remembered by all the old chiefs as "The Big Chief" and retains to this day as he did then their entire confidence and good will.
>
> It was pleasing to hear on every side the high opinion and respect in which the Indian commissioner is held by all the Indian officials, and the government is to be congratulated on securing the services of a gentleman of such high character, ability and fitness, and who possesses the confidence of the whole west for this important and responsible position.[16]

In Laird's lifetime the only "Royal party" to visit Calgary and to include a duke and a duchess was that of the Duke and Duchess of Connaught. The Duke, a son of Queen Victoria and uncle of King George V, was Governor-General of Canada at the time of the visit, which was in 1912; the occasion the first Calgary Stampede. The use of the term "Royal party" rather than "Royal couple" implies that there were more than two royals. Indeed, there was a third, Princess Patricia, daughter of the Duke and Duchess.

David Laird continued working until a short time before his death. He caught a bad cold and with no one to insist that he take proper care of himself, it turned to pneumonia, at that time an often-fatal disease. He died on 12 January 1914, two months before his eighty-first birthday.

When his son William and his daughter Louise heard that he was seriously ill, they immediately left Winnipeg for Ottawa, of course by rail. Not only did they have a long way to go, but a bitter blizzard in Northern Ontario stalled their train for a full day. Both food for the passengers and fuel to fire the locomotive's boiler rapidly ran short. Even hot water for tea was almost unobtainable, and the inside of the cars were nearly as cold as the outside. Louise and William did not reach Ottawa before her father had passed to his reward, but their sister Mary and her husband were able to do so.

The funeral was in Charlottetown, the service being held in the home of Laird's son-in-law, Premier J. A. Mathieson. In recognition of the loss which the whole Dominion had suffered, the federal government had the icebreaker *Earl Grey* carry the body directly from the mainland to the frozen-over harbor of Charlottetown instead of to the ice-free port of Georgetown. D. L. Mathieson quotes a letter from his sister (and Laird's granddaughter) Avila (Mathieson) Rogers:

> Lethe and Dora had not a great deal to add to our personal memories of Grandfather. They do remember that they, and Helen were sent over to Bentley's (a neighbor) on the day of his funeral. They remember the crowds lining the street, and all the Indians. I was kept at home (age 8) and watched the funeral procession from the window in the hall. I'll never forget those prancing black horses covered with black net, and with waving black plumes on their heads. There were four horses as I remember. And the crowds of people. Lethe remembers coming home from school and hearing the guns booming and people running to the wharf, as the Earl Grey came in the harbor bearing Grandfather's body.[17]

The three girls were all granddaughters of David Laird. Lethe — Miss Aletha Laird — was Rennie's daughter; the other two, Dora (Mathieson) Campbell and Helen (Mathieson) Chauvin were, like Avilla, children of Laird's elder daughter Mary Alice.

The roll-call of the official mourners (all male) provides only a hint as to the extent of the family connections. The list included D. Rennie Laird, son; Albert Laird of New Glasgow, brother; Hon. J. A. Mathieson, son-in-law; Alexander and Robert Laird of Bedeque, William Owen, Aeneas McDonald, L. A. and Walter Haszard, nephews, Charles and A.

W. Owen, brothers-in-law; David Laird, grandson. Absent through distance or for other reasons were sons Gordon, William, and Harold, brother William, son-in-law (and nephew) David H. Laird, and no doubt many others. Not even mentioned were female relatives: daughters, granddaughters, sister-in-law, nieces, and cousins of either sex.

After the service at the Mathieson home, conducted by Rev. Dr. T. F. Fullerton and Rev. G. C. Taylor, the funeral procession proceeded to the railway station and entrained for Sherwood cemetery, a few miles away, where a short graveside service was conducted by the Rev. Mr. Taylor.

Forty-one years after the Hon. David Laird's death, in the little community of New Glasgow, Mr. Justice Estey, Supreme Court of Canada, unveiled a plaque in memory of the man-whose-tongue-is-not-forked, to the Great Chief, to the Laird of the West. It reads:

HONOURABLE DAVID LAIRD

FOUNDED THE PATRIOT NEWSPAPER
CHARLOTTETOWN 1859
PRINCE EDWARD ISLAND LEGISLATOR
MINISTER OF THE INTERIOR
LIEUTENANT-GOVERNOR OF THE
NORTH-WEST TERRITORIES
INDIAN COMMISSIONER
BORN AT NEW GLASGOW, P.E.I., 1833
DIED IN OTTAWA, 1914

ERECTED BY THE GOVERNMENT OF CANADA
HISTORIC SITES AND MONUMENTS BOARD

One of the speakers was Dora (Mathieson) Campbell, David Laird's granddaughter. His niece, Elsie Laird, donated the hundred by eighty-foot site for the plaque.

Perhaps no more spontaneous tribute to David Laird has appeared in print than that of the missionary John McDougall. It was published within a few days of Laird's death in *The Albertan* and other newspapers.

> Editor Albertan: Will you kindly give me space to pay a modest tribute to one of Canada's noblemen who recently died in Ottawa? I refer to the Hon. David Laird.
>
> My first association with Mr. Laird was in 1877, when Treaty No. 7

was enterprised and accomplished. He was then lieutenant-governor of these territories and at that time also in association with Colonel Macleod, a commissioner in making the treaty. Later, in the spring of 1879, when we were driving from the mountains to Winnipeg, via Battleford, my brother and myself and our families were most hospitably entertained in the government house by Mr. and Mrs. Laird, and this was my second opportunity to become acquainted with this splendid man for as the years went by our intimacy grew and I learned to warmly admire his sterling character and to know him to be indeed a true patriot and a genuine Christian gentleman.

In one of my recent visits to Ottawa I had the pleasure of dining with him in his home in that city.

An incident which took place in our association in 1905 will remain with me as long as my memory lasts. We were at the Indian agency near Kamsack when I was taken suddenly sick and it was thought by some that my death was near. I was in constant pain and also very lonely when the door of my room opened and Mr. Laird entered with his Bible in hand and sitting down near me read the 103rd Psalm and then turning to the gospels he read a part of the 14th chapter of St. John and then with a tremulous "Good night" he left me. I seem to hear that "Good night" now and to see his tall form as he bent at the door of the upper chamber and I cannot help but think that somewhere and "by and by" we will again meet and then it will be "Good morning."

Yours faithfully,

John McDougall[18]

In his native province, David Laird is remembered as a legislator who helped mold its public school system, and who led the Island into Confederation only when he could secure equitable terms. He is also renowned as the Member of Parliament who with Donald Smith blew the whistle on Sir John A. Macdonald's Conservative government for its corrupt political machinations in connection with the building of the Pacific railway. In the West, he laid the foundations for the legal and educational systems of two great provinces. but mostly he is remembered for his part in negotiating the Great Treaties with the Indians. He was Minister of Indian Affairs for No. 5 and 6, Treaty Commissioner for No. 4, 7 and 8, and at least peripherally concerned, as Indian Commissioner, with No. 9 and 10.

If the Great Treaties have become somewhat tattered and eroded, such damage was none of David Laird's doing. Despite criticisms made of the treaties — and more than a century after their negotiation they are many and justifiable — their existence is one important reason why white settlement of the North-West proceeded with little violence and terror, and none of the genocide that marked the occupation of native lands in other

New World countries. Moreover, battered though they may be, the treaties still stand as obstacles to those who would exploit our native peoples and their resources to their own ends.

The registration of the Indian under the treaties or otherwise, initially made in connection with the annuities and land allocations for reserves, has also done much to preserve his identity as an individual and encourage his pride of ancestry and his self-respect. Whether he (or she) lives in the country or the city, on a reserve or off it, he/she can say with self-confidence and absolute certainty, for example, "I am a Cree Indian of the Ermineskin Band," or "I belong to the Wesley band of the Stoneys," not merely, "I am an Indian — more or less."

Few are the Indians in Canada today who would choose not to be Indian.

References

1. Elizabeth Laird to John W. Chalmers, 11 May 1979.

2. *Ibid.*

3. Morris Zaslow, *The Opening of the Canadian West* 1870-1914, p. 226.

4. "A Correspondent," "Men Who Have Arrived," *The Morning Post* (London), 10 October 1905.

5. R. J. Macpherson, "The Hon. David Laird, P.C., Commissioner of Indian Affairs for Manitoba and the Northwest," *The Westminster* (New Series), v. 3, no. 4, p. 186.

6. Elizabeth Laird, "Hon David Laird, Indian Commissioner at Winnipeg, 1898-1909," (unpublished typescript), pp. 1-2.

7. Macpherson, *op. cit.*

8. *Ibid.*

9. *Ibid.,* p. 187.

10. David Laird to Artemas Moffatt, 3 January 1903 (Public Archives of Prince Edward Island, No. 2645-1).

11. Elizabeth Laird, "Hon. David Laird. . . ," p. 2.

12. David Laird to David Rennie Laird, 1 May 1908.

13. David L. Mathieson to John W. Chalmers, 8 March 1979.

14. F. J. Newson, "Reminiscences of Seaside Hotel, Rustico Beach, P.E.I.," (unpublished typescript), p. 5.

15. Elizabeth Laird, "Hon. David Laird. . . ," p. 2.

16. Copied from *Calgary Herald,* "Appreciation of Good Work," no date.

17. Mathieson, *op. cit.*

18. John McDougall, "Tribute to Late Hon. David Laird," *The Albertan,* date unknown.

Genealogical Tables

The following tables are not intended to include all the ancestors, descendants, collateral relations, and in-laws of the Hon. David Laird, but only those, or most of them, mentioned in this work and in the references cited. Where possible, dates of births, deaths, and marriages have been indicated. Occasionally the material, gathered from different family sources, reveals discrepancies, in which cases the most probable data have been chosen.

Scottish-Born Lairds

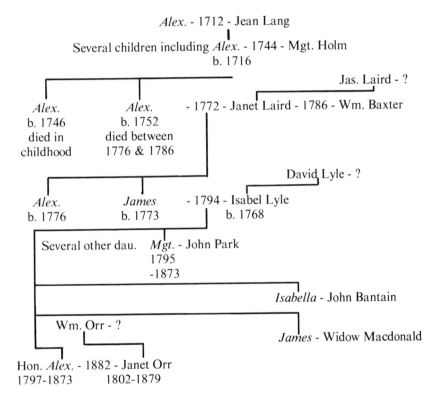

Alex. - 1712 - Jean Lang

Several children including *Alex.* - 1744 - Mgt. Holm
b. 1716

| *Alex.* b. 1746 died in childhood | *Alex.* b. 1752 died between 1776 & 1786 | | Jas. Laird - ? |
| | | - 1772 - Janet Laird - 1786 - Wm. Baxter |

| *Alex.* b. 1776 | *James* b. 1773 | | David Lyle - ? |
| | | - 1794 - Isabel Lyle b. 1768 |

Several other dau. *Mgt.* - John Park
1795
-1873

Isabella - John Bantain

Wm. Orr - ?

James - Widow Macdonald

Hon. *Alex.* - 1882 - Janet Orr
1797-1873   1802-1879

259

Family of Hon. Alexander Laird, Sr.

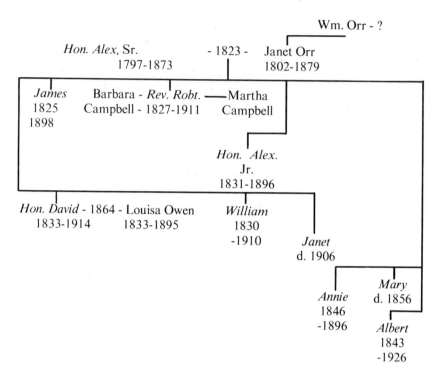

Family of Rev. Robert Laird

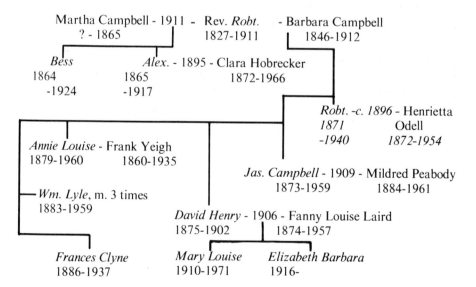

Family of Hon. David Laird

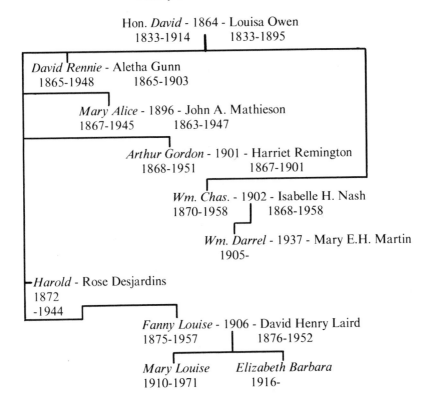

Hon. *David* - 1864 - Louisa Owen
1833-1914   1833-1895

David Rennie - Aletha Gunn
1865-1948   1865-1903

Mary Alice - 1896 - John A. Mathieson
1867-1945   1863-1947

Arthur Gordon - 1901 - Harriet Remington
1868-1951   1867-1901

Wm. Chas. - 1902 - Isabelle H. Nash
1870-1958   1868-1958

Wm. Darrel - 1937 - Mary E.H. Martin
1905-

Harold - Rose Desjardins
1872
-1944

Fanny Louise - 1906 - David Henry Laird
1875-1957   1876-1952

Mary Louise   *Elizabeth Barbara*
1910-1971   1916-

Family of David Rennie Laird

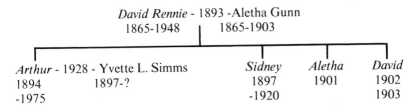

David Rennie - 1893 -Aletha Gunn
1865-1948   1865-1903

Arthur - 1928 - Yvette L. Simms   *Sidney*   *Aletha*   *David*
1894   1897-?   1897   1901   1902
-1975   -1920   1903

Thomas Owen Family

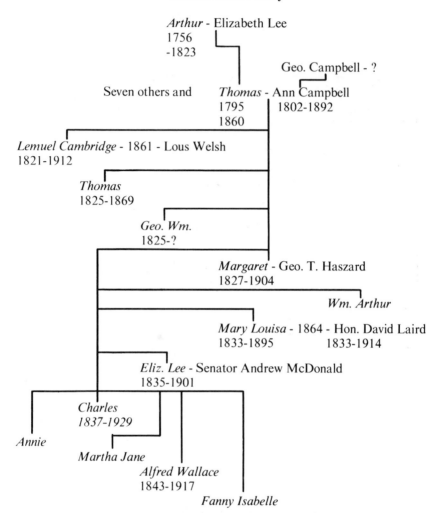

Hon. John A. Mathieson Family

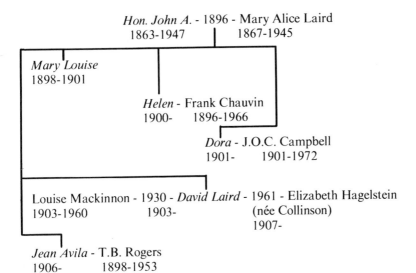

Hon. John A. - 1896 - Mary Alice Laird
1863-1947 | 1867-1945

Mary Louise
1898-1901

Helen - Frank Chauvin
1900-   1896-1966

Dora - J.O.C. Campbell
1901-   1901-1972

Louise Mackinnon - 1930 - *David Laird* - 1961 - Elizabeth Hagelstein
1903-1960   1903-   (née Collinson)
                                     1907-

Jean Avila - T.B. Rogers
1906-   1898-1953

Sources and Bibliography

Archival Resources

Invaluable were copies of letters, telegrams, and other material from sources listed in the acknowledgements. Unfortunately, some of the documents are photocopies of photocopies and do not include their depositories.

Family Papers and Records

One important source of information on David Laird's life was Laird family papers, including a large number of letters, newspaper clippings, and other documents, original or photocopies. Unfortunately, many of these indicate neither date nor source. Family members supplied data from family records, e.g., dates of births, deaths, marriages, etc. and family traditions which have been reduced to writing.

Unpublished Memoirs, Etc.

Fish, Aileen, "Treaty Number Seven," CBC radio script, undated.

Laird, David H., "Family of Alexander Laird of New Glasgow, Prince Edward Island," April, 1930.

Laird, David H., "Fort Livingstone, Saskatchewan," 2 October 1931.

Laird, Elizabeth, "Hon. David Laird, Indian Commissioner at Winnipeg, 1898-1909," undated.

Mair, Charles, "Mr. Mair's Account of the Meeting with the Sioux Chiefs," undated, unsigned manuscript on letterhead of Office of the Indian Commissioner, Regina, N.W.T., in Laird family papers, and PEI Archives.

Mathieson, Mary Alice, "Early Days in the North-West Territories," in Laird family papers, and Saskatchewan Archives.

Newson, F.J., "Reminiscences of a Seaside Hotel, Rustico Beach, P.E.I."

Published but Unsigned and Uncaptioned Materials

The files of the following publications, past and present, supplied a wealth of unsigned, uncaptioned but dated stories and editorial comment.

Calgary Herald.

Guardian of the Gulf (Charlottetown).

Highway 40 Courier.

North Battleford News-Optimist.

The Patriot (Charlottetown).

The Morning Post (London, England).

Regina Leader.

Saskatchewan Herald (Battleford).

Star-Phoenix (Saskatoon).

Winnipeg Free Press (Manitoba Free Press).

Winnipeg Telegram

Periodicals with Published and Captioned but Unsigned Materials

The Beaver, "Cumberland House," Spring, 1970.
   "Cumberland House 1774-1794," Winter, 1974.

The Colonist, "The Prairie Parliament," 1905 (exact date undetermined).

The Globe, "Hon. David Laird," 3 November 1876.

Saskatchewan Herald,
   "To Edmonton and Back Three Hundred Miles in an Open Boat," 25 August, 1979 (also in *Alberta Historical Review,* v. 18 no. 3).
   "The Administration of the North-West", 23 February 1880.
   "The Session," 15 March 1880.
   "Elective Councillors," 15 March, 1880.
   "The Lieutenant-Governor's Easter Tour," 29 November 1880.
   "Aid to Schools," 20 December 1880.
   "The Vice-Regal Journey," 4 September, 1881.
   "The Lieutenant-Governorship," 18 September 1881.
   "Citizens' Address to Governor Laird," 31 December 1881.
   "The Governor's Departure,"31 December, 1881.

Winnipeg Free Press, "In the Days of Governor Laird," 1905 (exact date undetermined).

Books, Articles, Reports, etc.

Alberta, *Indian Treaties Commemorative Program*

Baptie, Sue, "Edgar Dewdney," *Alberta Historical Review,* v. 16,no. 4.

Bartlett, John, *Familiar Quotations* (11th edition).

Bowman, Bob, "Confederation Table Still at Charlottetown," *Winnipeg Free Press,* 26 November 1967.

_____, "On this Day in 1877, foothills tribes signed over their territory," *Ottawa Citizen,* 22 September 1964.

Buckingham, Wm., and Ross, Geo. W., *The Life of Alexander Mackenzie.*

Canada, *Treaty No. 4 between Her Majesty the Queen and the Cree and Saul-teaus Tribes of Indians at Qu'Appelle and Fort Ellice.*

_____, *Copy of Treaty No. 6 between Her Majesty the Queen and the Plain and Wood Cree Indians and Other Tribes at Fort Carlton, Fort Pitt and Battle River with Adhesions.*

_____, *Copy of Treaty and Supplementary Treaty No. 7 Made 22nd Sept., and 4th Dec., 1877 between Her Majesty the Queen and the Blackfoot and other Indians of Bow River and Fort Macleod.*

_____,, *Treaty No. 8 Made June 21, 1899 and Adhesions, Reports, etc.*

Chalmers, John W., *Red River Adventure.*

_____, *Schools of the Foothills Province.*

_____, "Inland Journey," *The Beaver,* Autumn, 1972.

_____, "Treaty No. 6," *Alberta History,* v. 25, no. 2.

_____, Eccles, W.J., and Fullard, H. (editors), *Philips Historical Atlas of Canada.*

Complin, Margaret, "Calling Valley of the Crees," *The Beaver,* March, 1935.

Correspondent, A., "Some Men Who Have Arrived," *The Morning Post,* 10 October, 1905.

D'artigue, Jean, *Six Years in the Canadian North-West.*

Dempsey, Hugh A., *Crowfoot Chief of the Blackfoot.*

_____, *Jerry Potts, Plainsman.*

_____, (editor), William Parker Mounted Policeman.

Denny, Cecil E., *The Law Marches West.*

Erasmus, Peter (as told to Henry Thompson), *Buffalo Days and Nights.*

Fetherstonhaugh, R.C., "March of the Mounties," *The Beaver,* June, 1940.

Fischer, Lewis R., "The Shipping Industry of Nineteenth Century Prince Edward Island A Brief History," *The Island Magazine,* v. 4.

Fletcher, J.H., *Newspaper Life and Newspaper Men,* quoted in *the Guardian* (Charlottetown), 19 February 1949.

Forget, Mme., "Disappearance of the Buffalo and Starvation among the Indians," *The Colonist,* 1905 (exact date undetermined).

Forget, Amédée, "Government Aid to Schools," *Saskatchewan Herald* (government advertisement) 20 February 1880.

Franklin, John, *Narrative of a Journey to the Shores of the Polar Sea in the Years 1819, 20, 21 and 22.*

Fumoleau, René, *As Long as this Land Shall Last.*

Glover, R., "Cumberland House," *The Beaver,* December, 1951.

Grant, George M., *Ocean to Ocean.*

Griesbach, W.A., *I Remember.*

Hardisty, Richard, "The Blackfoot Treaty an eyewitness account," *Alberta Historical Review,* v. 5, no. 4 (reprinted from *Calgary Herald* 18 November 1933).

Harvey, D.C., "David Laird The Man Whose Tongue is not Forked," *The Grain Growers Guide,* 20 August, 1919.

Hughes, Katherine, "Hon. David Laird: One of Canada's Nation Builders," *The Globe,* (date undetermined).

_____, "Honourable David Laird," *The Canadian Magazine,* v. 27, no. 5.

Ironside, R.G. & Tomasky, E., "Development of Victoria Settlement," *Alberta Historical Review,* v. 20, no.2.

Kinnaird, George J., "An Episode of the North-West Rebellion," *Saskatchewan History,* v. 20, no.2.

Laird, Hon. David, "The Blackfoot Treaty," *The Globe,* 4 October 1877.

_____, "Governor Laird's Thanksgiving Day Address, 1879," (introduction by L.H. Thomas), *Saskatchewan History,* v. 5, no. 3 (reprinted from *Saskatchewan Herald* 15 December 1879).

_____, "North-West Indian Treaties," Historical and Scientific Society of Manitoba *Transactions* 1905.

_____, "Special Appendix C," North-West Territories *Sessional Papers* (No. 10) 1878.

Larmour, Jean, "Edgar Dewdney, Indian Commissioner in the Transition Period of Indian Settlement, 1879-1884," *Saskatchewan History,* v. 33, no. 1.

Letourneau, Roger, "The Grand Rapids Tramway: The First Railway in the Canadian Northwest," Historical and Scientific Society of Manitoba, *Transactions,* Series III, no. 32.

Looy, A.J., "Saskatchewan's First Indian Agent: M.G. Dickieson," *Saskatchewan History,* v. 32, no. 3.

MacGregor, James G., *Edmonton A History.*

MacKinnon, Frank, "David Laird of Prince Edward Island," *The Dalhousie Review,* v. 26, no. 4.

_____, The Public Life of the Hon. David Laird," *Charlottetown Guardian* and *The Patriot,* November, 1945.

Macpherson, R.J., "The Hon. David Laird, P.C., Commissioner of Indian Affairs for Manitoba and the North-west," *The Westminster,* v. 3, no. 4.

Mair, Charles, *Through the Mackenzie Basin.*

Mathieson, David L., "These distinguished men were no 'fork-tongued cheats'," *Edmonton Journal,* 23 December 1969.

McCook, James, "Frontiersmen of Fort Ellice," *The Beaver,* Autumn, 1968.

McDougall, John, "Tribute to Late Hon. David Laird," *The Albertan,* ? January 1914,.

McFadden, Molly, "Steamboating on the Red," Historical and Scientific Society of Manitoba *Transactions,* Series III, no. 7.

_____, "Steamboats on the Red," *The Beaver,* September, 1950.

McKee, G.A., *Edmonton School District No. 7 1885-1935.*

Murray, Jean E., "The Early History of Emmanuel College," *Saskatchewan History,* v. 9, no. 3.

Nix, J. Ernest, "Button Chief, A Native Hero," *Alberta History,* v. 29, no.1.

Oliver, E.H., *The Canadian North-West,* v. 2.

Oliver, Hon. Frank, "The Blackfoot Indian Treaty," *Maclean's Magazine,* 15 March 1931.

Peel, Bruce, *Steamboats on the Saskatchewan.*

Powell, Jack, "David Laird," *The Piper,* 1963.

Prince Edward Island, *Parliamentary Reporter 1870.*

Robertson, Ian R., "Pope, William Henry," *Dictionary of Canadian Biography,* v. 10.

_____, "The Bible Question in Prince Edward Island," *Acadiensis,* v. 5, no.2.

_____, "Party Politics and Religious Controversialism in Prince Edward Island," *Acadiensis,* v. 7, no. 2.

Russell, R.C., "A Minister Takes the Carlton Trail," *The Beaver,* Winter, 1959.

Sharp, Paul E., *Whoop-Up Country.*

Shave, Harry, "The Bells of the Turrets Twain," *The Beaver,* September, 1950.

Steele, Samuel B., *Forty Years in Canada.*

Stewart, A., "The First Half-Century: A Sketch of the Early Years of the Historical and Scientific Society of Manitoba," *Manitoba Pageant,* v. 24, no. 3.

Stewart, Robert, *Sam Steele of the Frontier.*

Story, G.M., "Cormack, William Eppes (Epps)," *Dictionary of Canadian Biography,* v. ix.

Thomson, Don W., *Men and Meridians,* v. 2.

"Timer, Old" (Williams, Stan), "Governor Held Vision of Growth for Edmonton," *Edmonton Journal,* 30 April 1955.

Turner, J.P., *The North-West Mounted Police,* v. 1.

Twilley, F.A., *Between the Hills,* extract in *Winnipeg Free Press.*

Vastokas, Ron, "The Grand Rapids Portage," *The Beaver,* August 1961.

Vickers, Reg, "Cluny treaty ceremonies," *The Globe and Mail,* 2 July, 1977.

Weadick, Guy, "Origins of the Calgary Stampede," *Alberta Historical Review,* v. 14, no. 4.

Wetton, Mrs. A.N., "Christmastide in Old Battleford," *Saskatoon Star-Phoenix,* 24 December 1958.

Wiebe, Rudy, "The Year We Gave Away the Land," *Weekend,* 5 July 1977.

Wilson, Clifford, "Indian Treaties," *The Beaver,* March, 1939.

Woodcock, George, *Gabriel Dumont.*

Zaslow, Morris, *The Opening of the Canadian West 1870-1914.*

Index